STRIKE!!

PAY THE
FORD WORKERS
WE'RE

Strike While the Needle is Hot

Josh MacPhee & Kennedy Block

Common Notions
Philadelphia

Introduction

Josh MacPhee

I didn't set out to collect strike records. As a self-employed artist who's always cobbled together a living doing odd jobs, I've never even been in a union. I've long admired them, seen them as foundational to the world I'd like to live in, but also twisted and bent through their endless struggle, quite literally, with their antithesis—capitalism. All to say, I love a good union fight, I do a fair amount of art and design for unions, but they've hardly been at the center of my world.

I became fascinated with the records in this book by accident. I was hoovering up any political music I could find for my *Encyclopedia of Political Record Labels* project, and it turns out that unions are one of the main "non-music" label entities that have produced and distributed vinyl records. In the US, and some European countries, unions began producing 10" shellacs in the 1930s and '40s, evolving into vinyl LPs in the '50s and '60s. Most are collections of historical labor songs, odes to a union's glorious past, and objects produced to bolster membership morale, maybe raise some money, or just to hand out to the rank and file at an annual convention.

In many countries a singular figure (or a couple figures) emerged as primary bards of labor; for instance in the US there is Paul Robeson and Joe Glazer, in Germany Ernst Busch, or in Canada Raymond Lévesque and Arlene Mantle. These artists would often work with unions to produce records specific to the union's history and its industry. Some of these might be strike records (and are included here), but most are not. For instance, Joe Glazer made records with the United Auto Workers, United Mine Workers (with songs such as "Dark as the Dungeon"), American Federation of State, County and Municipal Employees (AFSCME Sings with Joe Glazer), BRAC (The Brotherhood of Railway, Airline and Steamship Clerks, Freight Handlers, Express and Station Employees—the LP featuring jaunty hits such as "This Train's a Clean Train"), SEIU (Service Employee International

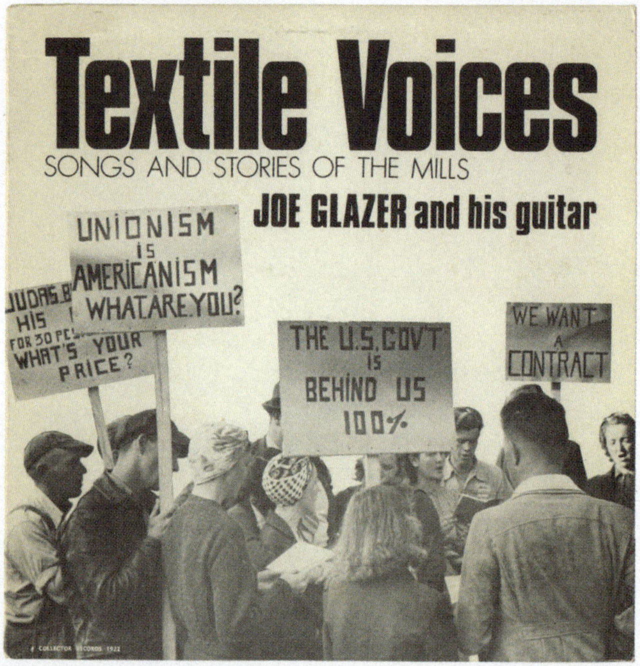
Textile Voices
SONGS AND STORIES OF THE MILLS
JOE GLAZER and his guitar
UNIONISM is AMERICANISM WHAT ARE YOU?
WHAT'S YOUR PRICE?
THE U.S. GOV'T IS BEHIND US 100%
WE WANT A CONTRACT

Songs of Steel & Struggle
The Story of the Steelworkers
Sung by Joe Glazer with the Charlie Byrd Trio

Service Employees International Union SINGS WITH Joe Glazer

UNION TRAIN
JOE GLAZER
MIKE AULDRIDGE, Dobro
ALAN BENNETT, Banjo

Union), United Steelworkers, and more. While Glazer was undoubtedly committed to organized labor, he was also clearly a hired gun.

While some unions and other non-state political groupings had produced records in the 1940s and '50s, it wasn't until the Civil Rights Movement that these records became direct tools of struggle. All of the major Civil Rights organizations began using vinyl records as both documentation and agitprop as early as the late 1950s, many of these records being at least partially funded and distributed by progressive unions (as an example, at least four different unions released MLK Jr. records in the 1960s). Many of these records are collections of songs like the Glazer records mentioned above (prime examples are the albums by the Student Non-Violent Coordinating Committee's musical group The Freedom Singers), others are field recordings of the movement, collaging together songs sung while marching, speeches, discussions at meetings, and even audio of police attacking protestors. More than anything that had been produced before, these audio documentaries brought the listener into the nitty gritty of the movement. It's hard to imagine life before cell phones, or even television, but in the 1950s and even into the early 1960s, the living rooms of many working class homes were organized around a "hi-fi" system, with listening to records as a central social activity (the record player replacing the piano of earlier generations, just as it would ultimately be replaced by the tv). Civil Rights documentary LPs (such as *Movement Soul* on ESP-Disk) were evidence that social movements could document themselves, and use that documentation as agitprop, not academic anthropology.

How this concept of vinyl agitprop jumped from the Black Liberation Movement in the United States to striking workers in Denmark or France is not exactly clear. As you'll see, few of the strike records are actually from the US. I suspect the missing link here is, in part, the international working class struggles of 1968, especially in France. In early May, initially students, then upwards of half the working class, went out on strike, bringing the entire country to a standstill and the brink of revolution. France has a robust union culture, but these strikes were autonomous, and the main unions actually opposed them and played an important role in disciplining workers back onto the assembly lines and into the status quo. This is the beginning of mass, autonomous political action taken by groups of individuals outside of either state structures or traditional unions.

I've collected almost two dozen

records from or about the French 1968 revolt, and I expect someone with a deeper knowledge and better French could double that. As a whole, these records parallel the sonic culture created by the US Civil Rights Movement. They include songs sung on the barricades; field recordings of protests, meetings, and speeches; and a relatively new form—experimental songs constructed out of all of these pieces. Although we haven't included these May '68 records here (they really demand their own project and publication), they are a spectre that haunts these strike records. They bridge the relatively centralized and formal union and Civil Rights Movement records of the 1950s and early '60s with the much more autonomous and decentralized output of the 1970s and '80s.

Many of the records here are cultural heirs to '68, either in their sound or visual design, while others have much more straight through lines. For instance, the 1973 LIP factory occupation, which produced multiple records, comes directly out of the earlier upheaval. Over in Belgium, *POUR*, a magazine that was inspired and birthed by these new autonomous politics of '68, not only provided media coverage and solidarity with strikers in multiple workplaces, but helped produce at least three vinyl records with them. They did layout and design—as well as arranging printing—for the sleeves, and then promoted the records (as well as the strikes) within the pages of the magazine.

Whether there are direct material connections or not, inspiration is rarely a singular and clear path. What this publication does show is that militant workers got the message that they could articulate themselves without mediation, and by the late 1960s were pressing their own records. It turns out that throughout the second half of the 20th century it was not at all uncommon for organized workers and unions to produce records to support their strike actions. Well, that might be a bit of an exaggeration, but the over seventy records included here shows that this certainly was not a lark. Using recorded sound and music was clearly a defined tactic of struggle, one used by workers in at least a dozen countries, and likely even more that we haven't found examples from yet.

* * *

If producing a record is a tactic, and winning a strike is the goal, then what is the strategy? From studying these records, it's clear that the hopes for them are sometimes singular, other times multiple, often overlapping, and almost always clearly understood and articulated by the workers and unions.

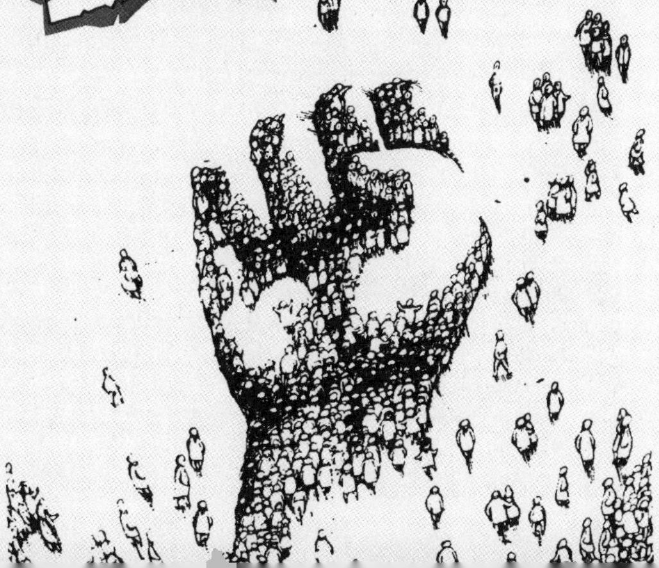

The records more often than not speak for themselves when you listen to them, but as most are quite hard to find, or in languages many of us don't speak, it's worth trying to lay out some of the intentions for the vinyl here.

There are two dominant reasons these records are produced: first, to raise public awareness of a strike, and second, to raise money to support the strike (and the strikers, who are by definition out of work and not being paid)—this latter reason is particularly acute for the wildcat strikes, where workers are not getting any support from an official union strike fund. That said, there are plethora of other intentions you can find for these records: to document a struggle after the fact, i.e., a "proof of existence"; to build capacity amongst the workers and their supporters—for example, learning how to work together, organizing and accomplishing increasingly complex projects, etc.; as an extension of this, to build confidence amongst workers by creating "permanent" documents of their struggle; to use as a tool to connect to other workers, often in different industries but facing similar macro economic pressures; and to reach audiences that might not read a pamphlet or a long-format political treatise, but are more than happy to pick up a record they might enjoy. A handful of records even come out of the practice of militant research, developed by the Facing Reality group in Detroit in the 1940s and '50s, then lifted up and expanded on by autonomous Marxists in Italy in the 1960s. The idea is simple: rather than prioritizing academic pursuits by outsiders, workers know their workplaces best, and can participate in the study of their own struggles, and learn from similar studies by workers in other struggles.

While the music and production of these records is surprisingly eclectic, there are some things most have in common. As we'll see, if workers' action produces a record, it is almost always a 7" single, either because the strike committee doesn't have the resources to produce something of a larger scope, or simply because most strikes don't last long enough to collect material to fill a full LP. The length of a 7″ single is roughly a third of an LP, and its packaging half the size and a fraction of the cost, and thus demands fewer resources to produce. In the pop music market, many singles were released in blank white sleeves, or with "company" sleeves that advertised the record label rather than the specific release. You'll find few of these here. Even if the format was small in stature, it was taken full advantage of. Almost all strike records came in picture sleeves, and many in gatefold sleeves—a double wide cover folded in half, giving the workers/union/solidarity committee twice the space to share information about the strike. In addition, it was not uncommon for the records to have additional information slotted into the sleeves: lyric sheets for sing-alongs, petitions to sign, even some oversized posters which could be hung up in apartments, or brought out to a picket line. These documents are likely as illustrative of a particular struggle as any union newspaper or pamphlet, and sadly haven't been given their due importance in research on worker organization. That said, this publication is at best a cursory overview of the field, a road-map to where we might look and dig deeper in the future.

I'm interested in the use of vinyl records as a form of agitprop—as can be exhaustively seen in my previously produced *An Encyclopedia of Political Record Labels*. The effects of my fetish for vinyl shouldn't be understated. Beginning in the late 1970s, and gaining serious steam by mid-1980s, the cassette became a much cheaper and more versatile tool for political organizing. If we had included cassettes and CDs here, the size of this book might have doubled, at least. Both formats are much easier to produce than vinyl, and much cheaper, especially in smaller runs. There are likely many, many homemade cassettes created by workers' strike committees that weren't distributed beyond the picket line. I've been able to find a half dozen without really spending much time looking. But what little research I've done has made it

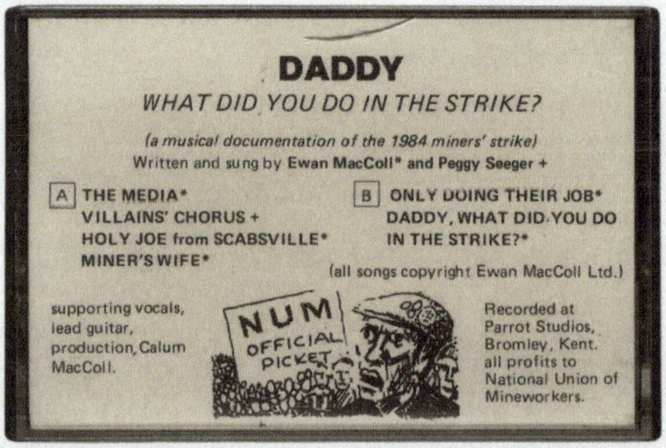

clear that a focus on cassettes and CDs is really another project altogether, and I stand by the decision to use vinyl as a curatorial tool here. Ideally someone else will pick up the thread and follow up with a deep dive into worker-produced cassettes and CDs. But for me, and in this book, the vinyl record functions as both a marker of financial investment and a commitment to mass distribution.

* * *

Co-editor Kennedy Block and I propose there are several ways to read this book. To look at any particular entry drops you into a specific strike, more than likely a fight that has been forgotten, at least by those who weren't active participants. Like the records themselves, the entries are modest time capsules, historical markers of punctuated class struggle. But when taken together, they tell a larger story, one of an arc of global conflict, of the gains of workers in the 1960s and '70s, and the re-entrenchment of capital in the '80s. We see fights for wages, shorter hours, and even worker ownership and control eclipsed by increasingly immiserated demands for factories not to shutter and pits not to close. It's a little brutal to listen to—in recorded real time—utopia slide into desperation, to see how neoliberalism stomped on the neck of hope for meaningful and fulfilling work, replacing it with a panicked need of workers to keep a roof over their heads.

It is likely no coincidence that the tectonic shifts towards neo-liberalism in workers' perceptions of what their struggles could accomplish appear to run parallel to another big shift, this one sonic. The earliest records you'll find in this book tend towards sounding like direct decendents of old left workers' choruses with their martial songs and anthems (a couple even include a version of "l'Internationale"). Over the course of the 1970s we see a shift towards the inclusion of more pop idioms into the music, first in the form of folk, and then rock, reggae, and finally hip-hop (or at least pop rap). While on the surface this may seem a natural progression, it exposes a much deeper and more complex process at work. While the labor music of the 19th and early 20th century might not be the most exciting to our contemporary ears, it developed out of generations of working class organization, both in the workplace but also the community. Songs such as "l'Internationale" and "The Red Flag" weren't just sung on picket lines, but in union halls, at pubs, worker's funerals, and solidarity marches. As there was little class mobility in the world, children would learn the songs from their parents, and in turn pass them down to their kids. So the shift towards pop music (primarily

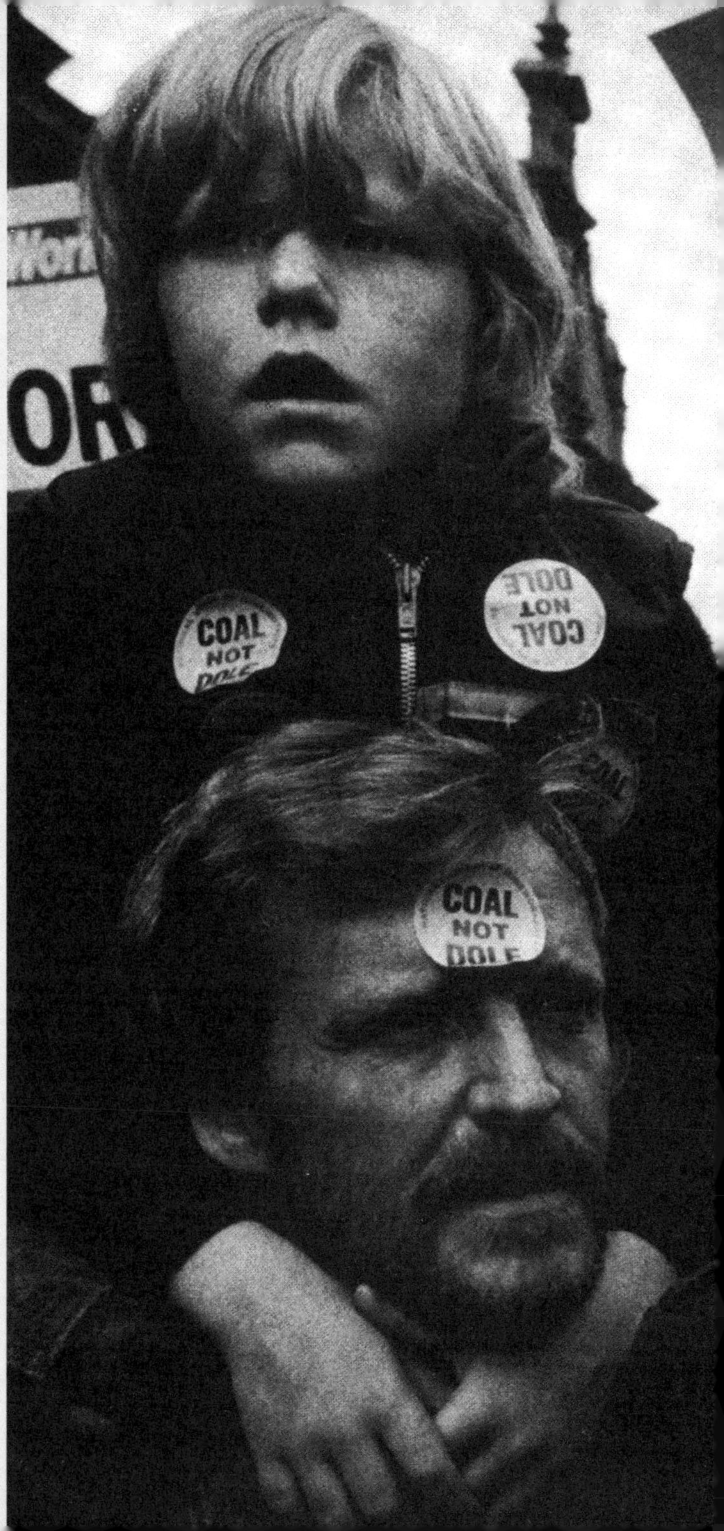

Anglophone pop) was not simply a stylistic one, but a shift in relationship to the songs themselves. Labor songs are a social form, to be performed and listened to in a community context. Pop music is a commodity, to be sold to individuals, who develop personal relationships to the music. This is likely why some of the later records come off as strange, or even worse, completely corny. The records fail musically, as well as fail to give voice to any sense of a coherent working class. And this was one of the projects of neoliberalism, the biopolitical replacement of any sense of collective working class identity with the atomized consciousness of individual consumers.

We're not labor historians, but hope something can be learned from the stories these records tell us. The last fifteen years have seen a huge upswing in militant labor organizing in the United States, from the Republic Windows and Doors occupation in Chicago in 2008 to the huge gains made by domestic workers across the country (such as the rise of Domestic Workers United and their successful fight to pass a New York State Domestic Workers Bill of Rights in 2010), to the increasingly successful campaigns to organize workplaces like Starbucks (Starbucks Workers United) and Amazon (Amazon Labor Union, affiliated with the Teamsters). Music and audio documentation haven't been a memorable part of these struggles so far, but in the social media-dominated attention economy we live in, it doesn't take much to imagine how music could play a larger role in publicizing worker action and encouraging broad support. But even if we set aside these larger promotional concerns for a moment, the records in this book exude the sheer joy of workers singing and marching together, fusing solidarity, and taking their lives into their own hands.

* * *

As is always the case, it feels strange to create a printed publication about music and culture that primarily takes the form of sound. Seeing (and/or reading) and hearing are very different activities. Sadly the vast majority of the records included here are difficult to find, if not nearly impossible, especially within the US. To work around this, we selected the most interesting and exciting tracks and crafted a mixtape! Search the Common Notions website (commonnotions.org) for *Strike While the Needle is Hot* to find a link. To listen to the records in full, your best bet is to search through YouTube. Happy hunting!

OH M.E. WAT DOE JE NOU?
Tekst en Muziek:
E. v.d. Horst
(45 BOV 2185)
45 rpm
RCS
1096
STEREO
STEMRA
BERTUS EN DE POSTERS
Produktie: Red Air
Opname: Rema-Bearcat
Studio's Rotterdam
MADE IN HOLLAND

3:38
GENERAL STRIKE
(J. KEIGHLEY)
THIS SIDE:
*Prisoner Publishing ©1983
SD004
D.O.A.
45 RPM STEREO

Streik bei Mannesmann
Szenische Kantate
GEMA
Langspielplatte
Stereo
Nr. S 30 E 100
pläne
LC 0972
A
Text: Erika Runge
Musik: Dietrich Boeckle
Hans Werner Henze
Niels Frederic Hoffmann
Thomas Jahn
Luca Lombardi
Wilfried Steinbrenner
Ausführende: Ensemble Hinz & Kunst

BUDKAVLEN
STREJK
Oktoberförlaget
SIDA A
33 VPM
STEREO
1. LUMP-LENAVALSEN
2. APRILVISA
3. MURARHANTLANGERSKORNAS STREJK
4. KRAVALLVISA FRÅN MÖLNDAL
5. MALMÖ VISA
6. RENHÅLLNINGSSTREJKEN
7. STUDENTKONSERTEN I STOCKHOLM
8. NY STUDENTSÅNG

FORD WORKERS SAY
£20 ON THE PAY
1hr OFF THE DAY
NO STRINGS
S/78/CUS
182 A

DIG THIS
Side 1
Poisongirls Cry
Poisongirls Voodoo Pappadollar
Mekons Flitcraft
Mekons Trouble Down South
Men They Couldn't Hang Jack Dandy
Men They Couldn't Hang Rawhide
FORWARD SOUNDS INTERNATIONAL

Womble 1
WAKE UP
Side One
The Redskins — Levi Stubbs' Tears
(Billy Bragg) Chappell Music
Billy Bragg — A Change Is Gonna Come
(Sam Cook) Abkco Music
The Neurotics — This Fragile Life
(Steve Drewett) Logo Songs
Side Two
Attila The Stockbroker — 40 Years
(Attila) Copyright Control
Kevin Seisay — All Smiles
(Kevin Seisay) Bewserp Music '86
Billy, Wiggy,
Neurotics & Attila —
Garageland
(Strummer/Jones)
Nineden Ltd

The GRIMETHORPE COLLIERY BRASS BAND with 7:84 THEATRE COMPANY ENGLAND
& G.C.H.Q. Trade Unions
7:84
John Tams
RAISE your BANNERS HIGH
TUC 784 A

MAI:
Side A
MAI 7701
(P) 1977
Streik!
1. Bergmannsvise (2:37) (russisk trad/Ellisif Wessel). 2. Hustadsangen (4:30) (T. Henriksen/G. Valderøy og T. Henriksen). 3. Judasmerket (1:34) (S. Fiskvik/anonym). 4. Vi husker Menstadslaget (1:50) (Ragnar Olsen). 5. Streikebryter Granerud (2:10) (T. Thorsen/J. Schwarz). 6. Tor i korridor (2:45) (A. Preus). 7. En sørgelig vise (2:25) (Klevstrand/R. Nilsen)

CSC
LIEGE
outien
AUX
AVAILLEURS
LIP
CFDT LIP
CGT LIP
CA LIP
NON AUX LICENC
NON AU DEMAN
disques

EMENTS
ELEMENT

Discography

EXIGENT DES
ET NON DES

ECONOMIE
REGIONALE

INSTITUT COOPÉRATIF DE L'ÉCOLE MODERNE
(Pédagogie FREINET)

I.C.E.M.

DOCUMENTS SONORES de la BT bibliothèque de travail

n° 5 LUTTES OUVRIÈRES AVANT 1914

FACE I • A Saint-Claude, Henri SERENO, ouvrier pipier, raconte...
Le travail, l'apprentissage, les grèves de 1906, le militant syndicaliste et la guerre de 1914.

FACE II • A Carmaux, du temps de Jean Jaurès, Rémy TERROUX évoque...
Les conditions de travail et de vie des mineurs, la "politique".
Il chante une chanson, émouvant témoignage des grèves de 1900.

(Photo Musée Jaurès - Jack-Photo)

Henri Séréno/Remy Terroux
<u>**Luttes Ouvrières Avant 1914**</u>
7" EP
I.C.E.M. Pedagogie Freinet (DSBT 5)
1972
France

One of around two dozen field recording records put out by the Cooperative Institute of the Modern School and Secular Education Cooperative (ICEM-CEL), which grew out of the international Modern School Movement and the theories of radical educator Célestin Freinet. A sound archive, this record includes interviews of two French laborers involved in workers' struggle prior to 1914. Side A is a recording with Henri Sereno, a pipe worker in Saint-Claude who discusses working conditions and the strikes he participated in in 1906. Side B is a recording with Rémy Terroux, who talks about the working and living conditions of miners, how they organized, and then sings a song that emerged from the miners' strikes in 1900. Although this record wasn't produced until the early seventies, it might be the only extant recordings of songs from the turn-of-century French labor movement, especially sung by participants!

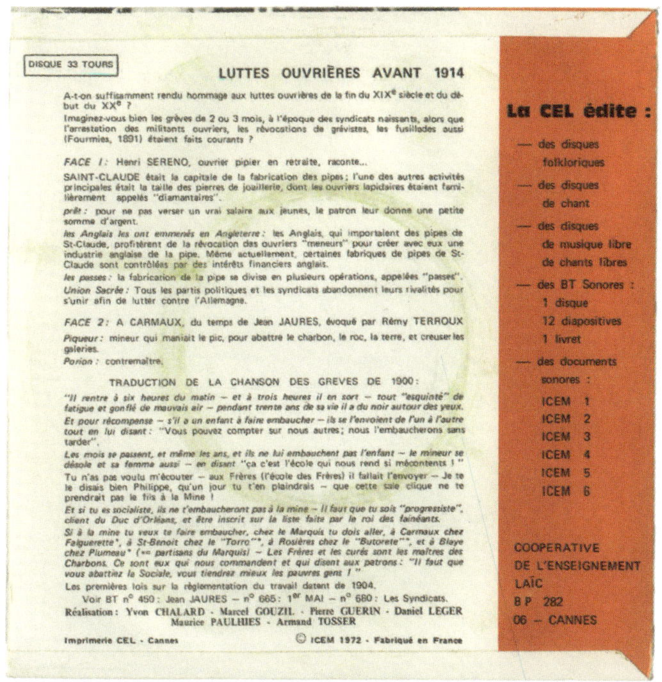

Chorale des Ouvriers de Trieux

<u>Trieux 1963: 79 jours de grève au fond de la mine</u>

7" single

Fédération régionale des Mineurs de CGT

1963

France

An early use of the vinyl record to support and document a labor strike. Miners in Trieux, in the northeast corner of France, occupied the mine they worked in for 79 days in protest of 258 workers being sacked and as part of the struggle to stop the mine's closure. The strike was quite popular, and François Corra, a member of the Communist Party of France and one of the leaders of the strike, was elected mayor of the town in 1965. The record contains two songs: on the A-side is an original composition in homage to the union—"La Chant de la Corporation," which the sleeve states was "composed at the bottom on the mine by Trieux workers on strike"—while the flipside is a rendition of "l'Internationale." Both are sung by the mine's workers' choir. Produced by and for the miners, a small box on the back of the sleeve states:

This disc can only be used in general assemblies or meetings, it is not for the general public.

TRIEUX 1963 :

79 jours de grève au fond de la mine

SAINTE - BARBE 1963 :

Le salut de la Corporation aux mineurs de Trieux, par A. Balducci

★———

LE CHANT DE LA CORPORATION

par la Chorale des Ouvriers de Trieux

★———

Fédération régionale des Mineurs de Fer C.G.T.

L'INTERNATIONALE

MONAURAL
TR00001
VIVA LA CAUSA!
SONGS AND SOUNDS FROM THE DELANO STRIKE
POR LOS HUELGUISTAS DE DELANO Y EL TEATRO CAMPESINO
NFWA
THUNDERBIRD RECORDS

El Teatro Campesino
Viva la Causa!
LP
Thunderbird (TR-00001)
1966
United States

Subtitled "Songs and Sounds from the Delano Strike," this record is just that, a collection of ten studio-recorded strike songs by the UFW's cultural group El Teatro Campesino on one side, and then a series of field recordings from the actual picket lines on the flip. The record itself is also an important historical document in the history of farmworker organizing. The Delano, California, grape strike was initiated in 1965 by the Agricultural Workers Organizing Committee, a largely Filipino union, but soon after they were joined by the National Farmworkers Association, a union made of mostly Mexican American laborers. At the end of the summer of 1966, the two unions merged, and became the United Farm Workers. This record is likely one of the first public-facing cultural productions of the new union. This is also true of El Teatro Campesino, which had been founded in 1965, and was based in Delano, and thus evolved parallel to the strike itself.

The record is a great tool to teach farmworkers—and those who want to act in solidarity with them—the songs of the nascent union, and in addition it also transports the listener onto the frontlines of the strike, documenting the struggle as it occurred. This is similar in character to a number of the early recordings documenting the US Civil Rights Movement.

Fausto Amodei
"Sciopero interno" b/w "Nei reparti della FIAT"
7" single
I Dischi del Sole (DS 210)
1969
Italy

An interesting record, these songs, written and performed by Italian militant and folk musician Fausto Amodei, are an explanation—in musical form—of the tactics of striking workers at the FIAT engine-building factory in Turin. The tactic of the *sciopero interno*, or internal strike, is described in detail:

We have found a method of action / to better harass the boss / the fastest and newest system / which is called the internal strike.

The B-side, "The departments of FIAT," is a detailed list of complaints about working conditions within the factory, clearly crafted out of extensive conversation with workers about their experiences on the production line. Not recorded at the behest of a union, but clearly born out of the experience of FIAT workers, the record functions both as a product of what Italian autonomists called "worker's inquiry" and as a pedagogical tool to share with other workers evolving strike tactics to stay ahead of the factory managers. In fact, this is a vinyl version of a long musical tradition in Italy, of traveling militant musicians who would move from one factory to the next, one field or vineyard to another, talking to workers, learning about their struggles and organizing, and using those conversations and experiences as the basis of songs to be sung to more workers moving forward—like itinerant griots aligned with the working class.

SCIOPERO
Due canzoni sindacali di Fausto Amodei per l'autunno caldo.
INTERNO
i dischi del sole
DS 210

Internal Strike

We found it
a method of action
to better annoy the boss
it is the quickest and most modern
system called the internal strike.
Internal strike
from inside the workshop
we lose little
and Agnelli goes to ruin
if we go on strike inside the gates
the one who loses is above all Agnelli.
As long as we are
two hundred strikers
throughout FIAT
it can no longer go on
a few people lose their pay
but everyone else produces nothing.
Internal strike
we drop the yield
and we lower
the piece rate down to 100
with the disruption of production
we will be able to beat the boss.
Internal strike
it means that essentially
today I fight
and not that I'm on holiday
but that I meet my comrades with the aim
of improving the fight the next day.
Internal strike
let's have an assembly
our leaders
they gets diarrhea
when seeing that without asking permission
we are already in charge in the factory.
Internal strike
we also march
our leaders
they stand there like fools
seeing that inside these walls
we are no longer afraid.
Come on comrades
let's strike internally
there is no devil
and there is no god almighty
that can hold us back
from moving forward and taking power.

In the Departments of FIAT

If you work in the deburring department
located at FIAT Grandi Motori
you only breathe rubbish
because there are no aspirators.
Jackhammers make a lot of noise
there is a lot of smoke which is the most disgusting
you can't see a few steps away
and you get a nice silicosis.
But Mr. Primus, a model doctor
he doesn't see that smoke he doesn't hear the hammer
if he does the statistics on your lungs then
afterwards he only shows them to the owners.
If you work in the Large Press department
you can't even find a substitute
certain reasons are not permitted
not even to take a minute break.
Who needs to go relieve themselves
he wets himself so everything is fine
and if then, let's just say he's ashamed
he can't do anything about it and must hold it.
And the chief engineer, who gets paid
fourteen lire per hour more
for that little money he feels obliged
to make you hold your pee and poo.
In the honing department
there is enough water to gargle with
if this water clears the air
on the other hand it causes rheumatism.
In a year you lose seven kilos
and you put in a lot of effort
the virile organs become weak
and the wife remains empty handed.
The doctors in white coats tell you:
"With all the car bodies you've already honed
it's clear that when you get home you're too tired
to make out again in private."
Okay, jokes aside, the problem remains
that these stories are all very true
but to gain workers' control
we fight in the factories and inside the neighborhood.

i dischi del sole
DS 210

SCIOPERO INTERNO

Due canzoni sindacali di Fausto Amodei per l'autunno caldo.

Sciopero interno

Abbiam trovato
un metodo d'azione
per romper meglio
le scatole al padrone
è il sistema più rapido e moderno
e che si chiama lo sciopero interno.
Sciopero interno
da dentro l'officina
noi perdiam poco
e Agnelli va in rovina
se si sta a scioperar dentro i cancelli
chi ci rimette è soprattutto Agnelli.
Basta che siamo
duecento scioperanti
tutta la FIAT
non può più andare avanti
ci rimette la paga poca gente
ma tutti gli altri non producon niente.
Sciopero interno
caliamo il rendimento
ed abbassiamo
il cottimo giù a cento
chè con lo scasso della produzione
noi riusciremo a battere il padrone.
Sciopero interno
vuol dire che in sostanza
oggi io lotto
e non che sto in vacanza
ma che incontro i compagni collo scopo
di migliorare la lotta il giorno dopo.
Sciopero interno
facciamo l'assemblea
ai nostri capi
gli viene la diarrea
nel veder che senza chieder permesso
noi comandiamo in fabbrica già adesso.
Sciopero interno
facciamo anche i cortei
i nostri capi
stan lì come babbei
nel vedere che dentro queste mura
noi altri non abbiamo più paura.
Forza compagni
facciam sciopero interno
non c'è demonio — e non c'é padreterno
che ci possa oramai più trattenere —
d'andare avanti e prendere il potere.

Nei reparti della FIAT

Se lavori al reparto sbavatura
che si trova alla FIAT Grandi Motori
tu respiri soltano spazzatura
perché mancano fin gli aspiratori.

I martelli pneumatici fan chiasso
c'è un gran fumo che è dei più schifosi
non si vede lontano qualche passo
e ti becchi una bella silicosi.

Però il signor Primus, dottore modello
non vede quel fumo non sente il martello
se fa le statistiche ai vostri polmoni
poi dopo le mostra soltanto ai padroni.

Se lavori al reparto Grandi Presse
non ci trovi neppure un sostituto
certe cause per lì non sono ammesse
che ti fanno assentar per un minuto.

Chi ha bisogno di fare i suoi bisogni
li fa addosso così va tutto bene
e se poi, putacaso si vergogni
non può farci un bel niente e se li tiene.

E il capo-macchina, che vien pagato
quattordici lire all'ora di più
per quei pochi soldi si sente obbligato
a farti tener la pipì e la pupù.

Al reparto per la pomiciatura
c'è tanta acqua da farci i gargarismi
se quest'acqua ti rende l'aria pura
d'altro canto procura i reumatismi.

In un anno perdete sette chili
ed avete un bel mettercela tutta
si fan deboli gli organi virili
e la moglie vi resta a bocca asciutta.

Vi dicono i medici in camice bianco:
« Con tutte le scocche che hai già pomiciato
« è chiaro che a casa poi sei troppo stanco
« per ripomiciare di nuovo in privato ».

Va be' scherzi a parte però resta il guaio
che queste storielle son tutte ben vere
ma per conquistare il controllo operaio
lottiam nelle fabbriche e dentro il quartiere.

prodotto dalle Edizioni del Gallo s.p.a.
20133 milano - via sansovino 13 - tel. 228192

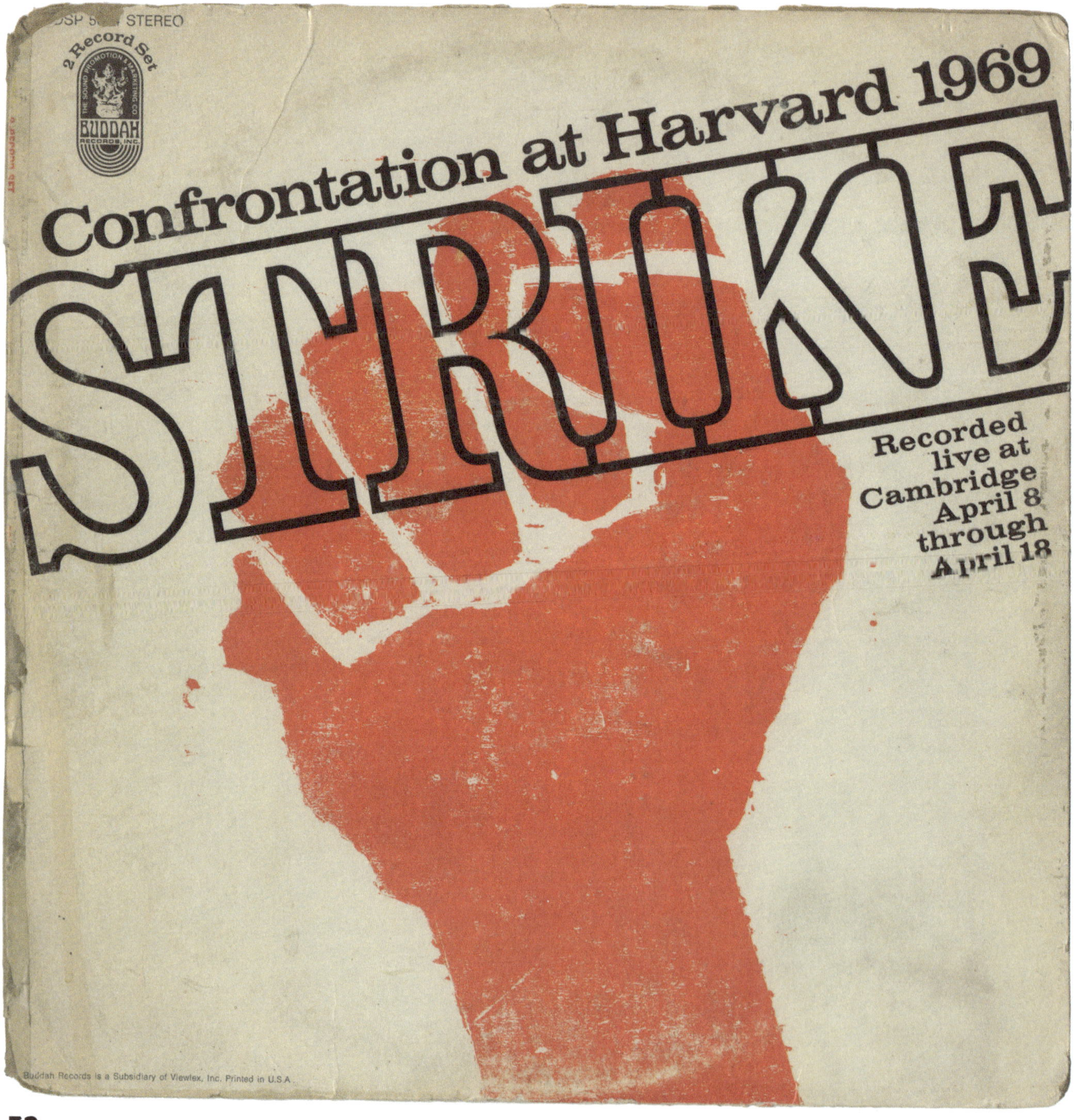
STEREO
2 Record Set
BUDDAH
RECORDS, INC.
Confrontation at Harvard 1969
STRIKE
Recorded live at Cambridge April 8 through April 18
Buddah Records is a Subsidiary of Viewlex, Inc. Printed in U.S.A.

Charles Osgood

<u>Confrontation at Harvard 1969: Strike</u>

2xLP

Buddah Records (BDSP 5044)

1969

United States

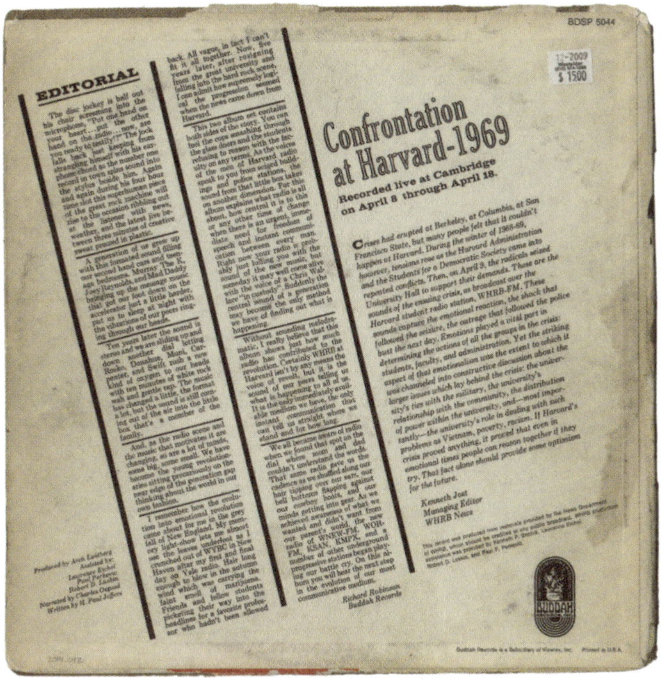

This two record set collects Charles Osgood's reportage on the 1969 Harvard University student strike, which he broadcast over WHRB (the Harvard radio station) from April 8-18, 1969. At the time Osgood was a rising tv and radio personality, regularly appearing on CBS News. The Harvard strike, organized in large part by the Students for a Democratic Society, or SDS, was one of the first major student strikes in the US, and not surprisingly followed within a year of the events in France in May 1968. The Harvard strike also preceded—by almost exactly a year—the nationwide student strikes of 1970, which started on May 1st in opposition to the US bombing of Cambodia (and thus expansion of the Vietnam War), then grew considerably after the National Guard killed students at Kent State, eventually evolving to include almost 900 campuses around the US. It was likely the largest strike in US history. Strangely, this much larger and broader strike did not generate any documentation via the vinyl record.

The Harvard records themselves are fairly traditional "news documentation," with reportage, interviews, and some field recordings merged together into a single document. Osgood is only 36 at the time of the recording, but sounds a world apart from the students, his clipped radio voice striking a hard contrast with the informal and meandering speech of the strikers. The whole thing makes for a fascinating capture of a moment of struggle, even if it's a tough listen at times.

Tony Hale & Roger Perks
"A Lament for a Lost Soul" b/w "A Plea for Public Support"
7" single
National Union of Teachers (TET 135)
1970
Great Britain

The National Union of Teachers (NUT) was the largest teacher's union in England and Wales (until it merged with the Association of Teachers and Lecturers in 2017 to form the National Education Union). This record contains a couple jazzy pop numbers which feature explicit calls for support for teachers. The lyrics are mostly a collection of anecdotes and complaints from teachers—narratives of being both disrespected and underpaid—and outside of its original context it only becomes clear this is a strike record when halfway through the B-side there's a lyric that states, "Please support your local teachers / we didn't go out on strike for fun." With no picture sleeve to provide additional context, it's hard to pinpoint exactly where this record is coming from. We do know that on February 18, 1970, almost 5,000 teachers in Birmingham went out on strike at over 450 area schools, so this record is most likely connected to that struggle in some way. Teacher militancy in the UK continued throughout the 1980s, with regional strikes occurring consistently, often in demand for relatively modest pay raises.

ALL RIGHTS OF THE MANUFACTURER AND OF THE OWNER OF THE RECORDED WORK RESERVED · UNAUTHORISED PUBLIC PERFORMANCE BROADCASTING AND COPYING OF THIS RECORD PROHIBITED
PRODUCED
FOR THE NATIONAL
UNION OF TEACHERS
TET 135
Side B
℗ 1970
A PLEA FOR PUBLIC SUPPORT
(Perks, Hale)
TONY HALE & ROGER PERKS

Typografer på Politiken
<u>Strejken på Politiken</u>
7" single
Demos (Dem 11)
1972
Denmark

On December 1st, 1972, 120 typographers at the newspaper *Politiken*—a Danish left-liberal newspaper which also published Ekstrabladet, the largest daily paper in the country—went on strike. The decision to strike came after months of negotiations and the firing of 17 typographers. *Politiken* refused to negotiate, and locked out the remaining 320 typographers and many of the paper's other workers. The strike ended when the company reinstated two of the fired typographers. The record features two songs with lyrics about the strike co-written by workers and Benny Holst (a politically committed folk singer and organizer of the leftist musical collective Agitpop) and performed by folk rock/country band Hvalsø-spillemændene. Much of the record focuses on how the newspaper presents itself to the outside world as a beacon of democracy and progressive values, but inside treats its workers as poorly as any capitalist firm.

The typographers were part of Dansk Typograf-Forbund (Danish Typographial Union), which in turn was part of the Graphic Workers' Cartel organized under the Danish Confederation of Trade Unions. The record also states that all proceeds from its sale will be given to the strike fund of women locked out of their jobs painting porcelain plates at the Den kgl. Porcelainsfabrik (who recorded their own record of strike songs in 1976, see page 98).

Strejken på
POLITIKEN

De strejkende typografer på Politiken har ønsket at Demos sender overskuddet ved salget af denne plade til de lock-outede porcelænsmalere på Den kgl. Porcelainsfabrik i Valby. Lock-outen startede d. 27. november fordi firmaet brød en indgået aftale med de damer, der maler juleplatter, om ekstra betaling for maling af dårlige juleplatter. Ved denne plades produktionsafslutning løb lock-outen stadigvæk. Bl. a. pågrund af LOs sendrægtighed er der udsigt til en lang konflikt.

Alting starter med vor solidaritet

Højt på hjørnet maner flaget
kamp for ret og menneskeværd
men derinde bag facaden
tæller kun profitbegær

Hør kultur og frisind skræppe
fra det gamle fuglebur
men spektaklet skjuler bare
kapitalens diktatur

Smukke ord fra maskemunde
taler sødt om sympati
bag ved masken: hårde kæbers
arbejdsgivertyrrani

Hvis vi ikke mer vil springe
rundt i deres rotteræs
kastes masken og de viser
klassefjendens gamle fjæs

De som leder og fordeler
gør det kun sålænge nogen
lar sig dele og forlede
til at opretholde roen

OMKVÆD:
Direktør og aktionærer
ligger nu som de har redt
kammerater, alting starter
med vor solidaritet

Mel.: Oh, My Darling Clementine.

POLITIKEN - en levende avis

På pladsen ved rådhuset ligger et hus
af mange beundret næsegrus
udadtil en avis om demokrati
indadtil en politik uden mening i
man sender arbejdet ud mens folkene fyres
kan det være sådan et blad det skal styres
vi har svært ved at se logikken
derfor strejker vi på Politiken.

I ledelsen indrømmes ikke fejl
deres motto må være stå fast vær stejl
indtil nu har de fyret sytten
men her kommer vi ind og vender bøtten
hvis du ikke vil være den næste i rækken
så hold ud kammerat vi må fortsætte strejken
du er til salg for en slik i butikken
støt strejken på Politiken.

Vi har sat artikler om uret og nød
kronikker om kampen for dagligt brød
annoncer for huse og heste og biler
miss Danmark der viser sin røv mens hun smiler
nu sætter vi dem stolen for døren
fra faktoren og til direktøren
vi kan se de er grebet af panikken
over strejken på Politiken.

De har rakt hånden ud de kan ta to mand tilbage
til gengæld skal vi så tage to mand af dage
det kan lyde som en gåde
men det skal selvfølgelig forstås på denne måde
at de får penge for at stå af
så ledelsen får det antal de vil ha
det ku være kønt, kan du se komikken
vi sku sælge os selv til Politiken.

Ordet er frit hvis du kan betale
trykpresse, folk, papir og lokale
bladhuse drives som andre butikker
her handles med ord sat op i rubrikker
frisind på tryk over disken
men herinde svinger de pisken
nu vil vi dirigere musikken
derfor strejker vi på Politiken.

Sytten er fyret siden september
strejken begyndte først i december
protester og forslag er fejet af bordet
nu er det slut med at be om ordet
nu må vi tale et sprog de forstår
bestyrelsen høster som ledelsen sår
vi sætter handling bag kritikken
når vi strejker på Politiken.

Den 1. december 1972 gik 120 håndsættere på A/S Dagbladet Politiken, som også udgiver Danmarks største dagblad Ekstrabladet, i strejke.

Strejkens forhistorie er lang og typisk. Efter en periode med forhandlinger i forbindelse med rationaliseringsbestræbelser fyrede huset efterhånden 15 mand under arbejdernes protester. Til trods for typografernes samarbejdsbestræbelser og til trods for, at sætteriet var så underbemandet, at man måtte sende arbejde ud i byen, fyrede man yderligere 2 mand på et helt usagligt grundlag, og en enstemmig strejkebeslutning var en kendsgerning. Firmaet afviste enhver forhandling om genantagelse af de to og svarede med at lockoute 320 typografer og et antal arbejdere i pakkeriet og indklagede de strejkende for arbejdsretten. Samtidig meddelte man, at man under ingen omstændigheder ville bøje sig for typografernes krav. Efter at konflikten havde løbet en uges tid, fremsatte man under stor publicity et tilbud om en slags menneskehandel: to ældre håndsættere skulle overtales til at fratræde mod et kontant vederlag, hvorefter man ville genansætte de to fyrede. Forslaget blev selvfølgelig afvist, også fordi sætteriet efter dette forslag stadig ville være underbemandet.

Efter 12 dages strejke hvorunder sympatitilkendegivelser og kontant hjælp strømmede ind til de strejkende, blev konflikten afsluttet med at de to fyrede blev genantaget. Nogle dage efter at arbejdet var blevet genoptaget idømte Arbejdsretten typograferne en bod på 30.000 kr.

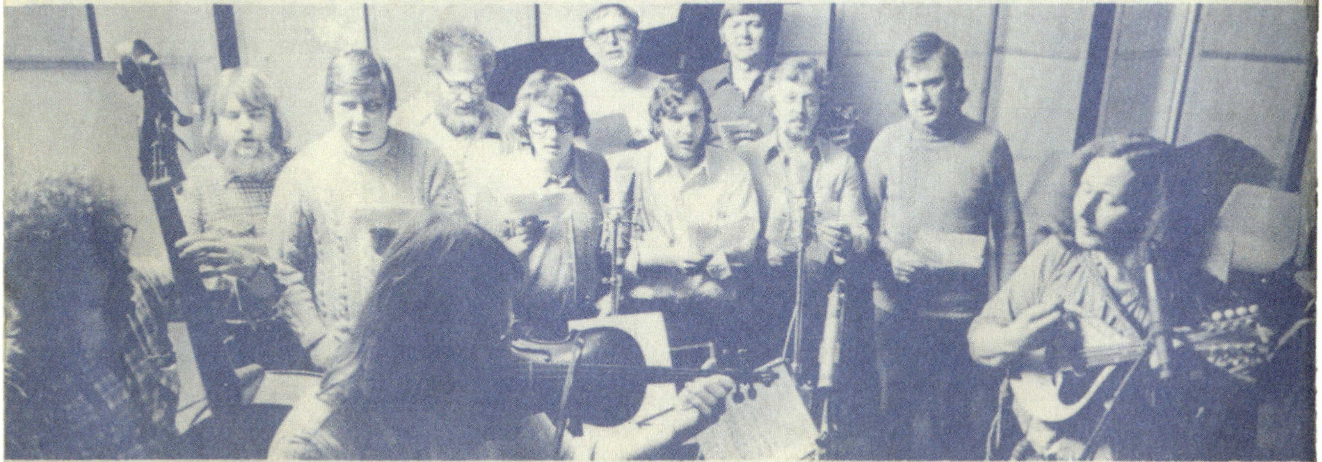

Musik: Benny Holst. Tekst: Typografer på Politiken og Benny Holst, Jesper Jensen og Per Schultz. Arrangement: Hvalsø Spillemændene. Sang: Typografer på Politiken. Musikere: Tom McEwan (trommer) og Hvalsø Spillemændene: Søren Berggreen (violin & piano), Jesper Hindø (bas), Steen Rasmussen (mandolin), Anders Roland (violin & guitar & mandolin). Lydteknik: Freddy Hansson. Lydstudie: Rosenberg. Pres: EMI. Omslag: Anne Rohweder. Fotos: Gregers Nielsen og Leni Schou. Tryk: Eksskolen. Produktion: Niels Frølich/Karsten Sommer.

Indspillet 17.12.1972. Vi siger tak til Ivar Rosenberg, Freddy Hansson (lydteknik), Nikolaj Steenstrup (lydass.), Eksskolen og EMI for hurtig hjælp da det gjaldt.

Demos Pris: 10 kr. Stereo 45 omdr. Demos 11

Socialistisk forlag og boghandel, Grønnegade 37, 1107 K. tlf. (01)14 15 37.

Various artists
Lakkokevät
LP
Eteenpäin (ETLP-310)
1972
Finland

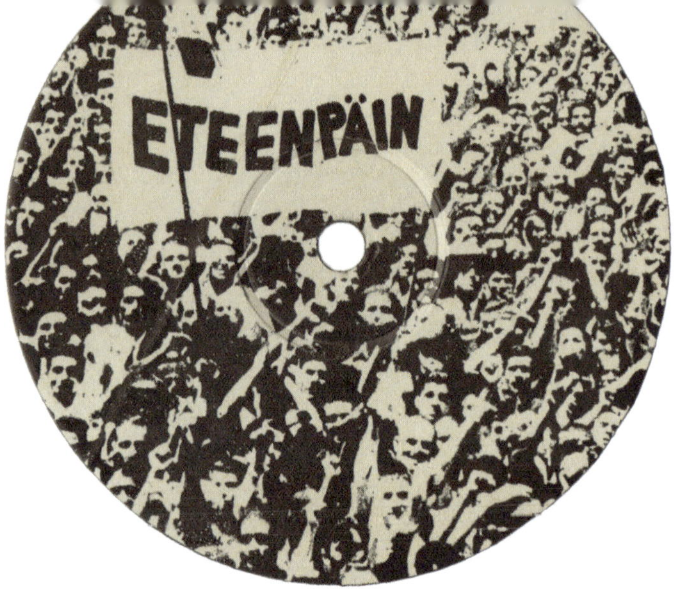

Lakkokevät roughly translates to "Strike Spring," here referencing an upheaval of labor militancy in Finland in the spring of 1971, the level of strike action approaching a general strike (which had been held in Finland in 1956). The record is an audio archive of the movement, with each track—whether it be an interview with a family in a working class home, a field recording of a picket line, or a song by the left-wing folk group Agit Prop—featuring the date and event it was recorded at. The recordings document roughly a month of activity, from early February through mid-March.

While the recordings here are very specific to their moment, more so than many of the records here, all of the framing materials included discuss the broader political and economic context of the strikes. From disappointment with the left-wing government elected in 1966, the devaluation of Finnish currency in 1967, and the increased push for Finland to join both NATO and the EEC (the European Economic Community, a forerunner of the European Union and European Common Market), the liner notes to the album clearly line out the broader framework for the actions documented on the record itself.

This makes sense given the label the record is on, Eteepäin! [Forward!], a far left political project similar in some ways to Demos, the Danish label that produced the typographers strike record on the pages 36-39. Eteepäin! was a sub-label of Love Records, one of the most influential Finnish independent labels, and was the imprint used to produce explicitly political and movement oriented records. While Love wasn't aligned with specific political parties, it is clear that they worked with left-wing and anti-imperilaist organizers to develop the Eteepäin! catalog (Love also had a sub-label called Cuba, dedicated to releases by Cuban musicians).

ÄNESTÄMME
EI
LAKKOKEVÄT

OXYGENOL
Kuusinen
onnenvuosi 71
TAISTELEEN
VOITTOON

Jaffina
TUKEKAA METALLIN TYÖLÄISIÄ
HINNAT KU-
RIIN—PALKKO-
JEN KOROTUS
REAALISENA!
TYÖPAIKOILLE
LÄHDETKÖ
PENNILLÄ
TÖIHIN?

The Hennessys
Who Will Cast a Stone? Songs for the Miners' Strike 1972
7" single
Sain (SAIN 22)
1972
Wales

The UK miners' strike of 1972 was a successful two month long battle over pay that had the National Union of Mineworkers (NUM) face off against the conservative government of Edward Heath. This record was put out on the Welsh folk-revival label Sain in support of the Welsh miners who took part in the strike. The Hennessys were a group of Celtic musicians from Wales who had relocated to Ireland: "'We have always,' they maintain, 'been conscious of the great financial aid given by the miners of Wales to the Irish Transport and General Workers when their Union was threatened by their employers in 1913. We hope that in making this record we can in some small way repay the miners for their support and generosity at that time.'" All proceeds went to the NUM strike fund. Half the songs are historical tales—one about the "Halfpenny Strike" of 1910 and another about the "Gresford Disaster" of 1934 where 265 miners died in an underground explosion and fire—drawing a through line from past miners' struggles across the UK.

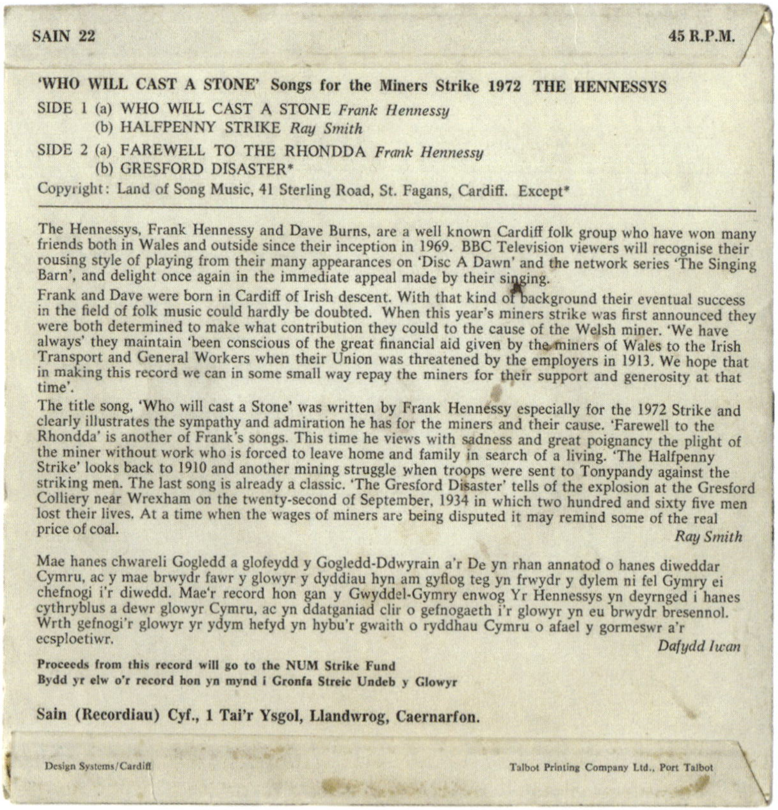
SAIN 22 45 R.P.M.

'WHO WILL CAST A STONE' Songs for the Miners Strike 1972 THE HENNESSYS

SIDE 1 (a) WHO WILL CAST A STONE *Frank Hennessy*
(b) HALFPENNY STRIKE *Ray Smith*

SIDE 2 (a) FAREWELL TO THE RHONDDA *Frank Hennessy*
(b) GRESFORD DISASTER*

Copyright: Land of Song Music, 41 Sterling Road, St. Fagans, Cardiff. Except*

The Hennessys, Frank Hennessy and Dave Burns, are a well known Cardiff folk group who have won many friends both in Wales and outside since their inception in 1969. BBC Television viewers will recognise their rousing style of playing from their many appearances on 'Disc A Dawn' and the network series 'The Singing Barn', and delight once again in the immediate appeal made by their singing.

Frank and Dave were born in Cardiff of Irish descent. With that kind of background their eventual success in the field of folk music could hardly be doubted. When this year's miners strike was first announced they were both determined to make what contribution they could to the cause of the Welsh miner. 'We have always' they maintain 'been conscious of the great financial aid given by the miners of Wales to the Irish Transport and General Workers when their Union was threatened by the employers in 1913. We hope that in making this record we can in some small way repay the miners for their support and generosity at that time'.

The title song, 'Who will cast a Stone' was written by Frank Hennessy especially for the 1972 Strike and clearly illustrates the sympathy and admiration he has for the miners and their cause. 'Farewell to the Rhondda' is another of Frank's songs. This time he views with sadness and great poignancy the plight of the miner without work who is forced to leave home and family in search of a living. 'The Halfpenny Strike' looks back to 1910 and another mining struggle when troops were sent to Tonypandy against the striking men. The last song is already a classic. 'The Gresford Disaster' tells of the explosion at the Gresford Colliery near Wrexham on the twenty-second of September, 1934 in which two hundred and sixty five men lost their lives. At a time when the wages of miners are being disputed it may remind some of the real price of coal.

Ray Smith

Mae hanes chwareli Gogledd a glofeydd y Gogledd-Ddwyrain a'r De yn rhan annatod o hanes diweddar Cymru, ac y mae brwydr fawr y glowyr y dyddiau hyn am gyflog teg yn frwydr y dylem ni fel Gymry ei chefnogi i'r diwedd. Mae'r record hon gan y Gwyddel-Gymry enwog Yr Hennessys yn deyrnged i hanes cythryblus a dewr glowyr Cymru, ac yn ddatganiad clir o gefnogaeth i'r glowyr yn eu brwydr bresennol. Wrth gefnogi'r glowyr yr ydym hefyd yn hybu'r gwaith o ryddhau Cymru o afael y gormeswr a'r ecsploetiwr.

Dafydd Iwan

Proceeds from this record will go to the NUM Strike Fund
Bydd yr elw o'r record hon yn mynd i Gronfa Streic Undeb y Glowyr

Sain (Recordiau) Cyf., 1 Tai'r Ysgol, Llandwrog, Caernarfon.

Design Systems/Cardiff Talbot Printing Company Ltd., Port Talbot

The Hennessys
Who will cast a Stone?
Songs for the Miners Strike 1972

IN AID
OF MINERS'
DEPENDENTS
MONO 45
SOS1
VERNE/FELDMAN
SIDE A
JOINT PRODUCTION
HOLYGROUND &
MULTICORD
THE MINERS' SONG
DAVIDGE
JOHN & CITY LIGHTS
ALL RIGHTS OF THE MANUFACTURER AND OF THE OWNER OF THE RECORDED WORK RESERVED · UNAUTHORISED PUBLIC PERFORMANCE BROADCASTING AND COPYING OF THIS RECORD PROHIBITED

John & City Lights

<u>In Aid of Miners' Dependents</u>

7" single

Holyground & Multicord (SOS 1)

1972

Great Britain

This is the earliest example I've found of people involved in the commercial popular music industry attempting to use their talent to support striking workers. The "John" in the band here is John Paul Joans (birth name Reginald John Davidge) who worked largely as a comedian, but had a brief career in the early '70s as a pop star, wth one charting single as well as a couple others on multiple major labels. City Lights is a one-time alternative name for his backing band, Hotlicks, which would very soon after change their name to 10cc.

Joans recorded this single in support of British miners who struck for seven weeks in 1972. Supposedly his label at the time, Polydor, wasn't interested, which is why it was independently released (although a version was pressed which states "Marketed by Polydor"). Unlike his other singles, which were popular on the BBC, this one was apparently shadow banned for its politics. This largely ended Joans' pop stardom. The labels on the record itself state "In Aid of Miners' Dependents" but as it wasn't released with a picture sleeve or any additional information, it's unclear if there was an intention to raise money for a specific strike fund, or even if the record was ever commercially released.

The music here also breaks the mold set so far, as not only were miners not involved in the production, but this is clearly a *pop* record. A slinky proto-disco funk beat (I wouldn't be surprised if this record hasn't been mined for its breaks) rolls in the background as Joans intones a downbeat spoken word text about the strike ("I recall every face with the blue mark of falling coal, now the pit is closed and the valley has lost its soul"). It's a somewhat jarring juxtaposition, making for a truly strange sonic experience, the two parts never quite gelling into a whole.

SdL/AS/11
UNDERGROUND
MILANO
LOTTA OPERAIA
ALLA CROUZET
A cura
del Consiglio di fabbrica
della Crouzet
Registrazioni
raccolte sul campo
da Franco Coggiola
ARCHIVI SONORI
A cura dell'Istituto Ernesto de Martino

Consiglio di fabbrica della Crouzet
Milano Lotta Operaia alla Crouzet
LP
Archivi Sonori (SdL/AS/II)
1972
Italy

On May 25, 1972, metalworkers from the engineering firm Crouzet led a city-wide general strike in Milan. The struggle began a year earlier when workers received a letter notifying them that the company planned to close and relocate their factory. They mobilized instantly, initially setting up pickets and then blocking the company from exporting product out of the factory. An escalation of the struggle eventually leads to the general strike, shutting down the entire Sempione neighborhood. This record documents the events, with audio recordings of workers discussing their situation and organizing strategy, field recordings of speeches and action on the picket lines (including the owner of Crouzet throwing a bottle in anger at striking workers), and workers' songs.

The label Archivi Sonori released a dozen other field recordings from sites of social struggle as geographically disparate as Venezuela and Angola. It was an extension of the Istituto Ernesto de Martino, founded in Milan in 1966 to preserve and promote Italian working class culture. The Institute was an important cultural node for the Italian left in the 1960s and '70s, particularly the revival of political folk music through labels such as i Dischi della Sole (see the 1969 Fausto Amodei record on pages 28–31). While it is unclear exactly if the Archivi Sonori records came out of the Italian autonomists' worker's inquiry movement, it was certainly a parallel project.

Il Canzoniere delle Lame di Bologna

<u>Alla Tenda Dei Metalmeccanici In Piazza Maggiore</u>

7" single

FLM (N. 6)

1973

Italy

This record features four union songs in solidarity with metal workers (members of the Federazione Lavoratori Metalmeccanici) fighting for a new contract who set up a protest encampment in the Piazza Maggiore, the central square in Bologna. The song titles say it all: "You Companion, and I, and You, and Us"; "Always Partisans, Even Tomorrow"; "Not Even a Mickey Mouse"; and "The Master's Screw Turns."

Canzoniere delle Lame (which translates to "The Songbook from Lame," a neighborhood in Bologna) was a political music project put together in 1967 by Janna Carioli and Gianfranco Ginestri. A unique effort, the two musicians remained the nucleus of the group, but over their 20 year run they worked with hundreds of activists, workers, and other musicians on more than two dozen records—many in solidarity with labor struggles, but also with Chile, Vietnam, and more.

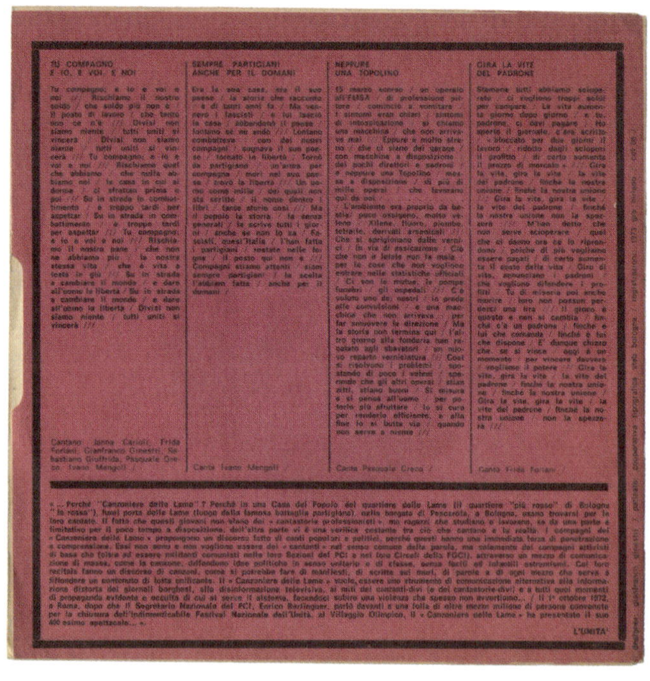

IL «CANZONIERE DELLE LAME» DI BOLOGNA
canta 4 canzoni sindacali (di solidarietà alla lotta per il rinnovo del contratto) presentate
ALLA TENDA DEI METALMECCANICI IN PIAZZA MAGGIORE
FLM
FLM
Disco stereo, N. 6, edito dalla FLM (Federazione Lavoratori Metalmeccanici) di Bologna / / L. 500 /
Cantano e suonano: Janna Carioli, Frida Forlani,
Gianfranco Ginestri, Sebastiano Giuffrida, Pasquale Greco, Ivano Mengoli, Patrizio Nocciolini /
Queste 4 canzoni sono state composte da lavoratori, da studenti e dal
"Canzoniere delle Lame" / Canzoniere di ricerca, composizione e spettacolo di canti popolari e politici /
Gruppo collaboratore dell'ARCI (Associazione Ricreativa Culturale Italiana) /
Telefono 051/38.76.07 / Via Zanardi, 164 / Quartiere Lame / Bologna /
Le musicassette e i dischi grandi e piccoli si richiedono in contrassegno alla Discoteca « Rinascita » / Via Botteghe Oscure, 3 / Roma

NON AUX LICENCIEMENTS
NON AU DEMANTELEMENT
18 juin
73
lip
CGT
un combat, un espoir.

Commission "Popularisation" de Travailleurs LIP & Claire Martin-Michon

LIP: un combat, un espoir

7" EP

Commission "Popularisation" de Travailleurs LIP (L 73.8.37)

1973

France

LIP produced watches and clocks in Besançon (eastern France, close to the Jura Mountains in Switzerland). The region is heavily Catholic and conservative, and workers had historically resisted unionization and rarely joined national strikes. This began to change in May 1968, when the workers voted to join the nationwide general strike. In the late sixties, the company struggled with profitability, and after going public, a majority stake was bought by Ebauches (a Swiss company that would eventually evolve into Swatch). Ebauches fired 1,300 workers in 1970, which rapidly radicalized the workforce. In 1973, when the company attempted to shut down the factory, the workers went out on a series of strikes, formed an action committee, and uncovered a secret plan to fire 450 additional workers. On June 12th, the workers decided to occupy the factory, and were so angry about the secret plan they took two administrators and a government inspector hostage. The police responded by raiding the factory. The extreme violence of the raid backfired, building immense local support for the workers. On June 18, the workers voted to seize the tools, parts, and stock of watches, and to run the company themselves.

The record collects direct recordings from that workers' general assembly on June 18, 1973. Interestingly, the recordings are interspersed with songs written and performed by Claire—also known as Claire Michon-Martin, a chanson singer from a union family known for her involvement in political movements—who crafted the lyrics from statements made by LIP workers in that very same assembly. Claire would go on to tour France throughout 1973 in support of the strike, and promoting the sale of LIP watches produced at the occupied factory.

The 7" itself is housed in an oversized trifold sleeve which is packed with photos, lyrics, cartoons, and information about the strike.

NON AU DÉMANTÈLEMENT, NON AUX LICENCIEMENTS.

Telles sont les deux revendications essentielles exprimées par les travailleurs de LIP et qui, classiques dans leur formulation, auront été le point de départ d'un conflit au retentissement i national.

Chez LIP en effet, et c'est une innovation, les travailleurs ont délibérément et avec détermina refusé une situation qui leur était imposée.

N'étant aucunement responsables, d'une gestion désastreuse, et n'acceptant, ni la carence Pouvoirs Publics permettant à un trust étranger de prendre — sans garantie — le contrôle entreprise française, ni la volonté de la direction d'un démantèlement de l'usine avec en laire les licenciements que toute restructuration implique, ils ont inventé de nouvelles formes lutte (remise en marche d'une partie de l'usine, vente de montres), inversé les rapports de f fait en sorte que le jour où une négociation sérieuse interviendrait, les représentants du pers s'assoient autour du tapis vert, en partenaires à part entière.

Au-delà du salaire de survie, qui, initialement justifiait la remise en marche de la production, i sont rendu compte rapidement que des valeurs non exprimées jusqu'alors apparaissaient, que responsabilités naissaient, que des rapports différents pouvaient exister, soit dans le travail ré dans une ambiance où l'homme tient la place essentielle soit au niveau de l'autre, du camarad peut s'exprimer librement, qui découvre ses possibilités, qui participe aux prises de décisions lectives.

Le conflit LIP, c'est aussi autre chose...

C'est la démonstration pour les travailleurs de partout que l'on peut innover dans l'action.

C'est la démonstration qu'il est possible ailleurs et avec les adaptations nécessaires, de renv les rapports de force.

C'est l'espoir caressé qu'un jour et dans un contexte économique différent de celui où vivons, le monde du travail sera prêt à prendre ses affaires en main.

LIP 1973, c'est par contre pour les « Princes » qui nous gouvernent, un exemple très mauvais est indispensable de briser et dont il faut à tout prix empêcher la propagation.

C'est pourquoi, toutes les forces dont ils disposent entrent en action afin d'effrayer, de divise pousser à la capitulation.

C'est pourquoi, en ce moment, l'issue du conflit n'apparait pas encore...

Mais quelle que soit cette issue, et dans l'esprit des travailleurs de LIP, elle ne peut être que torieuse, l'expérience vécue aura été exceptionnelle.

De par sa popularité, de par la solidarité extraordinaire rencontrée partout, de par sa dimer humaine, elle aura marqué d'une pierre blanche l'histoire ouvrière de notre pays et soulev immense espoir dans le cœur des travailleurs.

« Il n'y aura plus de licenciements chez LIP. Du travail il y en aura pour tous. Nous saurons en trouver ».

(M. Saintesprit, P.D.G. de LIP, février 1971)

« Le Conseil municipal de Besançon souhaite que tout soit mis en œuvre par les pouvoirs publics et notamment par M. le Ministre du Développement industriel et scientifique, et conservés les 1.300 emplois ».

(15 mai 1973)

« Ce serait
familles la p
des épreuve

« J'ai l'intime conviction que la maison peut être sauvée au prix d'une courageuse restructuration ».

(M. Schmitt, préfet du Doubs, 3 mai 1973)

« Les erreurs de gestion LIP n'autorisent pas le personnel à se faire justice lui-même ».

(Les patrons du Doubs, juillet 1973)

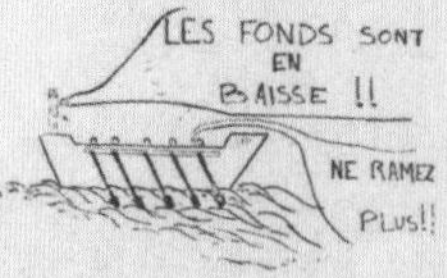

« Ce qui me scandaliserait, c'est que l'on commence par des licenciements ».

(M. Edgar Faure, juin 1973)

« L'attitude du patronat est scandaleuse ».

(Georges Séguy, juin 1973)

« Le désir de la majorité d'entre vous est de travailler ; le souci des administrateurs, de la direction et des cadres est de s'efforcer d'assurer le travail pour tous ».

(Maitre Pesson, administrateur provisoire, 18 mai 1973)

« Je ne manquerai pas d'intervenir efficacement après les élections dans le cas où je serais réélu ».

(M. Weinman, candidat U.D.R. aux élections législatives, 9 mars 1973 - Il a pourtant été réélu)

« Au train où vont
allons avoir des trou

(Fred LIP a

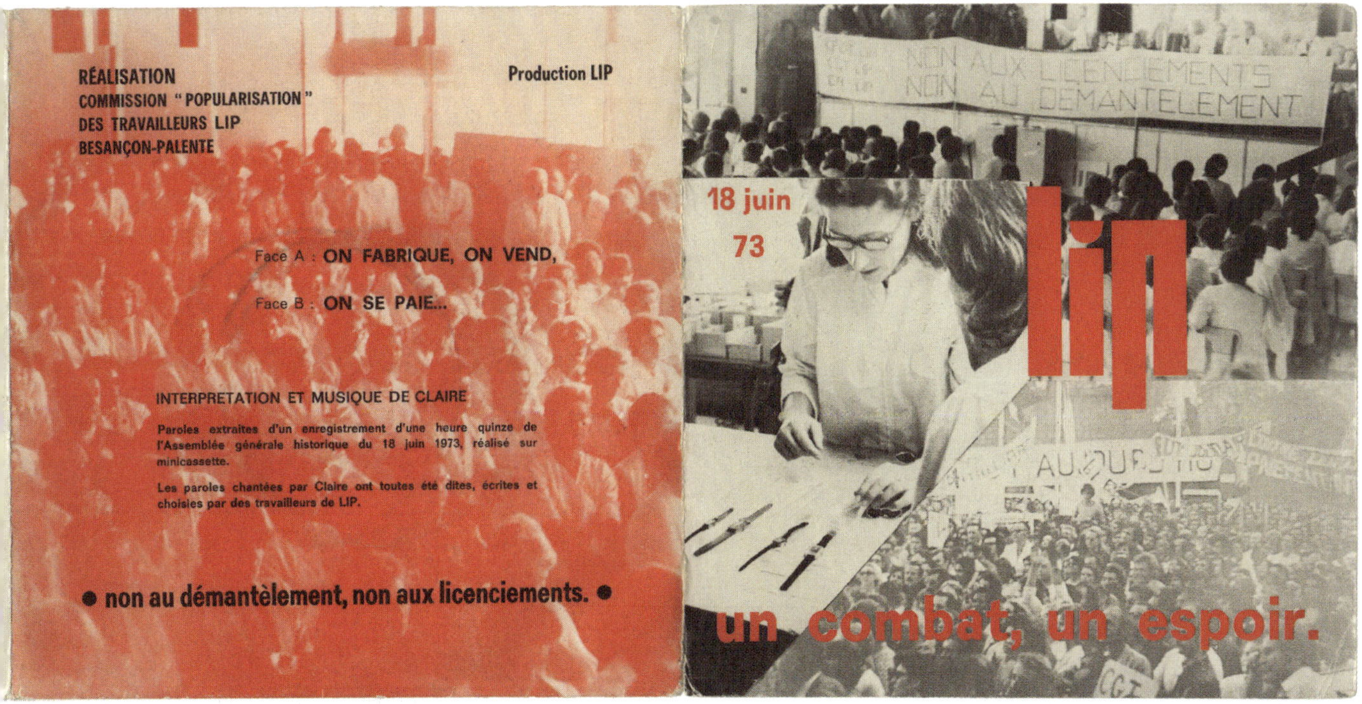

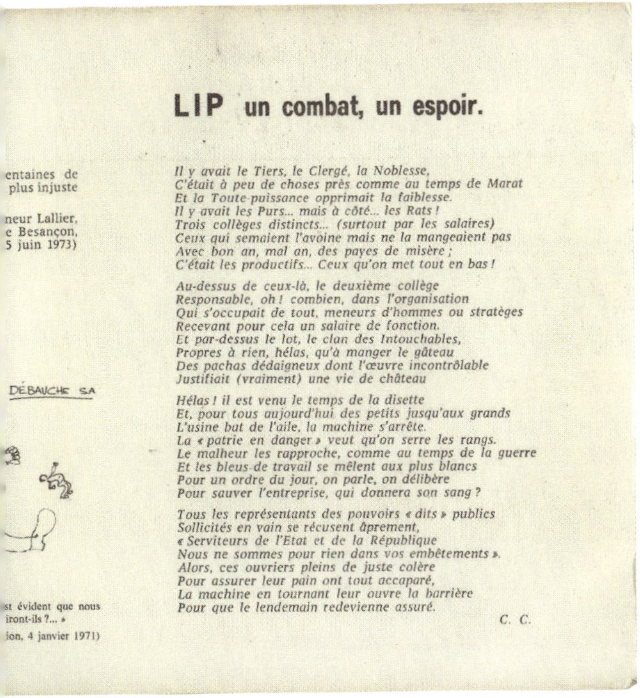

entaines de
plus injuste

neur Lallier,
e Besançon,
5 juin 1973)

DÉBAUCHE SA

st évident que nous
iront-ils ?... »
ion, 4 janvier 1971)

LIP un combat, un espoir.

Il y avait le Tiers, le Clergé, la Noblesse,
C'était à peu de choses près comme au temps de Marat
Et la Toute-puissance opprimait la faiblesse.
Il y avait les Purs... mais à côté... les Rats !
Trois collèges distincts... (surtout par les salaires)
Ceux qui semaient l'avoine mais ne la mangeaient pas
Avec bon an, mal an, des payes de misère ;
C'était les productifs... Ceux qu'on met tout en bas !

Au-dessus de ceux-là, le deuxième collège
Responsable, oh ! combien, dans l'organisation
Qui s'occupait de tout, meneurs d'hommes ou stratèges
Recevant pour cela un salaire de fonction.
Et par-dessus le lot, le clan des Intouchables,
Propres à rien, hélas, qu'à manger le gâteau
Des pachas dédaigneux dont l'œuvre incontrôlable
Justifiait (vraiment) une vie de château

Hélas ! il est venu le temps de la disette
Et, pour tous aujourd'hui des petits jusqu'aux grands
L'usine bat de l'aile, la machine s'arrête.
La « patrie en danger » veut qu'on serre les rangs.
Le malheur les rapproche, comme au temps de la guerre
Et les bleus-de travail se mêlent aux plus blancs
Pour un ordre du jour, on parle, on délibère
Pour sauver l'entreprise, qui donnera son sang ?

Tous les représentants des pouvoirs « dits » publics
Sollicités en vain se récusent âprement,
« Serviteurs de l'Etat et de la République
Nous ne sommes pour rien dans vos embêtements ».
Alors, ces ouvriers pleins de juste colère
Pour assurer leur pain ont tout accaparé,
La machine en tournant leur ouvre la barrière
Pour que le lendemain redevienne assuré.

C. C.

LUTTES OUVRIERES ACTUELLES
1973 - à propos de lip
CSC LIEGE
Soutien aux travailleurs LIP
NON AUX LICENCIEMENTS
NON AU DEMANTELEMENT
disques ICEM - CEL

Commission "Techniques Audiovisuelles" de l'Institut Coopératif de l'École Moderne

Luttes Ouvrieres Actuelles 1973: À Propos de LIP

LP

ICEM-CEL (Edition Spéciale N°1)

1974

France

Another of the two dozen or so educational records from ICEM (see pages 22-23), this one documents, explains, and generalizes the struggle for worker self-control at LIP through lightly annotated interviews with unionized and non-unionized workers. Obviously ICEM saw the struggle for worker self-management at LIP as offering educators a model to learn from: "The safety, calm, lucidity, and quality of the commitment of all workers in the face of a difficult reality and provocative or divisive actions impressed all observers of the LIP fight. How did the trade unions obtain and succeed with this education? This delegate provides some information on the structures put in place and the spirit in which they operate." To compound the intended pedagogical use of the record, half of the space on the sleeve's back is given to definitions of key terms used by those in the recordings.

The record was clearly produced with the support of the LIP workers, but it is unclear how it circulated amongst workers. ICEM-CEL records were intended as pedagogical tools and largely distributed through educational markets (and a subscription service), similar to the way Scholastic Records were distro'd in the US. This is backed up by the clear pedagogical framing on the back of the record sleeve, including an extremely helpful definition of terms such as "capital," "démantèlement" [dismantling], and "profit."

L'Enseignement Agricole
16 Octobre 1974: Journée Nationale de l'Enseignment Agricole Public
LP
L'Enseignement Agricole (supplément n° 33)
1974
France

This record documents a large-scale meeting and demonstration on October 16th, 1974 in Paris dubbed "National Day of Public Agricultural Education." The protest dovetailed with the beginning of a strike by the postal and telecommunications workers, with which it would combine along with other labor sectors into a nationwide general strike which brought France to a standstill through the end of the year.

The educators that were part of SNETAP-CGT, the National Union of Public Agricultural Technical Education, set their day of action to function in concert with a rotating strike action which multiple industries participated in to support the postal workers and create a rolling general strike. For their part, the documentation in the record implies that the teachers' demands were that they should be organized as part of the larger educational system—with the commensurate wages and benefits—no longer an appendage to the Ministry of Agriculture. For his part, the Minister initially refused to meet with the teachers, instead sending riot cops and locking them out of the Ministry.

As far as we can tell, this record was never sold, but instead distributed to rank and file union members by mail as a special edition of the publication *l'Enseignement Agricole* (the organ of the union SNETAP-CGT, the National Union of Public Agricultural Technical Education). A promotional flyer included discusses how the record was distributed and includes an order form. Inside are also instructions on how each copy comes with a double cover and booklet, and that these were produced so they could become an exhibition, or as they call it, "a readable and attractive union information panel."

Fédération d'Education Nationale
Syndicat National de l'Enseignement Technique Agricole Public
F.E.N. S.N.E.T.A.P

ANIMATEUR=ENSEIGNANT

6 ANS
sans Argent
C'EST TROP

ECROULEMENT
ASPHYXIE ...

DES
CONCOURS
POSTES
PISTONNE

EN VOILA ASSEZ

ANIMATEUR = ENSEIGN
STATUT DES ANIMATEURS

TITULARISATION DES
CHAUFFEURS... DES
ACTES... PAS DES
PROMESSES !!!

Dan & Judy Rose-Redwood
<u>**Original Huelga Songs**</u>
7" EP
Huelga Records (no catalog #)
ca. 1974
USA

This undated record of United Farm Workers (UFW) strike songs is a bit of a mystery. Dan and Judy Rose-Redwood were socially conscious folk singers primarily active in the early to mid-1970s, which is why we've dated this record around 1974. Huelga Records was created to release this 7" and otherwise has no footprint. The Rose-Redwoods must have worked directly with the UFW to produce the record, as it was distributed (and the cover likely designed by) Taller Grafico, the UFW cultural arm and storefront in Keene, California. Although not recorded for a specific strike, the record is a selection of four "Huelga songs."

HUELGA RECORDS

UNITED FARM WORKERS

ORIGINAL HUELGA SONGS

WRITTEN AND SUNG

by

DAN & JUDY • ROSE-REDWOOD

1. Take Back The Land
2. Song For Romulo
3. La Lucha Continuara
4. Thunderbird

L'ARCI-UISP E IL «CANZONIERE DELLE LAME» DI BOLOGNA

presentano un disco di canti sindacali

in occasione delle manifestazioni di solidarietà con

LE OPERAIE DELLA «RAQUEL» DI BOLOGNA

Il Canzoniere delle Lame di Bologna
"Noi siam quelle della Raquel" b/w "Tu Compagno"
7" single
L'ARCI-UISP (N. 10)
1974
Italy

Another record by Canzoniere delle Lame. Side A is the workers of the Raquel knitwear factory in Bologna singing "Noi siam quelle della Raquel" [We Are Raquel] with Canzoniere delle Lame. Contextual information about this strike is scarce, but it appears as if workers at the clothing factory were fired, and in response occupied the factory—or at least occupied and blocked the entrance, in protest and in demand of reinstatement.

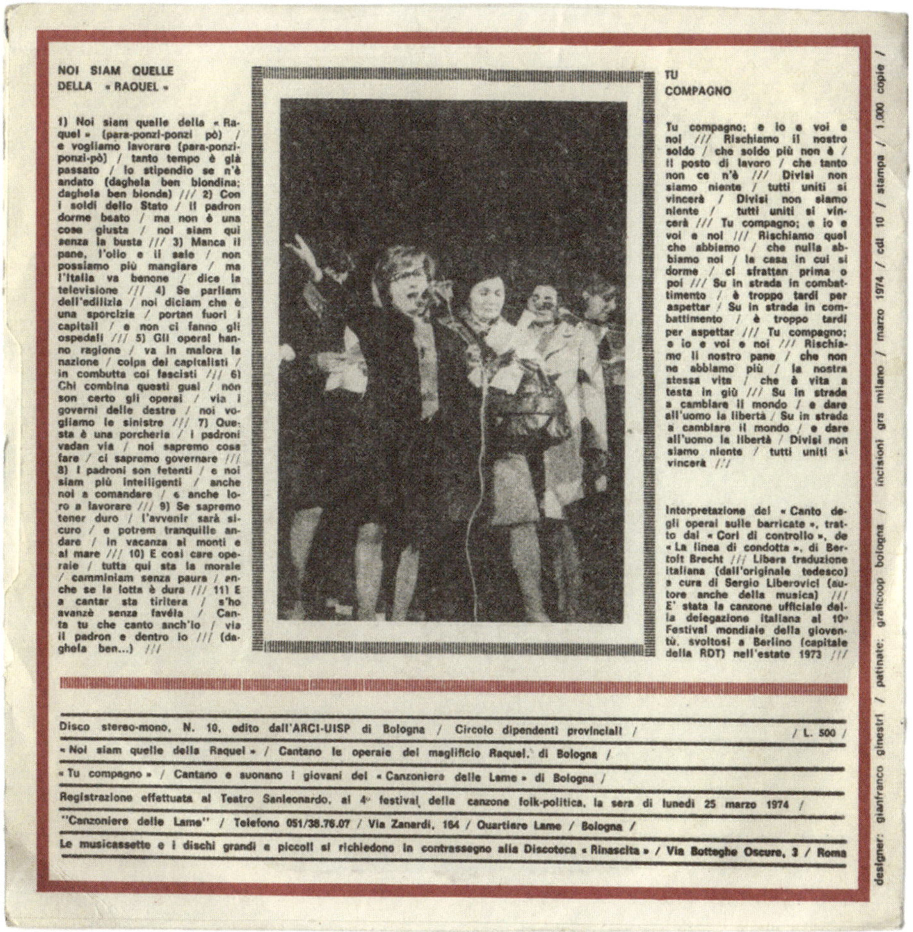

NOI SIAM QUELLE DELLA « RAQUEL »

1) Noi siam quelle della « Raquel » (para-ponzi-ponzi pò) / e vogliamo lavorare (para-ponzi-ponzi-pò) / tanto tempo è già passato / lo stipendio se n'è andato (daghela ben biondina; daghela ben bionda) /// 2) Con i soldi dello Stato / il padron dorme beato / ma non è una cose giusta / noi siam qui senza la busta /// 3) Manca il pane, l'olio e il sale / non possiamo più mangiare / ma l'Italia va benone / dice la televisione /// 4) Se parliam dell'edilizia / noi diciam che è una sporcizie / portan fuori i capitali / e non ci fanno gli ospedali /// 5) Gli operai hanno ragione / va in malora la nazione / colpa dei capitalisti / in combutta coi fascisti /// 6) Chi combina questi guai / non son certo gli operai / via i governi delle destre / noi vogliamo le sinistre /// 7) Questa è una porcheria / i padroni vadan via / noi sapremo cosa fare / ci sapremo governare /// 8) I padroni son fetenti / e noi siam più intelligenti / anche noi a comandare / e anche loro a lavorare /// 9) Se sapremo tener duro / l'avvenir sarà sicuro / e potrem tranquille andare / in vacanza ai monti e al mare /// 10) E così care operaie / tutta qui sta la morale / camminiam senza paura / anche se la lotta è dura /// 11) E a cantar sta tiritera / s'ho avanzè senza favéla / Canta tu che canto anch'io / via il padron e dentro io /// (daghela ben...) ///

TU COMPAGNO

Tu compagno; e io e voi e noi /// Rischiamo il nostro soldo / che soldo più non è / il posto di lavoro / che tanto non ce n'è /// Divisi non siamo niente / tutti uniti si vincerà / Divisi non siamo niente / tutti uniti si vincerà /// Tu compagno; e io e voi e noi /// Rischiamo quel che abbiamo / che nulla abbiamo noi / la casa in cui si dorme / ci sfrattan prima o poi /// Su in strada in combattimento / è troppo tardi per aspettar / Su in strada in combattimento / è troppo tardi per aspettar /// Tu compagno; e io e voi e noi /// Rischiamo il nostro pane / che non ne abbiamo più / la nostra stessa vita / che è vita a testa in giù /// Su in strada a cambiare il mondo / e dare all'uomo la libertà / Su in strada a cambiare il mondo / e dare all'uomo la libertà / Divisi non siamo niente / tutti uniti si vincerà ///

Interpretazione del « Canto degli operai sulle barricate », tratto dai « Cori di controllo », de « La linea di condotta », di Bertolt Brecht /// Libera traduzione italiana (dall'originale tedesco) a cura di Sergio Liberovici (autore anche della musica) /// E' stata la canzone ufficiale della delegazione italiana al 10° Festival mondiale della gioventù, svoltosi a Berlino (capitale della RDT) nell'estate 1973 ///

Disco stereo-mono, N. 10, edito dall'ARCI-UISP di Bologna / Circolo dipendenti provinciali / / L. 500 /

« Noi siam quelle della Raquel » / Cantano le operaie del maglificio Raquel, di Bologna /

« Tu compagno » / Cantano e suonano i giovani del « Canzoniere delle Lame » di Bologna /

Registrazione effettuata al Teatro Sanleonardo, al 4° festival della canzone folk-politica, la sera di lunedì 25 marzo 1974 /

"Canzoniere delle Lame" / Telefono 051/38.76.07 / Via Zanardi, 164 / Quartiere Lame / Bologna /

Le musicassette e i dischi grandi e piccoli si richiedono in contrassegno alla Discoteca « Rinascita » / Via Botteghe Oscure, 3 / Roma

designer: gianfranco ginestri / patinate: graficoop bologna / incisioni grs milano / marzo 1974 / cdl 10 / stampa / 1.000 copie /

Various artists
Stöd de Strejkande Hamnarbetarna
LP
Proletärkultur (PROLP 474)
1974
Sweden

This record emerges out of a huge upswing in autonomous worker action in Sweden in 1974. As the record sleeve states, in the first quarter of 1974 more workers participated in wildcat strikes and actions than in the entirety of 1973. One of the most important and militant of these actions was by the dockworkers, who on May 9-11th, shut down the port in Gothenburg. The strike was not about money, or even directly about job security, but rather about the nature of worker organization itself. The Swedish Employers Association (SAF—like a cartel of bosses and business interests) wanted to negotiate the contracts of all dockworkers through a single union, the Transportation Workers Union (who were members of the Swedish Trade Union Confederation—LO), even though they only represented a small fraction of the workers on the docks. In response, workers blocked the entire port, shutting down imports and exports, as well as fighting off scab labor the SAF and LO kept trying to bring in. Although it had broad public support, the strike ultimately failed, as the SAF and LO worked behind the workers' backs, negotiating in bad faith.

The record itself is taken from a series of 3 evenings of solidarity concerts held by the communist group KFML(r) [Communist League Marxist-Leninist (Revolutionary)] and features artists active in the group and on the party's record label Proletärkultur [Proletarian Culture], including Knuta Nävar, Röda Ropet, and Dan Berglund. The back of the cover features a great overview of the strike in a grid of nine captioned photos, a powerful pedagogical tool for understanding the events while listening to the music.

»STÖD DE STREJKANDE HAMNARBETARNA«
Inspelning från tre visaftnar på Marx-Engelshuset i Göteborg den 9-11 maj 1974 till stöd för de strejkande arbetarna i Svenska Hamnarbetarförbundet.
Tre kronor från varje sålt exemplar går till Svenska Hamnarbetarförbundets strejkfond.
KPML (r)
VÄXJÖ

Trustee Bert Svensson from the Hamnarbetarförbundet [Dock Workers' Union] section 4 informs the temporary dock workers about the union's overtime blockade, which leads them to stop work.

The blockade, however, was not respected by these scabs, who made their way down to the quay during the conflict.

Strike guards effectively blockaded all quay sections. Here is Lundby Harbor on one of the first strike days.

The fact that the employers were furious with the blockade became clear to the strike guards when a chief official was sent to drive them away.

Information about the strike is spread in this way (via posted signs). This picture is from a terminal in Skandia Harbor.

Collections for the strikers were started all over the country. This picture is from Helsingborg.

Strike guards block the road against an unsympathetic truck driver, who is trying to bringing goods onto the quay.

This is what one of the worst hate writers against the strikers looks like. It's Nils Viktorsson from Arbetet (s).

Trustee Karl Axel Kandevik, Hamnarbetarförbundet, informs strikers in Skandiahamnen about the agreement concluded between Transport and Stuvarförbundet, which arouses justified anger.

Förtroendeman Bert Svensson från Hamnarbetarförbundets avdelning 4 upplyser de tillfälliga hamnarbetarna om Hamnarbetarförbundets övertidsblockad, som dessa helt sluter upp i.

Blockaden hörsammades dock ej av de här svartfötterna, som letade sig ner till kajen under konflikten.

Strejkvakter bevakade effektivt alla kajavsnitt. Här i Lundbyhamnen en av de första strejkdagarna.

Att arbetsköparen hetsade upp sig över bevakningen fick strejkvakterna också erfara, när en chefstjänsteman skulle köra iväg dem.

Information om strejken spreds bl a på det här sättet. Bilden från en terminal i Skandiahamnen.

Insamlingar för de strejkande drogs igång över hela landet. Bilden från Helsingborg.

Strejkvakter spärrar vägen för en oförstående chaufför, som kommer med gods.

Så här ser en av de värsta hetsskribenterna mot de strejkande ut. Det är Nils Viktorsson från Arbetet (s).

Förtroendeman Karl Axel Kandevik, Hamnarbetarförbundet, informerar strejkvakter i Skandiahamnen om avtalet som slutits mellan Transport och Stuvarförbundet, vilket väcker berättigad harm.

Sid 1
Den g
G Frödi
Strejk
H Ande
Ballac
NJA-gru
Katju
Trad
Rallar
R Nilsso
Åkare
R Nilsso
En val
N Ferlin

Sid 2
The C
Trad
Worki
Trad
Riksd
C M Bel
Måsac
Ö Sund
Visa t
D Bergl
De mi
D Bergl

»STÖD DE STREJKANDE HAMNARBETARNA«

demokratiska rätten att få sluta avtal för si egna medlemmar.

CHEZ HANREZ, ÇA CONTINUE ...

GAM & Hanrez Workers
<u>Chez Hanrez, ça continue. . .</u>
7" single
Self-produced (G. 003)
1975
Belgium

The top of the lyric sheet included in the record states:

For 8 weeks, the workers of Ateliers Hanrez have been on strike for the reinstatement of their comrade René Andersen, a combative union activist, dismissed for inaccurate and abusive reasons.

Andersen had been the lead organizer of a slate of union members organizing to be elected to replace the existing corrupt union leadership. His centrality to the struggle is further communicated by the record sleeve, a one-color printed and folded piece of paper, which features a photo of workers mobilizing in the street in front of graffiti which states, "Rene is with us!" After eight weeks of striking, corrupt union officials organized and pushed for a new vote to end the strike, which they won by a very slim majority. Anderson (whom union officials offered a job as part of their campaign to end the strike) and the more militant workers were ultimately proven right to have struck, as within months the company began laying off dozens of workers.

The Hanrez workshops were a Belgian state industry that originally produced steam engines but evolved to make various machines for use in heavy industry. There is no information on the record itself about when it was made, but the record was produced with the militant musical act GAM, or Groupe d'Action Musicale, and in the liner notes of

DERRIERE LE RIDEAU.

Chanson composée après l'assemblée générale des travailleurs, le 7 mars. Lors de cette réunion, alors que 60% des ouvriers venaient de voter pour continuer la grève, le "dirigeant syndical" proposait à René un emploi dans l'organisation syndicale.
Une manière comme une autre d'essayer de casser la grève...

Refrain:
Derrière le rideau, il faut qu'il se cache
Derrière le rideau, de peur que les ouvriers se fachent.

I. Trahisfrère a appelé René: "j'ai une bonne place pour toi,
Si tu abandonnes la lutte, si tu renonces au combat".

Refrain: ....

II. René répond à Trahisfrère: "ta place, je n'en veux pas;
Je me battrai avec mes frères, leur colère, c'est mon combat".

Refrain:
Levons le rideau sur ces sabotages,
Levons le rideau sur son vrai visage.

FACE I : CHEZ HANRE

Depuis 8 semaine
pour la réintégrati
cal combatif, licen

Refrain:
Chez Hanrez, chez H
Grève des ouvriers,
Faites rentrer René
Non Urbain, car dem
On peut tous être d

I. A tous les ouvr
Qui entrent travail
Nous allons expliqu
Qu'il ne faut pas c
Car ce serait laiss
Mains libres aux PD
Pour voler notre li

II/ Pendant les ass
Si tu oses proteste
Si tu oses discuter
Te voilà licencié
Mais nous ne voulon
REster des sourds-m
Prenons tous le drc

Lundi 10 mars: p
obligé les travaill
coeur, mais....(Ref

Chez Hanrez,
Faut continu
Liberté de p
Liberté d'pa

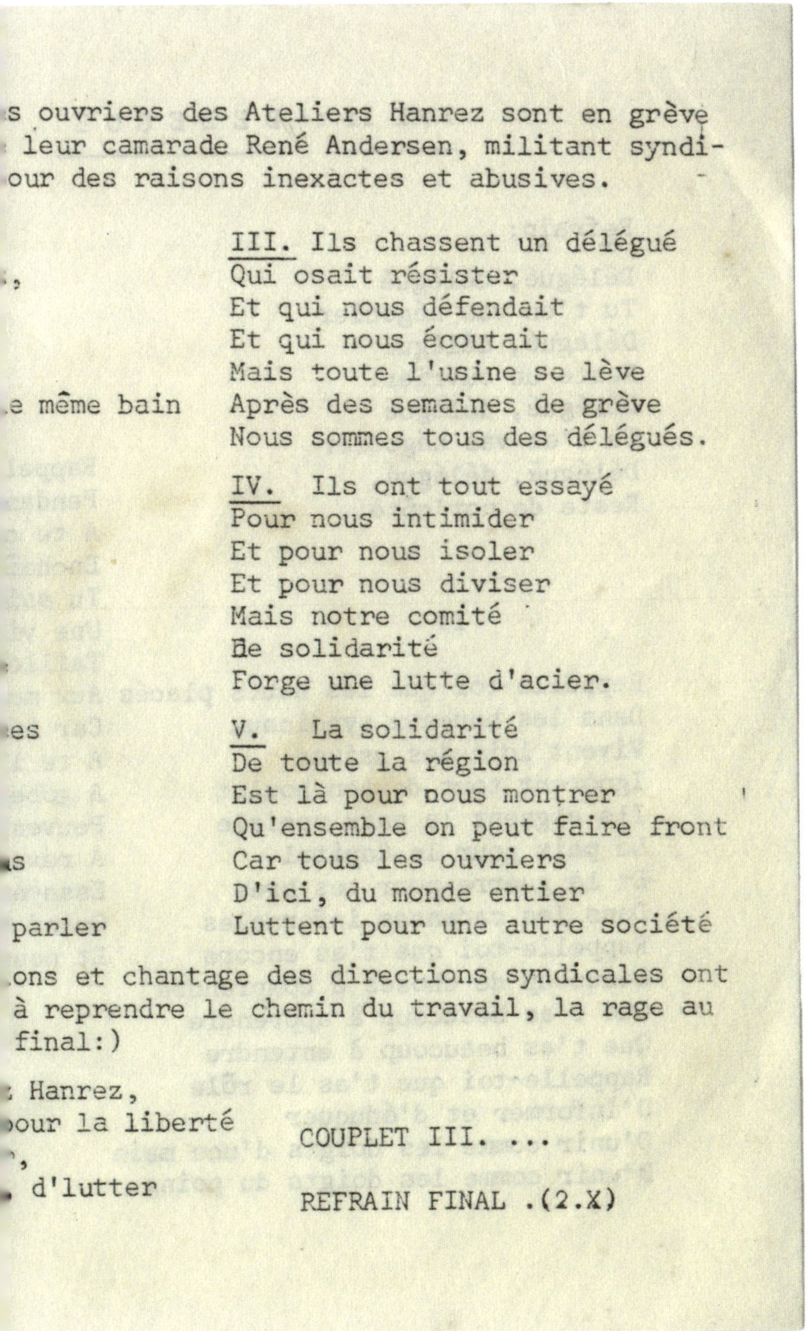
s ouvriers des Ateliers Hanrez sont en grève
leur camarade René Andersen, militant syndi-
our des raisons inexactes et abusives.

III. Ils chassent un délégué
Qui osait résister
Et qui nous défendait
Et qui nous écoutait
Mais toute l'usine se lève
e même bain Après des semaines de grève
Nous sommes tous des délégués.

IV. Ils ont tout essayé
Pour nous intimider
Et pour nous isoler
Et pour nous diviser
Mais notre comité
De solidarité
Forge une lutte d'acier.

es V. La solidarité
De toute la région
Est là pour nous montrer
Qu'ensemble on peut faire front
s Car tous les ouvriers
D'ici, du monde entier
parler Luttent pour une autre société

ons et chantage des directions syndicales ont
à reprendre le chemin du travail, la rage au
final:)

Hanrez,
our la liberté
COUPLET III. ...
d'lutter
REFRAIN FINAL .(2.X)

one of their other LPs they discuss writing these songs in February of 1975. The songs are complex, dense, yet jaunty results of worker's inquiry, the first marked as being "made by workers," the next a ditty written after a general assembly that recreates a moment of heroism from a worker in face of trickery from union officials. The songs are obviously made outside any union support or structure, and put out not on any official record label, but quickly self-produced with the aid of GAM. They chronicle specific grievances from the strike, lessons learned, goals and theory, and were likely sung at union officials as much as with and for workers. Spoken interludes cut in on one track to make everything crystal clear:

> [we were] pressured and blackmailed [back to work by the union]. To all workers / who come to work / we will explain / that we must not give in / cause that would leave the CEO's hands free / to steal our freedom

Comité de grève
FGTB-CSC
CHANTS
DE
LUTTE
On occupe,
on produit,
on vend,
pour l'emploi
pour le contrôle
pour la mise sous
statut public
DISQUE DE
SOLIDARITE
80 F
VAL-SAINT-LAMBERT
SERAING, PRINTEMPS 1975

GAM
Chants de Lutte
7" single
Comité de grève FGTB-CSC (no catalog #)
1975
Belgium

One of three records included here featuring GAM, or the Groupe d'Action Musicale. Here they've constructed two of the three songs by setting words by striking workers to existing folk songs. The music created is just as that sounds, a rousing folk intended to encourage sing-alongs.

In this instance the strikers are from a glass blowing factory at Val-Saint-Lambert, which they occupied for six months. Their actions and motives are clearly articulated by the text on the oversized envelope sleeve:

We occupy,
we produce,
we sell,
for employment,
for control,
for public ownership.

Chausson Strikers & Germinal
"Chantent & Luttent" b/w "Vive la grève des Chausson"
7" single
Self-produced (no catalog #)
1975
France

This record documents an action on June 29, 1975 when striking workers from Chausson (a French bus manufacturer)—with the aid of workers from Câbles de Lyon, also on strike—blocked trucks from entering or exiting the factory in Gennevilliers (outside of Paris). The factory was occupied by the police to stop strikers from taking it over, effectively locking the workers out. Side A is a rowdy field recording of the protests, scored live thanks to the participation of the band Germinal, and including a crew of Morroccan workers playing North African instruments. It's a really enjoyable listen. The flip side is a written song, performed by Germinal, which tells the story of the strike, the workers' grievances, and the actions they've taken.

The insert, written by Germinal, is very clear, direct, informative, and worth reprinting at length:

This 7" was recorded to support the struggle of Chausson workers last spring. First designed as financial support for the strike, it is today one of its testimonies. In Chausson-Gennevilliers, in May–June 1975, the strike was long and hard. In the occupied factory, the workers—mostly immigrants—collectively take charge of organizing their struggle. An elected strike committee is the united expression of the militance of the strikers. The workers also popularize their struggle: leaflets, posters, interventions in markets, meetings, calls for support and solidarity. Various cultural groups, including

Usine CHAUSSON
VIVE LA GREVE

Germinal, take part in this campaign launched by the strikers themselves.

On June 28, the C.R.S. (French riot cops) occupy the factory. On the 29th, the workers demonstrated in front of the doors, supported by the people of Gennevilliers and strikers from the Câbles de Lyon. These, with darbukas, bass drums, and tambourines, dance and sing, in the faces of the cops, slogans echoed by everyone. With our instruments, we join them.

The party will last all day. The first side of the disc, recorded on site, captures one of the most enthusiastic moments. Thanks to the contact established during the strike (in particular with comrades from the strike committee) we created a song which tells the story on the B-side: "Long live the Chausson strike." As for us—and, as much as possible, in liaison with other cultural groups—we intend to continue this type of work, minus errors and inadequacies, where the people live, work, struggle and express themselves, so that a culture will be created which belongs to them and bears witness to their multiple battles against the economic, political, and cultural oppression of the bourgeoisie.

Ce disque a été enregistré
pour soutenir la lutte des ouvriers de Chausson
au printemps dernier.
D'abord conçu comme soutien
financier à la grève,
il en est aujourd'hui un des témoignages.
A Chausson-Gennevilliers, en mai-juin 1975,
la grève a été longue et dure.
Dans l'usine occupée,
les travailleurs — en majorité immigrés —
prennent collectivement en main
l'organisation de leur lutte.
Un comité de grève élu
sera l'expression unitaire
de la combativité des grévistes.
Les ouvriers popularisent aussi leur lutte :
tracts, affiches, collectes,
interventions sur les marchés, meetings,
appellent au soutien et à la solidarité.
Divers groupes culturels, dont « Germinal »,
prennent part à cette campagne
lancée par les grévistes eux-mêmes.
Le 28 juin, les C.R.S. occupent l'usine.
Le 29, les ouvriers manifestent devant les portes,
soutenus par les habitants de Gennevilliers
et des grévistes des Câbles de Lyon.
Ceux-ci, avec darboukas,
grosse caisse et tambourins...,
dansent et chantent, au nez des flics,
des slogans repris par tous.
Avec nos instruments, nous nous joignons à eux.
La « fête » durera toute la journée.
La première face du disque, enregistrée sur place,
en donne un des moments les plus enthousiastes.
Grâce au contact établi au cours de la grève
(notamment avec des camarades du comité de grève)
nous avons créé une chanson qui en raconte l'histoire
(deuxième face du disque :
« Vive la grève des Chausson »).
Quant à nous — et, autant que possible,
en liaison avec d'autres groupes culturels —
nous entendons poursuivre ce type de travail,
erreurs et insuffisances en moins,
là où le peuple vit, travaille, lutte et s'exprime,
afin que puissent naître des œuvres culturelles
qui lui appartiennent
et témoignent de ses multiples combats
contre l'oppression tant économique,
politique que culturelle de la bourgeoisie.

GERMINAL.

Le 29 Juin 1975, à Gennevilliers

Les ouvriers de CHAUSSON
bloquent les camions ;

avec leurs camarades
des CABLES DE LYON.

Ils chantent
et ils dansent leur LUTTE,

avec le Groupe GERMINAL

au nez des C. R. S.

qui occupent l'usine

Various artists
<u>**Solidarité PTT: Chantons tout le long de la grève**</u>
7" EP
Expression Spontanée (ES 20)
1975
France

This record is the document of the massive 1974 strike of the workers at the Postes, Télégraphes et Téléphones (PTT), the state administered post office and telecommunications company. In October the workers at the postal sorting centers go on strike, and by October 23rd, the movement had grown to 10,000 striking workers marching through the streets of Paris. One of the main demands of the strike—initially put forward by the ORA, or Anarchist Revolutionary Organization, a caucus in the larger union—is the end of the use of auxiliary workers, who were brought in increasingly since the 1960s and paid sometimes as low as half the rate of full-time workers (sound familiar, all you adjunct professors out there?). The struggle is marked by its militancy, with significant participation and leadership from both anarchist and communist workers. Part of this militancy is seen in the non-hierarchical participation of the rank-and-file workers, with massive popular assemblies held each day, with all workers encouraged to voice their concerns and ideas—as opposed to closed door negotiations between union leaders and management. The CFDT and CGT briefly support a solidarity railroad strike, but eventually the union forces the PTT strikers back to work in December, ending the strike after forty-five days. There is an immense amount of writing and analysis about this strike by French radicals, sadly very little of it is available in English.

The record itself documents the struggle, and the day to day grievances of the workers. Unlike many other records here, there are no professional musicians involved, and all the lyrics are written by the workers themselves, and sung over traditional labor and folk melodies: "We're tied up, no right to speak / And we must beg to go pee."

Solidarité PTT
CHANTONS
TOUT LE LONG
DE LA GRÉVE
CFDT PTT
26 rue de Montholon 75439 PARIS CEDEX 09
CCP 1665-26 PARIS

OPPONER
ALFA BLUES
TILL MIN MAKE
Utgiven av Alfa Laval -
arbetarna i Tumba

Opponer
"Alfa Blues" b/w "Till min make"
7" single
Opponer (Opp 2)
1975
Sweden

Swedish progg group Opponer worked directly with striking Alfa Laval workers in Tumba to produce this single (with the Alfa Laval-Arbetarnas Stödfond union). Metal workers at Alfa Laval, one of the largest companies in Sweden, were negotiating for a small cost-of-living pay increase, and representatives of the company simply walked out on the workers' representatives. This provoked 450 workers to engage in a weeklong sitdown strike—a photo of the vote to strike graces the cover of the record. The band engaged with workers to craft lyrics and music around the struggle, producing the jaunty blues rock number "Alfa Blues" on the A-side. The B-side, "Till min make" [To My Husband] is not directly connected to the Alfa Laval strike, but labor-related, focusing on the conditions of workers at the state-run mining company LKAB.

STREJK
Strejkvisor
BUDKAVLEN

Budkavlen
<u>**Strejk Strejkvisor**</u>
LP
Oktober (OSLP-509)
1975
Sweden

Budkavlen have assembled here an impressive collection of sixteen Swedish strike songs from the peak of worker struggle at the turn of the 19th to 20th century. Budkavlen themselves are an interesting archival project. The group developed out of the Visgruppen inom Arkivet för folkets historia, the song group of the People's History Archive (a physical space and collection in Stockholm which ran from 1970 through 2000, and was open to all that supported its motto: "The people are the driving force of history"). Dedicated explicitly to retreiving songs from people's history (a similar project in many ways to Violetta Parra's *nueva canción* movement in Chile, or even Alan Lomax's work in the US), the group performs, records, and annotates songs that emerged out of working people's lives and movements.

Most of the songs here emerged from different labor struggles across the country, the record functions as a sonic catalog of worker uprisings: The great bakery workers strike in Stockholm of 1873; the Sundsvall sawmill strike of 1879; the Norberg miners revolt in 1891-92; the masons strike of 1888, which included the women that worked as mason assistants carrying 60 kilos of bricks up scaffolding all day; the Stockholm dockworkers strike of 1903; the Stockholm sanitation workers strike of 1905 (which has three songs dedicated to it); the 1908 Malmo municipal workers strike.

The music presented here is mostly fairly straightforward folk, which makes the songs listenable and even enjoyable, but minimizes the sense of their use on the picketlines, or as agitprop at the time they were written. The band balances this out by providing significant context, such as a great short piece of writing about how music was used by the workers, including being printed up as song sheets which would be sold out in public by striking workers to build strike funds.

Telefonsentralmontørene with Vømmøl Spellmannslag & Folk Flest

<u>Slå Tilbake Voldgiften</u>

7" single

Plateselskapet Mai (MAI:52)

1975

Norway

As much as it's focused on the strike of 250 switchboard operators, this record is a challenge to the use of arbitration by the state and the right of companies to impose "no strike" clauses in contracts. To Anglophone readers, the appearance of Vømmøl Spellmannslag is likely meaningless, but this progg group sold over 50,000 copies of each of their first two albums, which in a country the size of Norway made them superstars (the comparable scale of these sales numbers in the US would be roughly 3 million records each). Even more interestingly, the band was affiliated with the AKP(m-l), or Arbeidernes Kommunistparti [Worker's Communist Party], a hard Maoist political grouping. Vømmøl Spellmannslag's songs were largely about the ways industry and capital were transforming daily life in northern Norway, but the lyrics were peppered with references to Marx, Lenin, Mao, and even celebratory of Stalin. This would be like Fleetwood Mac singing about the Cultural Revolution in China. In addition, Plateselskapet Mai was an explicitly communist and cooperative record label, and Vømmøl Spellmannslag's sales success was used to fund the recording and production of all the other records on the label, including this one.

This record was made directly with the telephone switchboard workers, who you can hear on the chorus on the B-side (with music provided by the group Folk Flest). All royalties from the record were given to the Telefonsentralmontørene strike fund.

TELEFONSENTRALMONTØRENE
VØMMØL SPELLMANNSLAG
FOLK FLEST

STRIKE

In the last six months, a militant strike movement has swept across the country. The cleaning women, the meat industry workers, the lift fitters and the telephone switchboard fitters have gone on strike. There have been strikes at Norsk Hydro and Bergens Jernstøperi. These strikes have strengthened the unity within the working class and the unity between the workers and other groups, e.g., students. Well-developed strike support work has shown that the workers have broad support for their demands and that "party fat cats in LO and DNA" are no longer perceived as advocates for working people. MAI has asked one of the leaders in this autumn's strike movement, Leif Johannessen, who was chairman of the elevator fitters' PR committee, to explain what the strike weapon means in the struggle of the working class.

Capitalist society is filled with contradictions. The struggle between the two main classes, the workers and the capitalists, is an expression of these contradictions. This battle continues unabated.

In order to live, the workers must sell their labor power to the capitalists who own the means of production. How they will live and how much they will get for their toil depends on their ability and willingness to fight. Workers participate throughout their lives, more or less consciously, in this conflict.

A strike is a pointed form of this struggle and it is one of the working class's most important weapons to get its demands implemented.

The strike reveals contradictions that were previously hidden. Workers who throughout their long life may have fought for themselves and their people through faithful and persistent work in the trade union movement and young people who hardly know what a trade union is, are awakened to a new realization of their position in society, they become class conscious.

The intensified struggle develops and triggers solidarity between workers and is one of the most important elements in the struggle, but escalation also brings out the weak and the traitors.

A strike is therefore also the story of heroes and sacrifice, will and steadfastness, and of faithfulness and courage on the one hand and of betrayal, intrigue, bribes, corruption, cowardice, and snitching on the other.

The strike also concerns those who are close to the strikers and therefore illuminates people's characteristics and conditions when they must confront difficulties and challenges.

The strike intervenes deeply in the power relations in society and therefore often becomes a struggle against state power, revealing the class nature of the state.

The strikes intervene deeply in human and social conditions and are therefore filled with both external and internal drama and tension. What the artists can convey to us is both the bare history of the struggle and the human side, with all the emotions that are driven forward and developed between people in conflict.

Strikes are a education in war, but also a beacon on the road to a classless society where the fundamental causes of strikes have been removed.

—Leif Johannessen.

STREIK

Det siste halve året har en voldsom streikebevegelse gått over landet. Rengjøringskvinnene, kjøttindustriarbeiderne, heismontørene og telefonsentralmontørene har streiket. Det har vært streiker ved Norsk Hydro og Bergens Jernstøperi. Disse streikene har styrket enheten innenfor arbeiderklassen og enheten mellom arbeiderne og andre grupper, f.eks. ungdom under utdanning. Et velutvikla streikestøttearbeid har vist at arbeiderne har en brei oppslutning om krava sine og at «partipampan i LO og DNA» ikke lenger oppleves som talsmenn for arbeidsfolk. MAI har bedt en av lederne i høstens streikebevegelse — Leif Johannessen som var formann i heisemontørenes PR-komité — om å forklare hva streikevåpnet betyr i arbeiderklassens kamp.

Det kapitalistiske samfunnet er fylt av motsetninger. Kampen mellom de to hovedklassene, arbeiderne og kapitalistene er et uttrykk for disse motsetningene. Denne strid pågår uavbrutt.

Arbeiderne må for å leve, selge sin arbeidskraft til kapitalistene som eier produksjonsmidlene. Hvordan de skal leve og hvor mye de skal få for sitt slit, avhenger av evnen og viljen til kamp. Arbeidsfolk deltar gjennom hele livet, mer eller mindre bevisst i denne konflikten. *Streik* er en tilspisset form for denne kamp og den er ett av arbeiderklassens viktigste våpen for å få gjennomført sine krav. *Streiken* avdekker motsetninger som tidligere lå skjult. Arbeidere som gjennom et langt liv kanskje har stridd for seg og sine gjennom trofast og iherdig arbeide i fagbevegelsen og unge mennesker som knapt vet hva en fagforening er, vekkes til ny erkjennelse og sin samfunnsmessige stilling, de blir klassebevisste.

Den skjerpete kamp utvikler og utløser solidariteten mellom arbeidsfolk og er et av de viktigste elementer i striden, men opptrappingen av kampen bringer også fram i dagen de svake og forræderne.

Streik er derfor også historien om helter og oppofrelse, vilje og standhaftighet og om trofasthet og mot på den ene siden og om svik, intriger, bestikkelser, korrupsjon, feighet og angiveri på den annen.

Streiken angår også de som står de streikende nær og forteller derfor om menneskers egenskaper og forhold når vanskeligheter og prøvelser møter dem.

Streiken griper dypt inn i selve maktforholdet i samfunnet og blir derfor ofte en kamp mot statsmakten, ofte avsløres derfor klassestatens karakter.

Streikene griper dypt inn i menneskelige og samfunnsmessige forhold og fylles derfor av både ytre og indre dramatikk og spenning. Det kunstnerne kan formidle til oss er både den nakne kampens historie og det personlige menneskelige, med alle de følelser som drives fram og utvikles mellom mennesker i konflikt.

Streik er skole i krig, men også lys på veien mot det klasseløse samfunn der de grunnleggende årsaker til streik er fjernet.

Leif Johannessen.

FTQ - CONSTRUCTION 1975
AVEC TES OUTILS
FACE A
Paroles: Les gars du Chantier
Musique: Luc Cousineau
Une production: Luc Cousineau &
Don Habib

Luc Cousineau
Avec tes Outils
7" single
FTQ-Construction (FTQ-1)
1975
Canada

Coming in a generic paper sleeve, this record gives the listener little initial context when heard outside of its moment. Cousineau was a popular Quebecois singer-songwriter, and this record is his support for the construction workers that walked off the jobsite in May 1975, refusing to build the infrastructure for the 1976 Olympics in Montreal. It's a bit hard to parse, but the workers appear to have been supporting their union leadership, which was being brought up on corruption charges. Since the head of the union was eventually convicted of extortion, racketeering, and drug trafficking, the strike seems dubious, yet it's hard to imagine a comparable musician in the US recording a popular song dedicated to Jimmy Hoffa and it being released by the Teamsters.

LE DISQUE DE
L'AUTOMNE SHOW
MICHEL CHARTRAND
GUY BISAILLON
LOUIS LABERGE
LOUISE FORESTIER
RAYMOND LEVESQUE
PAULINE JULIEN
GEORGES D'OR
CLAUDE DUBOIS
DENISE FILIATRAULT
LA SEMILLA
JACQUES MICHEL
CLAUDE GAUTHIER
PRISCILLA
GILLES HUNTER
YVON CHARBONNEAU
ON VA PASSER
A TRAVERS!

Various artists
<u>L'Automne Show</u>
LP
Rival (RV-1)
1975
Canada

The Autumn Show was a "24-hour super show" thrown a year into a historic strike against American-owned United Aircraft. The strike was led by workers at its Longueuil, Quebec plant with the United Autoworkers of Canada (UAW). Solidarity spread across the province and south of the border into the US, with support strikes and marches totaling 100,000 participants. "Today agents, technicians, and record companies are adding links to the great chain of solidarity which surrounds United Aircraft strikers," proclaims the back of the sleeve. Jane Fonda even paid a visit! Not to be outdone by celebrity, the sleeve credits not only include the 60 or so artists who made up the show but also the 60,000 audience members, whose hooting and clapping are well preserved in the live recording. The record also captures performances by almost a dozen Quebecois musicians as well as speeches by workers and union officials. Both the concert and the record were used as fundraising tools for the strike fund.

About 7 months after this record was released, 34 workers occupied the factory. Despite being beaten bloody and evicted within a day, the militant action was viewed as a turning point, which led finally to an agreement favorable to the strikers. The entire struggle was used as a wedge for the next provincial election and brought the Parti Québécois to power. And for once a political party delivered: a year later they passed legislation banning the use of scabs during legal strikes, guaranteeing strikers the right to return to work, and more.

Consiglio di fabbrica della Filati Lastex

Bergamo Redona Filati Lastex alla riscossa

LP

Archivi Sonori (SdL/AS/12)

1975

Italy

A sound archive collected from within Filati Lastex, an occupied elastics textile factory. The record just drops you into the action, with no distinct tracks or framing, but instead a seamless collection of chants, speeches, interviews, and songs. Thankfully it came with a 20 page booklet documenting the struggle, with context and transcriptions of some of the recordings. The occupation started when the company and the regional industrial association negotiated with the union in bad faith, and the album takes the listener through the struggle to the final segment of the record, labeled: "The victorious conclusion of the struggle and the resumption of work, interviews, and songs." Like all Archivi Sonori records (see the *Milano Lotta Operaia alla Crouzet* LP from 1972 on pages 48-49), the production values here are quite high, with conscious editing and ordering of material, and the inclusion of the accompanying booklet. While the workers at Filati Lastex clearly participated in the creation of this document, it is unclear what role they played in its actual production, or if the record was distributed back into the factory.

Cultura di classe
SdL/AS/12
Bergamo Redona
Filati Lastex
alla riscossa
ricerca in una fabbrica occupata 22 nov. 1974/4 luglio 1975
A cura
del Consiglio di fabbrica
della Filati Lastex
Registrazioni sul campo di
Mimmo Boninelli
Giuliana Bertacchi
Cesare Bermani
Luisa Betri
Franco Coggiola
Carlo Leidi
ARCHIVI SONORI
A cura dell'Istituto Ernesto de Martino

SdL/AS/12

BERGAMO REDONA
FILATI LASTEX ALLA RISCOSSA

Cultura di classe

SdL/AS/12

Facciata A

Slogans dalla manifestazione del 28 maggio 1975.

Le lotte della Lastex dal 1962 al 1970.

Il padrone Menegatto. Interviste e canzoni
(«Mene-mene-gatto»; «Filati Lastex alla riscossa». «Noi della Lastex»).

La difesa del posto di lavoro.

Occupazioni e svaghi nella fabbrica occupata.
Interviste e canzoni («Bandiera bianca la vogliamo no». «O Pinotta bella Pinotta»).

Facciata B

«Menegatto vuoi la rovina di noi».

La solidarietà esterna e i risvolti familiari della lotta.
Interviste e canzoni.
(«Andiamo compagni». «Gh'è chi 'l fa i storie»).

La conclusione vittoriosa della lotta e la ripresa del lavoro.
Interviste e canzoni.
(«Non ti potrò scordar Filati Lastex». «Filati Lastex alla riscossa»).

ARCHIVI SONORI

A cura dell'Istituto Ernesto de Martino

Fotografia di Carlo Leidi, impaginazione Studio Steiner, stampa Grafica Cremonese, produzione Edizioni Bella Ciao s.r.l. Milano, via Melzo 9, novembre 1975

DEN SYNGENDE STREJKES
KOR OG ORKESTER

Arbejdere på Den Kongelige Porcelænsfabrik
<u>Den Syngende Strejkes Kor og Orkester</u>
7" EP
Demos (Demos 33)
1976
Denmark

The record sleeve states clearly:

The songs on this record were recorded at a joint meeting in the canteen at Den Kongelige Porcelainsfabrik in Copenhagen, on the morning of Monday, 8-23-1976. About 1,000 workers were present, who at the time had been on strike for 9 weeks to get the demand for a decent minimum wage met.

Den Kongelige Porcelainsfabrik produced the Royal Copenhagen brand of intricately patterned porcelain plateware, one of Denmark's most celebrated export goods. The songs in question are traditional folk and labor tunes, given new lyrics (printed on the back of the sleeve) which tell the story of the strike and outline the specific tactics used against the striking women by the courts and their bosses. At the time it was the longest strike in Danish history. The entire profit from sales of the record went to the strikers via a support committee.

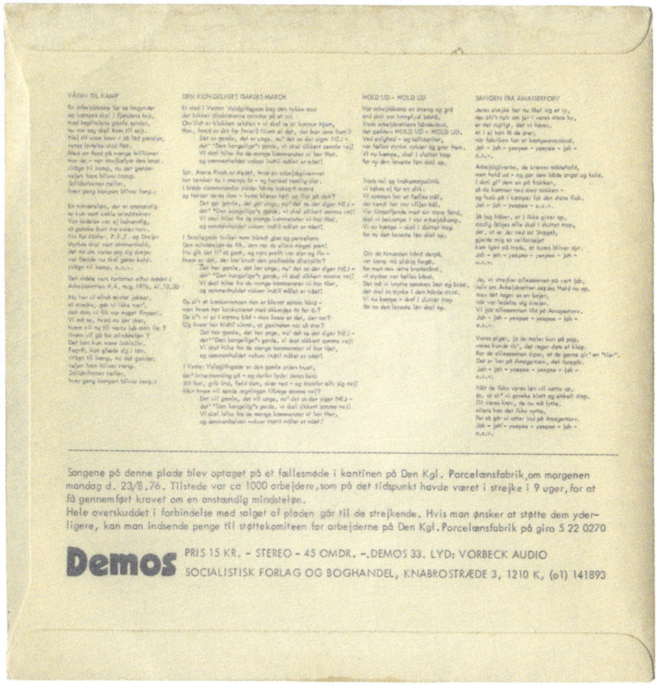

Les Ouvrières d'Obsession
<u>Histoire d'O...bsession Travail Liberté</u>
7" single
General Confederation of Labor (no cat. #)
ca. 1976
France

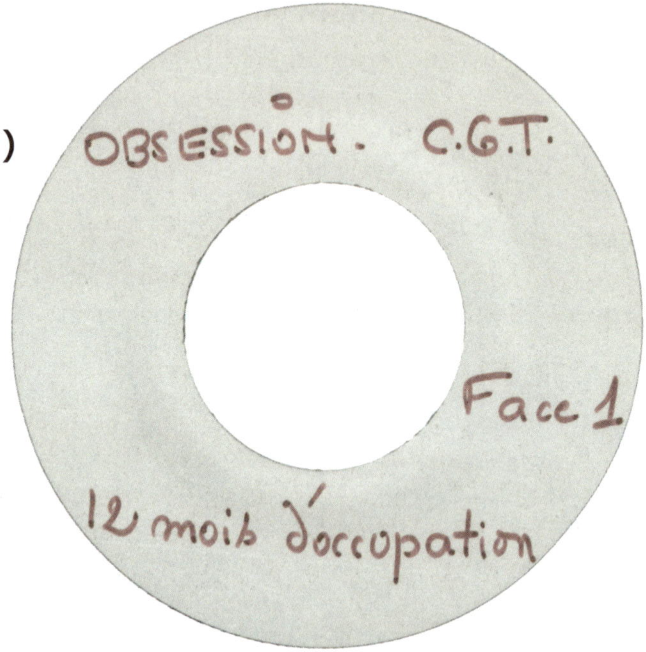

Obsession was a lingerie brand, and in 1975, following a wave of other closures in the textile industry in France, its parent GILMO filed for bankruptcy and fired 255 workers, essentially shutting down its three factories. In response, the women occupied one of them for over two years. "This struggle is led almost exclusively by women," recounts a worker in the recording. "We must of course take into account schedules: baby bottles, after school, public transport for evening shifts; because few women have a family vehicle!" The factory never reopened (and was ultimately demolished in 2011) but the women secured training to find other jobs. This record—produced by the workers' union, the General Confederation of Labor—mixes political monologues from workers with popular (and older, French Revolution-era) songs reworked with struggle-specific lyrics. The title, "Histoire d'O...bsession" is also a tongue-in-cheek pun, referencing the 1975 film *Histoire d'O,* based on the soft porn novel *The Story of O.*

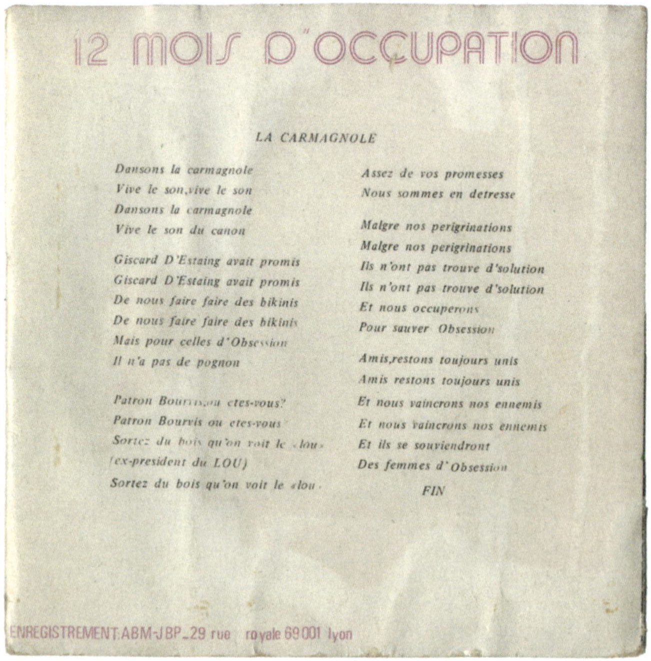

histoire
CGT
fsm
d"
travail
liberté
...bsession
dessin maqette michaud herick 78

pläne
S 30 E 100
Streik bei Mannesmann
Szenische Kantate
Text: Erika Runge
Musik: Dietrich Boekle
Hans Werner Henze
Niels Frederic Hoffmann
Luca Lombardi
Thomas Jahn
Wilfried Steinbrenner
Künstlerische Projektleitung
Hans Werner Henze

Various artists
Streik bei Mannesmann: Szenische Kantate
LP
Pläne (S 30 E 100)
1976
West Germany

This record is a collectively composed cantata (a musical version of a short drama in verse) of a then-recent wildcat strike and its fallout at Mannesmann steelworks in Duisburg, West Germany. The original strike resulted in the firing of 116 workers, but also developed into a strong, successful struggle with union support. This record was not made by the workers, nor is it a fundraising tool for the strike, instead it is constructed as a pedagogical object. A collaboration between journalist Erika Runge and a series of musicians (including noted German experimental composer Hans Werner Henze), the cantata was written for the 10th World Festival of Youth and Students held in Berlin (GDR) in 1973, which was organized to forge links between students, artists, and the working class. (The record label, Pläne, was based in Dortmund, West Germany, but it was an open secret that it was actually funded by the GDR.)

Included in the LP is an extensive insert with questions to ask when using this record as part of curriculum: Why do the workers resort to occupation? What forms of struggle preceded it? What attitude of the workers is expressed by the music? These questions are centered around the idea that "political and aesthetic education must coincide. . . . Music understanding can be trained on the concrete subject [of the strike], where music has a clear, functional relationship to the content." The back of the insert is a short essay expounding on the benefits of making modern music about workers' struggle:

> The musicians once again find their work subjectively satisfying and meaningful; instead of playing in front of empty rows of chairs and a crowd of professionals they play in front of a receptive, grateful, and discussion-happy audience.

In short, this record is part of the Marxist tradition attempting to sort out a more exacting relationship between culture and class consciousness.

Groupe Expression & the workers of Mangé

Les Fonderies L. Mangé et Cie: Occupées Depuis 8 Mois

7" EP

Self-produced (8477)

1977

Belgium

The first of two records about workers' occupations of the Mangé Foundry near Liège, Belgium. On August 27, 1976, workers decide to occupy the foundry after the company failed to pay their wages. On October 1st, the foundry declares bankruptcy under false pretenses in order to avoid paying the workers, and so they continue the occupation, now as a struggle to prevent the closure of the foundry. This record describes itself as one in a procession of tactics workers used to "break the wall of silence around their struggle." They had previously forced Radio-Télévision Belge (RTB)—the Francophone public broadcasting service—to report on the struggles; blocked a highway intersection under the gaze of an RTB cameraman; burst into the offices of economic officials; launched a raft on a river as part of their publicity actions; and, "Today, the workers have made this record."

The sleeve was designed and produced by the political journal *POUR*, a Belgian New Left publication founded in 1973 which took a radical political line connecting anti-authoritarianism and Marxism via a direct focus on people's struggles. This cover is a multi-folded, giant sheet of paper filled with photos, graphics, lyrics, and information about the occupation. Included are some great nuggets:

Somville, one of the bosses, is locked into the factory and forced to attend a staff meeting where there are also CSC and FGTB delegates, representatives of the secretariat to the regional economy and the Mayor of Embourg.

Les Fonderies L. Mangé et Cie
Fondées en 1895
4920 Sauheid-Embourg.
RUE J. DEFLANDRE, 2
occupées depuis 8 mois
FGTB

Historique

Déjà, avant les vacances, plusieurs arrêts de travail avaient eu lieu aux Fonderies Mangé pour protester contre le non-paiement des salaires.
Le 27 août, quand les travailleurs s'aperçoivent d'un découvert de 40 millions, ils occupent l'entreprise. Ils l'occupent toujours, depuis maintenant huit mois.
Il s'agit d'une entreprise viable qui a été gérée d'une manière catastrophique. Mais les travailleurs refusent de faire les frais de la mauvaise gestion des patrons et de se retrouver au

chômage. Pour empêcher la fermeture de l'entrepris
faillite frauduleuse est prononcée le premier octobre
travailleurs popularisent leur lutte, nouent des conta
entreprises en lutte de la région par toute une série d'

a

c les
:

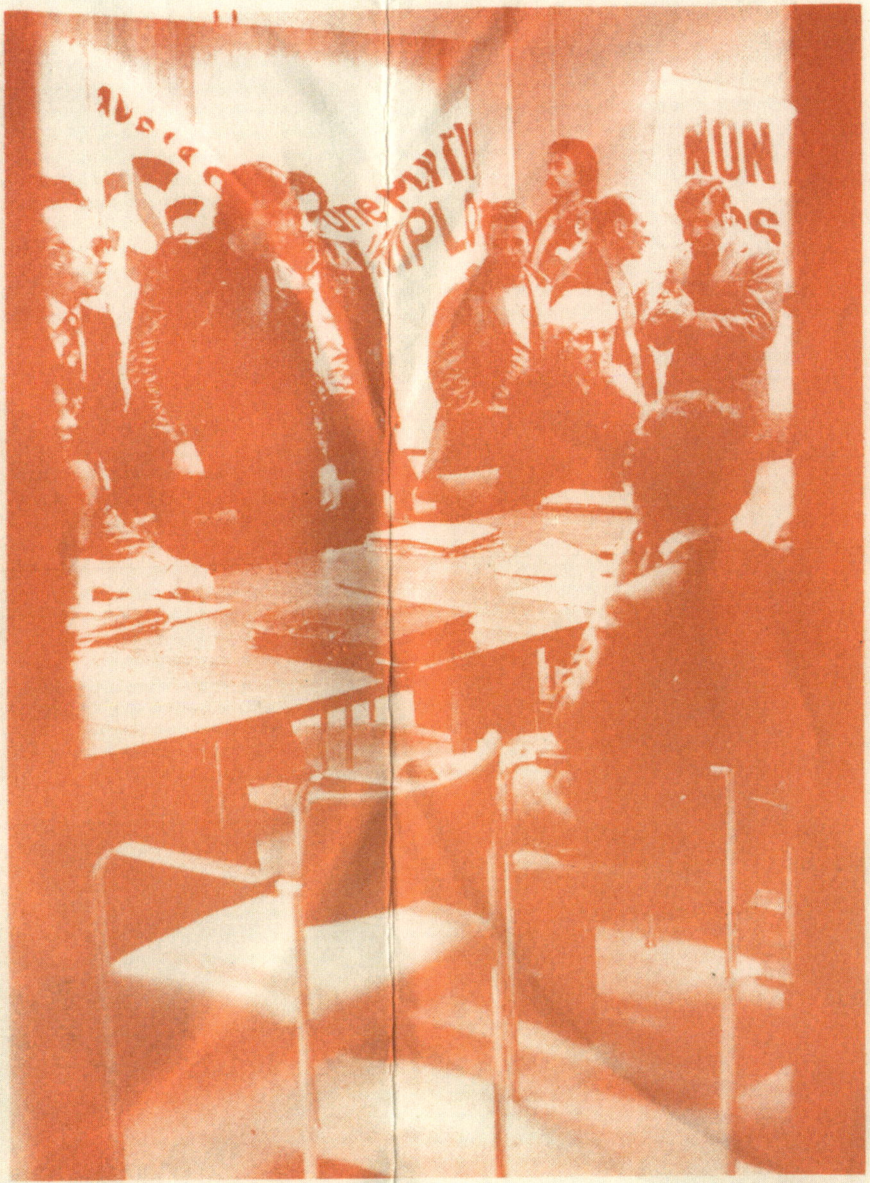

- l'autoroute Chênée-Beaufays est barré
arrêtées
- un radeau est lancé sur la Meuse
- un bus de la société des tramways liég
à transporter les ouvriers chez Gol à qui
de la fermeture,
- Somville, un des patrons, est séquestr
une assemblée du personnel où se trou
délégués CSC et FGTB, des représentan
l'Economie Régionale et le bourgmestr
Finalement, Gol en période électorale p
crédit de fabrication de 5 millions au cu
Mais ce n'est que du bois de rallonge et
semaines, le problème reste entier.
Aucun acheteur sérieux ne s'est présen
pourtant les commandent continuent à
Les travailleurs touchent, au début de 1
salaire. Sûrs de la rentabilité de leur ent
salaire en dépôt pour garantir leur produ
Autour de Mangé, c'est le silence. Un si

es voitures

est détourné et sert
primient leur refus

bligé d'assister à
galement des
Secrétariat à
nbourg.
d'accorder un
de la faillite.
quelques

entreprise et
er.
eurs arriérés de
e, ils mettent leur

voulu par Gol.

Pourtant les travailleurs forcent la RTB à diffuser des informations sur le développement de leur lutte, ils barrent le carrefour de l'autoroute de Luxembourg à Embourg sous les regards du cameraman de la RTB, ils font irruption le 1er avril dans les bureaux de l'Economie Régionale Wallonne à Bruxelles, enfin c'est l' « Arts Center », le building de l'ERW qui a reçu récemment la visite des travailleurs de Mangé...

Aujourd'hui, les travailleurs ont réalisé ce disque. C'est sur chacun de nous, travailleurs de la région de Liège et de partout dans le pays, syndiqués, chômeurs qu'ils comptent pour briser le mur du silence dressé autour de leur lutte.

« Nous refusons d'être chômeurs, disent-ils dans une lettre ouverte au bourgmestre d'Embourg, et de perdre notre emploi. Nous sommes convaincus que les Fonderies Mangé constituent une des dernières fonderies du bassin industriel Liégeois et de la région walonne. Il n'est ni pensable ni acceptable qu'elles disparaissent, que ce travail parte à l'étranger et que les entreprises importent toute la fonte dont elles continuent à avoir besoin ».

FACE 1

1. Les Fonderi

Notre pauv' Wallonie
se trouve bien démunie
on ferme ses industries
partout on licencie
mais nous n' voulons pas
perdre notre emploi

Ah non nous n'partirons p
L' chômage nous n'en vou

Ils nous laissent les trogn
d'une mauvaise gestion
Ils nous mettent dehors
sans se soucier d' not' so
mais nous n' voulons pas
perdre notre emploi

Ah non nous n' partirons
L 'chômage nous n'en vou

Faut-il prendre un avion
pour qu'la télévision
parle de notre action
mais nous nous contente
de garder l' patron
de réveiller Gol

Ah non nous n' partirons
L' chômage nous n'en vou

'angé

Voila sept mois qu' ça dure
s'ils comptent sur notre usure
ils s' foutent le doigt dans l'œil
ils peuvent en faire leur deuil
car nous n' voulons pas perdre
perdre notre emploi

Ah non nous n' partirons pas
L'chômage nous n'en voulons pas

L'usine peut fonctionner
ça nous l'avons prouvé
nous les gars d' chez Mangé
on n' demande qu'à travailler
car nous n' voulons pas
perdre notre emploi

Ah non nous n' partirons pas
L'chômage nous n'en voulons pas
2 ×

FACE 2

1. Allo! (le ministère de l'économie régionale wallone)

Allo, l'ERW,
Monsieur Desamory,
pourquoi tu n'as pas fait
ce que tu nous avait promis?

A la fonderie Mangé
Les moules sont pas terminés
Les mouleurs sont allés voir
L'heure où ils devront pointer

2 X

Nous avions bien du boulot
Mais à cause des rigolos
Qui jouaient à la gestion
Le travail part pour de bon.

Les politiciens wallons
Tardent à prendre une décision
Il faudra peut-être ma mère
Occuper le ministère

2 X

Allo, le Ministère du Travail,
Monsieur Califice,
qu'as-tu fait de tes bons offices?

Si tu veux faire not' bonheur
Califice, Califice,
Si tu veux faire not' bonheur
Donnes du travail aux travailleurs

Y' a déjà trop de chômeurs
Califice, Califice,
Y' a déjà trop de chômeurs
Ferme pas la porte aux travailleurs

La, la, la, la, la, la
La, la, la, la, la, la
La, la, la, la, la, la
La, la, la, la, la, la

Y' a déjà trop de chômeurs
Califice, Califice,
Y' a déjà trop de chômeurs
Ferme pas la porte aux travailleurs

Allo, l'ERW,
Les travailleurs en ont ras-le-Gol
Merci!

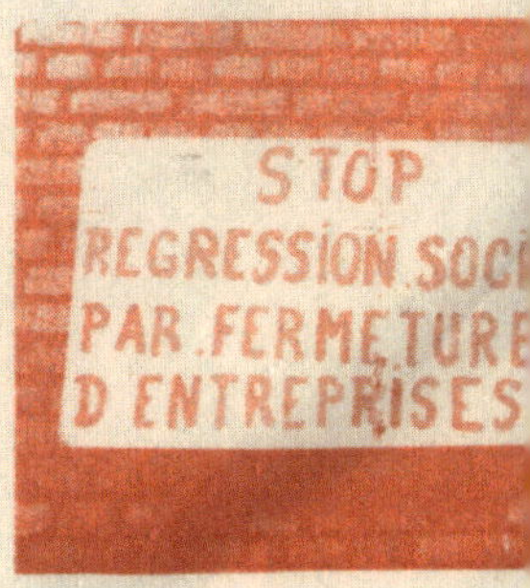

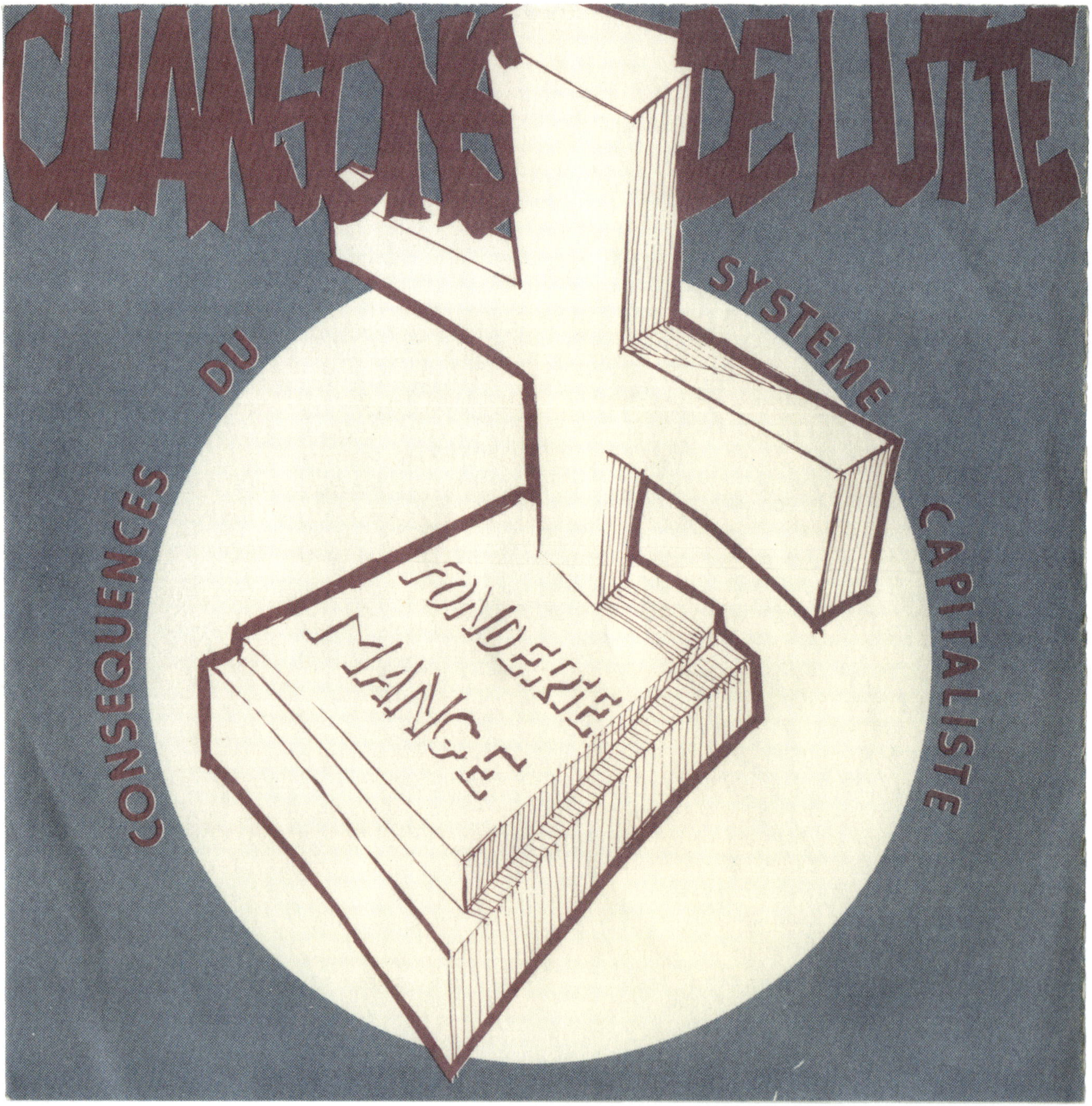
CHANSONS DE LUTTE
CONSEQUENCES DU SYSTEME CAPITALISTE
FONDERIE MANGE

Groupe Expression & the workers of Mangé

Chansons de Lutte

7" EP

Disque Fonderies Mangé (no catalog #)

1977

Belgium

Subtitled "Conséquences du Système Capitaliste," this second record of struggle songs assembled by Groupe Expression has a more populist outlook. As stated on the sleeve: "This second disc is a new call for solidarity because more than ever they need your militant support." In June 1977 the national employment office refused to grant workers pay for their time working whilst occupying the factory—basically claiming that they are unemployed and not due wages, all while working full-time.

The cover is much simpler, following the conventions of pop records, with a single graphic on the front (a tombstone with "Fonderie Mangé" written on it). This graphic is a cleaner interpretation of the same image which had been painted on a banner and hoisted onto the factory, which is featured in the photos on the first record's sleeve. If the front cover is emotionally dark, the back provides its antithesis, a giant raised fist emerging out of a guitar neck. (A version of this guitar/fist logo was also featured on the previous record sleeve.) It's not just the cover that is more outward looking, the songs are more diverse, with two folk and workers' songs being flanked by a rock song ("L'Usine Occupée"—The Occupied Factory) and a take on a tango ("L'Autogestion"—Self-Organization).

Les Wabco
<u>8 Semaines de Lutte!!</u>
7" single
Disques Vendémiaire (vdes019)
1977
France

Unlike most of the strikes represented through these records—where we've been able to dig up suplementary information—we've had a very difficult time finding out additional context for a 1976-1977 strike at Wabco (Westinghouse Air Brake Manufacturing Company). A US company, Wabco had two plants in France, employing a combined 1,850 people. From this record it is clear that workers with the CFDT went out on strike for eight weeks over a large and complex set of demands, and the strike won them most of those demands. The record itself is a self-styled document of the struggle, with a "history of the conflict with audio documentation" on the A-side, and strike songs (titled "And the Wabcos shouted.... And the Wabcos sang") performed by the workers on the B-side. The record was produced in association with the CFDT, and was likely intended as a document for militant workers and union members. The label, Vendémaire, was an explicitly leftist record company run by the anarchist and former Renault auto worker Jean-Pierre Graziani, releasing a wide range of militant music, from international solidarity records to free jazz to Corsican nationalist songs.

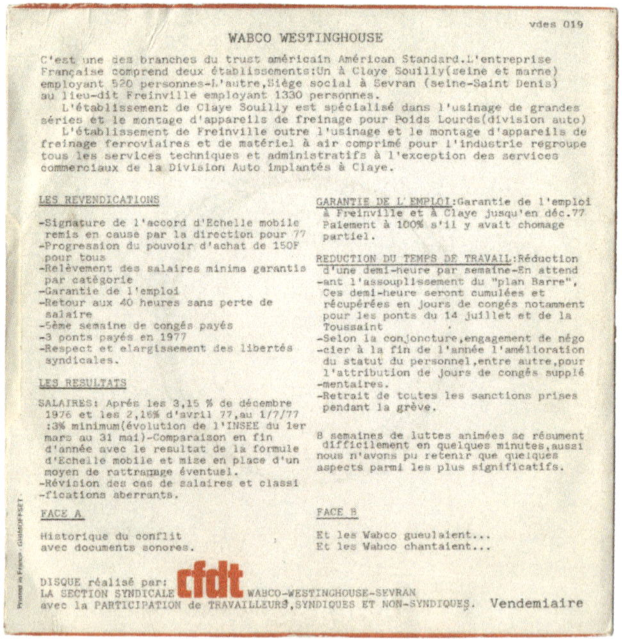

vdes 019

WABCO WESTINGHOUSE

C'est une des branches du trust américain Américan Standard.L'entreprise Française comprend deux établissements:Un à Claye Souilly(seine et marne) employant 520 personnes-L'autre,Siège social à Sevran (seine-Saint Denis) au lieu-dit Freinville employant 1330 personnes.

L'établissement de Claye Souilly est spécialisé dans l'usinage de grandes séries et le montage d'appareils de freinage pour Poids Lourds(division auto)

L'établissement de Freinville outre l'usinage et le montage d'appareils de freinage ferroviaires et de matériel à air comprimé pour l'industrie regroupe tous les services techniques et administratifs à l'exception des services commerciaux de la Division Auto implantés à Claye.

<u>LES REVENDICATIONS</u>

-Signature de l'accord d'Echelle mobile remis en cause par la direction pour 77
-Progression du pouvoir d'achat de 150F pour tous
-Relèvement des salaires minima garantis par catégorie
-Garantie de l'emploi
-Retour aux 40 heures sans perte de salaire
-5ème semaine de congés payés
-3 ponts payés en 1977
-Respect et elargissement des libertés syndicales.

<u>LES RESULTATS</u>

SALAIRES: Aprés les 3,15 % de décembre 1976 et les 2,16% d'avril 77,au 1/7/77 :3% minimum(évolution de l'INSEE du 1er mars au 31 mai)-Comparaison en fin d'année avec le resultat de la formule d'Echelle mobile et mise en place d'un moyen de rattrapage éventuel.
-Révision des cas de salaires et classi-fications aberrants.

<u>GARANTIE DE L'EMPLOI</u>:Garantie de l'emploi à Freinville et à Claye jusqu'en déc.77 Paiement à 100% s'il y avait chomage partiel.

<u>REDUCTION DU TEMPS DE TRAVAIL</u>:Réduction d'une demi-heure par semaine-En attend-ant l'assouplissement du "plan Barre", Ces demi-heure seront cumulées et récupérées en jours de congés notamment pour les ponts du 14 juillet et de la Toussaint
-Selon la conjoncture,engagement de négo-cier à la fin de l'année l'amélioration du statut du personnel,entre autre,pour l'attribution de jours de congés supplé-mentaires.
-Retrait de toutes les sanctions prises pendant la grève.

8 semaines de luttes animées se résument difficilement en quelques minutes,aussi nous n'avons pu retenir que quelques aspects parmi les plus significatifs.

<u>FACE A</u>

Historique du conflit
avec documents sonores.

<u>FACE B</u>

Et les Wabco gueulaient...
Et les Wabco chantaient...

DISQUE réalisé par:
LA SECTION SYNDICALE cfdt WABCO-WESTINGHOUSE-SEVRAN
avec la PARTICIPATION de TRAVAILLEURS,SYNDIQUES ET NON-SYNDIQUES. Vendemiaire

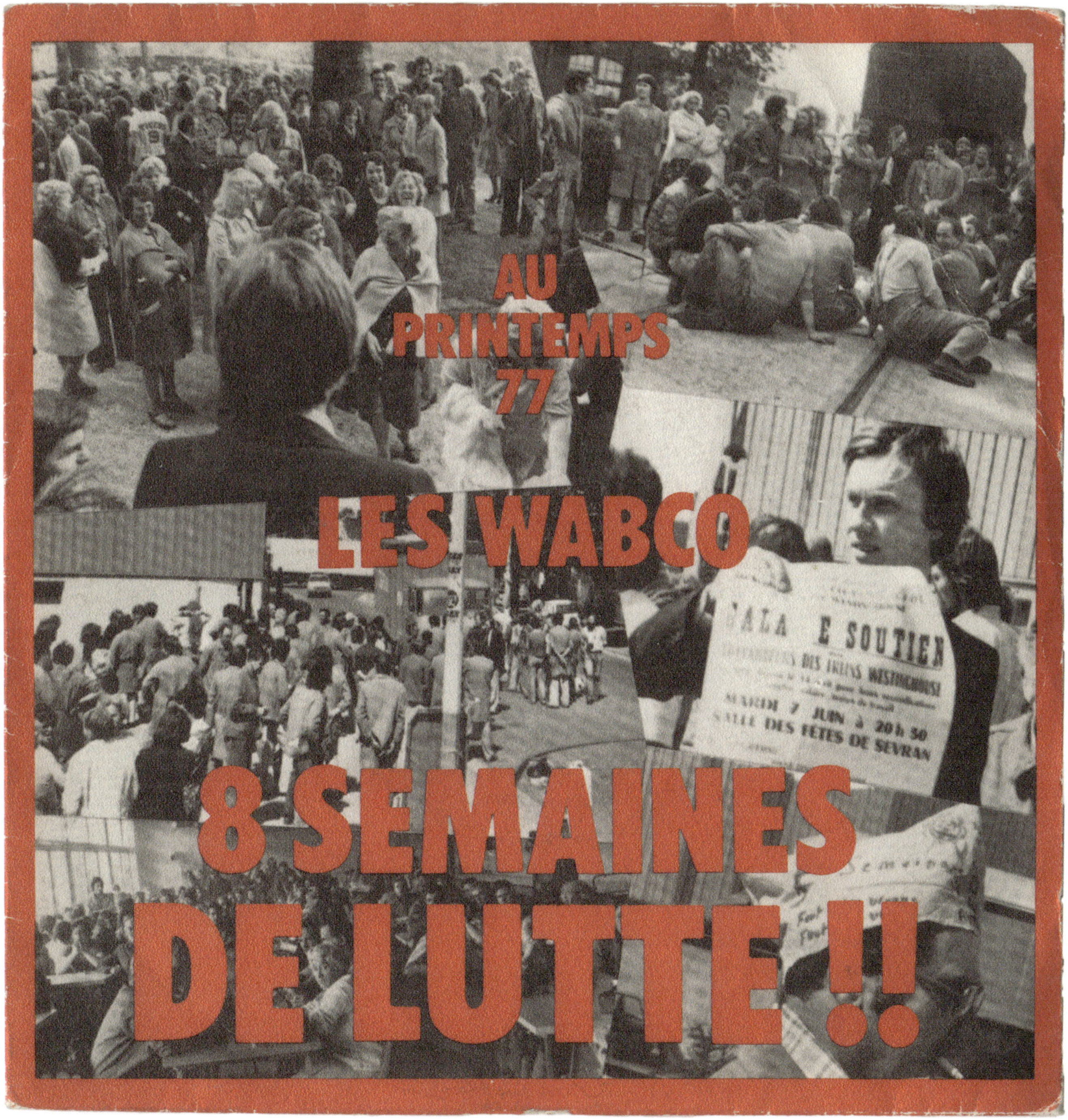
AU
PRINTEMPS
77
LES WABCO
8 SEMAINES
DE LUTTE !!
MARDI 7 JUIN à 20 h 30
SALLE DES FÊTES DE SEVRAN

BT
KLUBBEN
DET GRAFISKE PERSONALE
B.T.
Klubben - det grafiske personale
Tirsdag 1. februar 1977
Hvem lukkede Berlingeren?
Den kendelse
og Det Berlingske
blev ikke afsagt
Styrk solidariteten med
ADVARSEL
Ledelsen lukkede Berlingeren!
Til bladets aviskunder
Når Berlingske Tidendes ledelse nu græder krokodilletårer over ikke at kunne få deres aviser på gaden, skal der ikke herske tvivl om placeringen af ansvaret herfor.
1000 grafiske medarbejdere møder hver dag og står klar ved maskinerne. De vil gerne i gang. Det er blot et tryk på en knap. Teknisk set.
Hvad ønsker Berlingske?
AVISER ELLER INVALIDE-PENSIONISTER
retten er gået i tærerne
Direktør Oluf Poulsen, Berlingske Tidende
B.T.-Klubben

Jan Toftlund & Fællesakkorden/Den Røde Lue
"De Gemmer Sig Bag Løgne" b/w "Balladen om Berlingeren"
7" single
B.T. Klubben (BTK-1)
1977
Denmark

To explain this record, we need go no further than the sleeve, which states unequivocally:

Produced to aid the graphic workers in their fight against:
—Increasing the pace of work
—Extension of working hours
—Reduction of days off
—Dismissal of 300 workers
—Deterioration of income

B.T. Klubben was the union of graphic workers at the *B.T.* tabloid, one of the longest running newspapers in Denmark (founded in 1916). The background here is the conversion to computer technology to increase prepress productivity. Prior to 1977, *B.T.* was viewed as one of the best places to work, but in January of '77 management dropped all previous labor agreements, doubled the speed of work, and fired over 300 people. The union resisted, and almost 1,000 were sacked the next day. This led to workers forming a picket line, blocking access to the paper's production facility. The police were sent in to break the picket, and in response protests in support of the workers broke out across the country, and other workers at *B.T.* joined the strike. In May the strike was settled, largely in the workers' favor, at least in the short term. Everyone fired would be reinstated, but over time the workforce would continue to be cut and the few workers remaining would be trained to do the work of dozens via computers. This technological replacement of specialized typesetters and prepress workers happened across the globe, causing significant labor resistance, yet we've only found two records documenting this, and both are from Denmark.

All the musicians here are committed leftists, Toftlund is a singer/songwriter in the Leonard Cohen mold, Fællesakkorden is a rock group that released an album on Forlaget Tiden (record label of the Danish Communist Party), and Den Røde Lue was a long running prog act with records on Forlaget Tiden and Demos, as well as being part of the campaigns to stop Denmark from joining the EF (a predecessor to the EU) and NATO (both causes garnering massive popular support from the left).

Various artists
Streik!
LP
Plateselskapet Mai (MAI 7701)
1977
Norway

Not emerging from a specific strike, this compilation of 14 songs is an homage to the strike more broadly, developed as a tool for the militant labor organizing then sweeping Norway. More specifically, many of the songs focus on the role of the strikebreaker and the police in suppressing labor action, in particular in the wake of the successful Linjegods (freight transportation company) strike in 1976.

The label, Plateselskapet Mai, was founded in 1973 as an audio wing of the leftist publishing house Oktober Forlag, itself a project of the Norwegian Arbeidernes Kommunistparti—AKP(m-l), the Maoist Workers Communist Party. Many of the songs express this radicalism, in direct opposition to the leadership of the Norwegian Confederation of Trade Unions and the social democrat Labour Party [Arbeiderpartiet].

The tracks here are a combination of labor classics such as the Joe Hill song "Casey Jones" (performed here by the feminist folk group Reis Kjerringa) and "Til streik!" (an anthem of the Spanish antifascist movement, penned by anarchist Chicho Sánchez Ferlosio), as well as songs about the early 20th century history of the Norwegian labor movement. The song "Vi husker Menstadslaget" is about one of the most dramatic labor conflicts in modern Norwegian history, the battle of Menstad in June 1931 at Norsk Hydro's Menstad plant. A brief struggle between police and strikers saw law-and-order forces overwhelmed by the demonstrators, who threw stones and iron piping before retreating.

Of special interest are a couple songs about more recent Norwegian worker militancy. "Svartfoten på brygga" [Blackfoot on the Pier] by Almennigen, a folk-progg group from Trondheim, documents the victorious Oslo Brewery strike of the winter of 1977 (and is set to the tune of the Irish rebel song "Come Out, Ye Black and Tans"). "Hustadsangen," also by Almennigen, is a battle song against strike breakers and the police during the Fiskmatbedrift strike in 1976/77 in Hustad, a village in Trondheim.

STREiK !
"STREIK"
ARBEIDERKLASSENS
VIKTIGSTE VÅPEN
POLITI
VI
FORDØMMER
STREIKE-
BRYTARE
POL
MAI

Jacques Brunet
Les Piqueteurs de la Gloire
LP
Self-produced
1977
Canada

When you're in the heat of a struggle it's easy to forget that the context—even if it feels self evident at the time—will quickly fade, if not completely disappear. To that point, here we have an entire album in support of striking workers—yet outside of what can be discerned from the song lyrics, no information about the strike itself is included on the record sleeve. The picketers on the front are rendered as silhouettes and hence flattened symbols—there aren't even slogans on the picket signs. The musician or band isn't named either, on the sleeve or on the labels of the record itself. The only contextual info is revealed diegetically in the backside graphic: a picket sign with the tracklist written on it (and nothing else) leans against brick, and rendered behind it in graffiti: "by the strikers of Radio-Mutuel, on strike from January '77." The emphasis is clearly on the music itself, technically accomplished folk rock with prog flourishes that traces a narrative arc of the strike over the course of nine songs.

Radio-Mutuel had stations across Eastern Canada and was the oldest and one of the largest private radio networks in Quebec. On January 26, 1977, workers in five Mutuel stations represented by the Confédération des syndicats nationaux (CSN) went on strike, joined two months later by Canadian Union of Public Employees (CUPE) workers at a Quebec city station. They stayed out on strike for just under two years, and later learned that union members had been wiretapped by the police the entire time! Discogs lists the musician as Jacques Brunet, with an unidentified band, while a YouTube video of one of the songs states, "this album, having served as a defense fund, was composed by Radio-Mutuel strikers."

LES PIQUETEURS
DE LA
GLOIRE

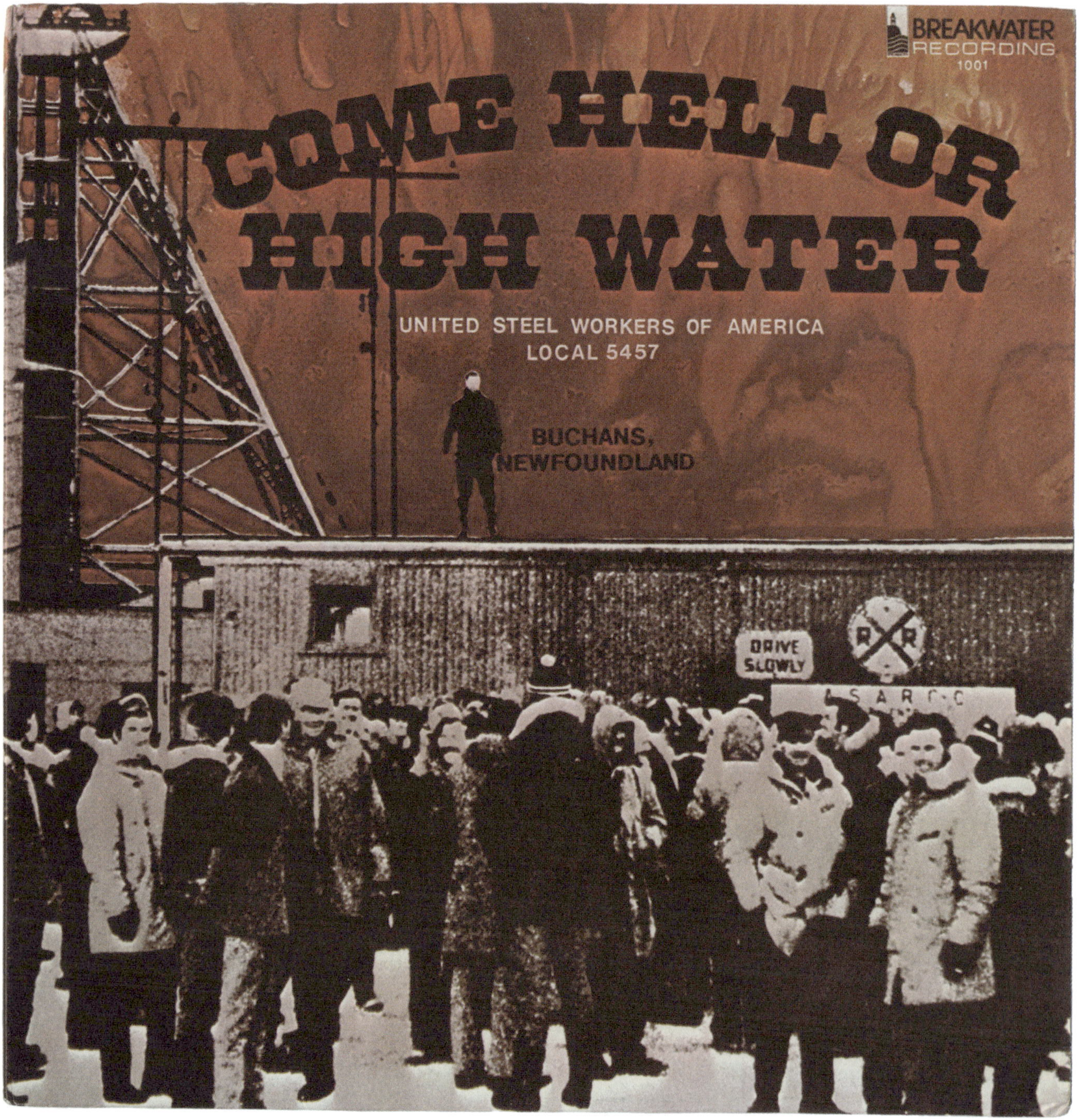
BREAKWATER
RECORDING
1001
COME HELL OR
HIGH WATER
UNITED STEEL WORKERS OF AMERICA
LOCAL 5457
BUCHANS,
NEWFOUNDLAND
DRIVE
SLOWLY
R R

United Steel Workers of America Local 5457
<u>Come Hell or High Water: Songs of the Buchans Miners</u>
LP
Breakwater Recording
1977
Canada

Subtitled "Songs of the Buchans Miners" this record is just that, a recreation—as opposed to field or contemporaneous studio recording—of twelve songs that arose from a successful 1973 strike of hardrock miners (United Steel Workers of America, Local 5457) in the company town of Buchans, Newfoundland, against the multi-national American Smelting and Refining Company (ASARCO). On the back of the record sleeve, Peter Narvaez of Newfoundland University's folklore department goes into great detail chronicling the initial development and circulation of the songs:

When [local poet] Angus submitted 'All Because of ASARCO' shortly after the 1973 strike commenced, some of the union members with musical ability developed an instrumental and vocal arrangement for the text and recorded a cassette which they then broadcast through the roof-speaker of a car that accompanied the marchers. The blaring speaker of Vice President Ivan Hodder's 'Yellow Peril,' as the car was fondly nicknamed, functioned as a musical background for the marchers who soon learned the lyrics and heartily vocalized their protests in song. This procedure was so successful that it continued throughout the duration of the strike. As significant events occurred, Angus would sit at his kitchen table and purposefully create serious parodies to popular Newfoundland melodies which would later be learned and sung by the marchers. The familiarity of the airs that Angus selected accelerated the speed with which unionists learned the songs and used them as relevant vehicles of protest.

Beyond the extensive liner notes of the sleeve, included within is a pocket-sized lyric publication designed to look like a union membership book—they obviously want these songs to be an active part of future struggles and believe in their strength. In this context, it's interesting that the record was not released by the United Steel Workers, but instead by a small, local Newfoundland label called Breakwater, which released only one other album, a collection of Newfoundland fiddle tunes.

BREAKWATER RECORDING
Side A
1001
1. Cock of the North (1:01)
2. The Christmas of '49 (2:17)
BREAKWATER
3. All Because of ASARCO (3:25)
4. The Victims (3:08)
5. The Buchans Strike (3:25)
6. Solidarity Forever (1:55)
Copyright © 1977 by Breakwater Books Limited.

BREAKWATER RECORDING
Side B
1001
1. Newfoundland Forever (2:46)
2. Unity Forever (2:42)
BREAKWATER
3. Our Leader Our President
Don Head (2:50)
4. The Bold Union Boy (4:21)
5. Aftermath (2:10)
6. Drunken Miners (1:17)
Copyright © 1977 by Breakwater Books Limited.

COME HELL OR HIGH WATER
LOCAL 5457
UNITED STEELWORKERS OF AMERICA
USA
AFL-CIO-CLC
BUCHANS
PRAY FOR THE DEAD
AND
FIGHT LIKE HELL
FOR THE LIVING
Signed: MOTHER JONES 1902

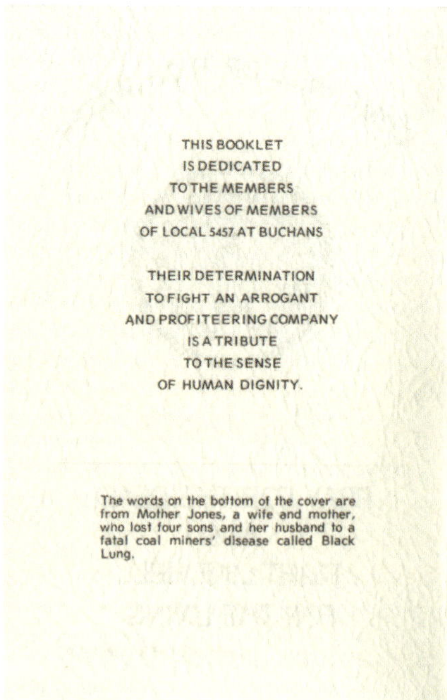
THIS BOOKLET
IS DEDICATED
TO THE MEMBERS
AND WIVES OF MEMBERS
OF LOCAL 5457 AT BUCHANS
THEIR DETERMINATION
TO FIGHT AN ARROGANT
AND PROFITEERING COMPANY
IS A TRIBUTE
TO THE SENSE
OF HUMAN DIGNITY.
The words on the bottom of the cover are from Mother Jones, a wife and mother, who lost four sons and her husband to a fatal coal miners' disease called Black Lung.

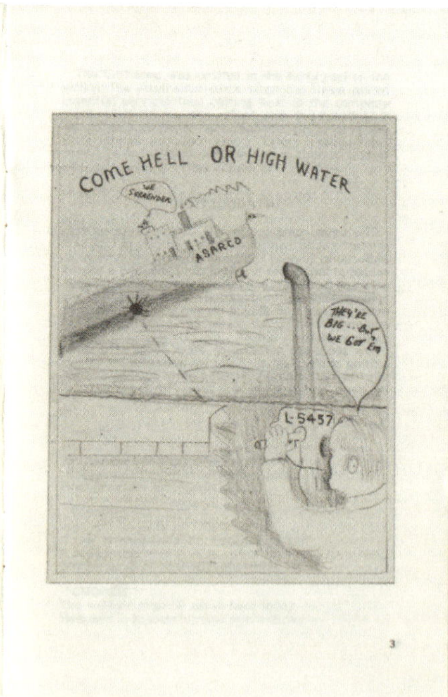
COME HELL OR HIGH WATER
ASARCO
L-5457
3

SONGS OF THE BUCHANS MINERS

In 1969 Canadian folklorist Edith Fowke stated that "Canadian workers have been less militant and less inclined to sing about their grievances than their neighbours to the south", and "the United Steelworkers are one of Canada's largest and most aggressive unions, but they report only one song". Recent history, however, has outdated these observations. In 1973 a strike of hardrock miners (United Steelworkers of America, Local 5457) in the company town of Buchans, Newfoundland, against the multi-national American Smelting and Refining Company (ASARCO), fostered a series of very militant union songs. Through a poetical formulation of significant issues these creations inspired solidarity within the community labour force and bolstered the workers' determination to achieve major concessions, which they ultimately attained, from an often intransigent management. Sung daily by hundreds of strikers and their families as they marched through the town, the moving songs re-created on this record still convey the drama and emotions which tore apart a community from March 15 to October 2.

The marching and singing strategy of 1973 was built upon the grim memories of the strike experience of 1971. That five month confrontation, which many judged as a defeat for the union, was characterized by a slow but steady ebbing of union morale. During the course of the 1971 conflict a lifetime resident of Buchans, Hazel Flight, wrote the "Buchan's Strike" (Side A, Band 5) in collaboration with her sister Fronie. As Hazel remembers, the immediate inspiration for the song arose when her father, like many other union members, "was preparing to move his family elsewhere as making a living was very far from sight". One unionist recollects that when another strike was called in 1973, this time "we wanted to show them that we meant business". Thus, assembling at the union hall in groups that sometimes numbered two and three hundred persons, strikers, wives, children and sympathizers marched up to the picket line at the company gate every morning and noon in order to face the management and staff of ASARCO.

However, many union members believed that just facing the staff was insufficient. They considered it important to develop the impact of the marching ritual through the use of songs. Angus Lane, a unionist and a well know local poet, helped fulfill this need. Some of his fame in Buchans was based on his rhymed portrayal of an historical incident in the "Christmas of '49" (Side A, Band 2) which graphically described some of the difficulties employees had experienced in their attempts to leave the mines during the Christmas season in the days before 1956, when the ASARCO railway was the only access to and from the town. When Angus submitted "All Because of ASARCO" shortly after the 1973 strike commenced, some of the union members with musical ability developed an instrumental and vocal arrangement for the text and recorded a cassette which they then broadcast through the roof-speaker of a car that accompanied the marchers. The blaring speaker of Vice President Ivan Hodder's "Yellow Peril", as the car was fondly nicknamed, functioned as a musical background for the marchers who soon learned the lyrics and heartily vocalized their protests in song. This procedure was so successful that it continued throughout the duration of the strike. As significant events occurred, Angus would sit at his kitchen table and purposefully create serious parodies to popular Newfoundland melodies which would later be learned and sung by the marchers. The familiarity of the airs that Angus selected accelerated the speed with which unionists learned the songs and used them as relevant vehicles of protest.

The majority of Angus's union poems along with the "Buchans Strike" by Hazel and Fronie Flight and the internationally accepted "Solidarity Forever" by Ralph Chaplin were later published in a booklet entitled **Come Hell or High Water** by the union local as a testimony to a successful strike effort and as an encouragement to organized labour. A copy of this historic songbook is enclosed in the jacket of this record. As the songs in the latter portions of the songbook indicate, the feelings between management and union members were often bitter, leading to violent clashes that resulted in the physical injury of workers, the destruction of company property (for example the "caboose" at the company gate depicted on the cover of the album was subsequently burned) and the indictment of union President Don Head for defying a court injunction which limited the number of union pickets to four and provided access to company property for management personnel and office staff. As carried by the news media, Head's statement "come hell or high water, law or no law, nobody is going to cross that picket line until the company names a date for a resumption of negotiations" became a rallying cry for the strikers but was eventually used as evidence against him in provincial court. The union was greatly encouraged, however, by the act of confidence it received from hundreds of supporters throughout the Province and Canada whose contributions quickly paid their President's conviction fine of $5,000. The turbulence of these days was partially relieved by the studious efforts of Howard J. Dyer, Commissioner for the Industrial Inquiry Commission, whose basic settlement recommendations were finally adopted by both parties after three months of delays by an obstinate ASARCO. These later events of the strike are poetically summarized in "Aftermath", a song which was composed (after the printing of **Come Hell or High Water**) by Angus for the victory banquet (Side B, Band 5).

As a re-creation of the original strike renditions, the music on this record owes its greatest debt to union member Harold Skanes, who as the musical impresario of Buchans for the last thirty years has tutored many musicians in his band the "Buchaneers". Although the personnel and musical styles of the group have often changed during this period, the Buchaneers have continued to be a viable musical force in the community and all the musicians playing union songs on this album have been members of that band at one time or another. The first item on the disc "Cock of the North" (Side A, Band 1), with the excellent accordion lead of Don Bursey, reflects the musical repertoire of the early Buchaneers with its emphasis on traditional Newfoundland dance tunes. The musical accompaniments for most of the vocals here demonstrate the continuing importance of button accordion in local Newfoundland performances as well as the flavour of country music as conveyed by Harold's adept mandolin picking and the solid rhythm guitar backup of his son Len. The twentieth century heritage of country music, so much a part of the musical scene in Atlantic Canada, influenced Harold at an early age via the airwaves of WWVA, Wheeling, West Virginia, which beamed clearly into Buchans every night. It was the rhythm and blues and rock styles of the Buchaneers of the sixties, however, that has been the most important influence for Sandy and Bill Ivany, featured vocalists on these recordings. Sandy, Recording Secretary for the union local and strong lead vocalist, not only sang Angus Lane's lyrics during the strike but helped shape them as well through his practical editing of the texts for singing purposes. The tight harmonies provided by Bill Ivany, a former Buchaneers electric guitarist, and his rousing lead vocal in the traditional "Drunken Miners" (Side B, Band 6) as played and sung by the Ivany family rock group, "Unity", reflect a newer musical dimension in the Buchans of today.

Before closing it should be mentioned that the struggle of the strike of '73 has also inspired a major artistic stage production in the highly acclaimed drama "Buchans — A Mining Town" written and performed by the Newfoundland Mummers Troupe in 1974 and 1975 to packed audiences across Canada.

As the recordist and producer of this record I wish to express my sincerest gratitude to the people of Buchans for the kindness, warmth, hospitality and patience they have afforded my wife Ann Anderson and myself in our numerous visits to the community. The heartfelt sincerity of these performances is an inspiration for working people everywhere.

Peter Narváez
Folklore Department
Memorial University of Newfoundland

Personnel

Don Bursey, button accordion; Bill Ivany, acoustic guitar, harmony vocals, lead vocal on "Drunken Miners"; George Ivany, organ and harmony, vocal on "Drunken Miners"; Gerald Ivany, electric bass and harmony on "Drunken Miners"; Kitty Ivany, harmony on "Drunken Miners"; Sandy Ivany, lead vocals; Angus Lane, monologist on "Christmas of '49" and vocal on "Solidarity Forever"; Harold Skanes, mandolin and vocal on "Solidarity Forever"; Len Skanes, acoustic guitar and vocal on "Solidarity Forever".

Recorded on location in Buchans, Newfoundland by Peter Narváez on: November 8, 1975; June 6, 1976; and August 14, 1976
Producer: Peter Narváez
Mixdowns: Peter Narváez, Neil Rosenberg, Rick Harris
Production Assistance: Memorial University of Newfoundland Folklore and Language Archive
Technical assistance: Kenneth S. Goldstein
Photography: cover photos donated by Don Head
Front cover design and art: Ian Stewart in co-operation with Extension services, Memorial University, Newfoundland.

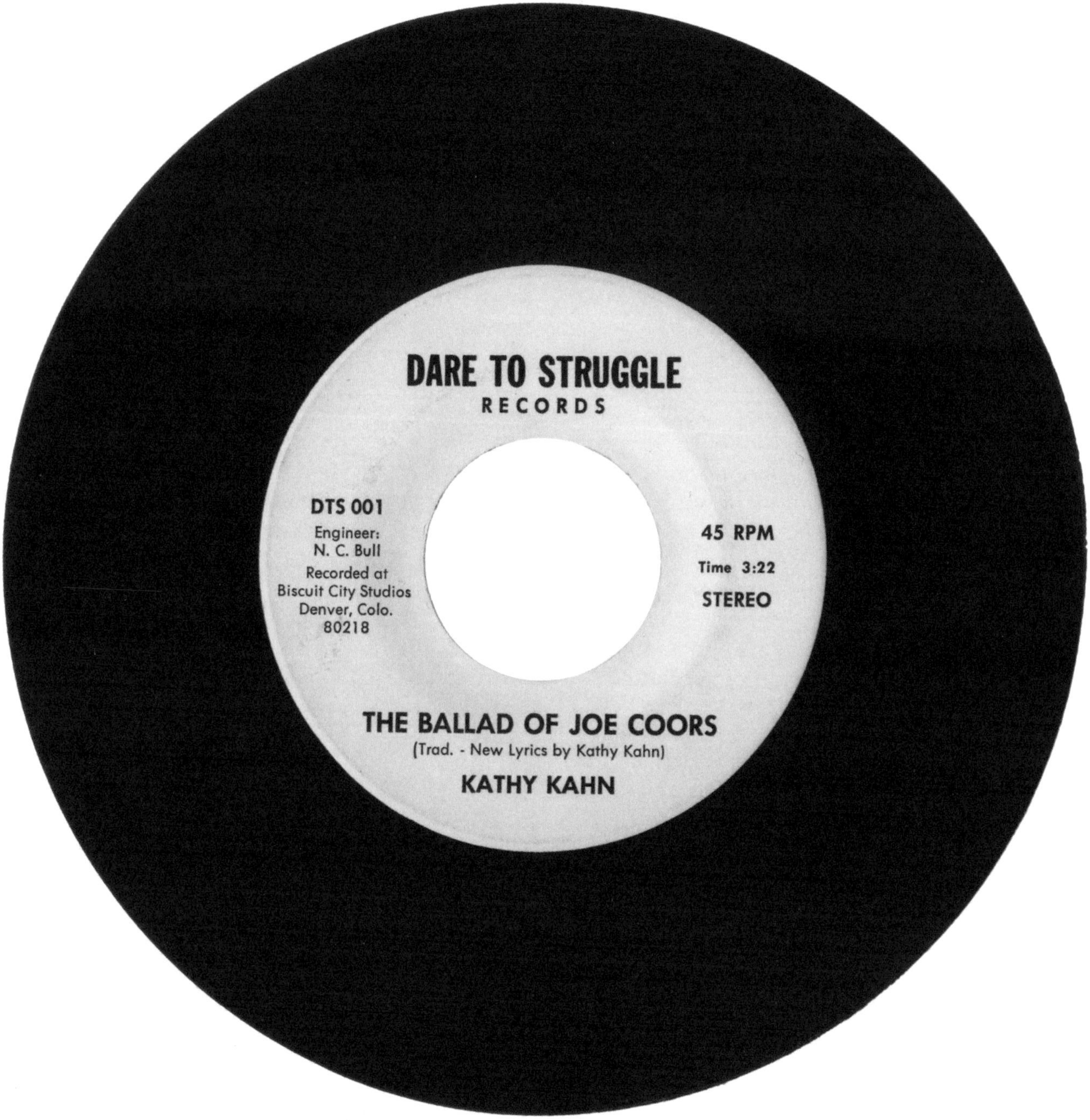
DARE TO STRUGGLE
RECORDS
DTS 001
Engineer:
N. C. Bull
Recorded at
Biscuit City Studios
Denver, Colo.
80218
45 RPM
Time 3:22
STEREO
THE BALLAD OF JOE COORS
(Trad. - New Lyrics by Kathy Kahn)
KATHY KAHN

Kathy Kahn and Danny McMahan
<u>Coors Brewery Strike Songs</u>
7" single
Dare to Struggle Records (DTS 001)
1977
USA

The strike at Coors' brewery in 1977 was preceded—and outlasted—by a well organized boycott by Latinx groups in the late 1960s that was spread across the US via other anti-racist, feminist, and gay liberation organizations. Coors' founder, Joseph Coors, was a virulent racist and homophobe with an immense amount of money and the political connections that come with it. To give you a snapshot, potential workers had to undergo an "are you gay or a communist" litmus test in their interviews. Rather than pay, the strike by Brewery Workers Local 36 was over these political and social concerns, as well as discriminatory hiring and disciplinary practices. The strike was beaten after nine months with a combination of scab labor and anti-union organizing, which led to a vote to decertify the union. The supporting boycott against Coors served, however, as connective organizing tissue between gay activists and the Teamsters (who had organized Coors distribution workers in San Francisco), with a general queer revulsion towards Coors lasting for years after the strike and official boycott had ended.

The insert makes a sophisticated argument for broad solidarity via Joe Coors' influence in politics generally, and provides multiple points of contact, both for how to get involved and for how to send money to the strike fund. The songs were written and performed by Kathy Kahn, "who has been arrested twice on the Coors picket line. She sings on picket lines, at concerts and in jails," and Danny McMahan, "a brewery worker and member of [AFL-CIO] Local 366. He spent two months in New Mexico organizing the Coors boycott." Kahn is also the wife of the folk musician Si Kahn. One standout track is a less than 30 second ditty, sung in chorus, about scabs, and easy to imagine belted out on the picket line. The name of the record label, Dare to Struggle, sounds like a front for a party that emerged from the New Communist Movement, but it appears to be a standalone entity, created to release this record. The 7" was recorded at Biscuit City Studios in Denver, an otherwise apolitical folk and bluegrass studio.

OHC and the Gappers, George Chriba

Ford Workers On Strike

7" EP

Ford (UK) Workers' Combine

1978

Great Britain

In 1978, despite a profitable year for Ford, workers were offered a measly 5% pay rise. This was sadly in line with the Labour government's pay guidelines. On September 22nd, 15,000 workers walked out in a wildcat strike, organized by the Ford Combine—workerist miltants, many of whom were part of Big Flame (a UK Marxist organization heavily influened by the Italian extraparliamentary political party Lotta Continua, which it's worth noting also released vinyl records in support of their struggles). The strike grew to 57,000, forcing the Transport and General Workers' Union & Amalgamated Engineering Workers' Union to make it official two weeks later. The strike lasted about two months and was successful, against both the bosses and the government. Workers got a 17% raise and inspired a wave of similar actions across the country.

"£20 on the pay, 1 hour off the day, no strings," was a popular slogan printed on the B-side of the record itself. "Will John Peel play it?!" is printed sideways in small type along the front edge of the sleeve. With the BBC towing the government line, Peel—one of the only DJs on British radio that played popular music—might have been the worker's main hope for being heard on a national broadcast. Continuing the propaganda line, all proceeds from the record were to raise funds "for our leaflets, etc." (as opposed to the usual call to fill a strike fund). The songs—including George Chriba's spirited lo-fi rock number "Johnny Strika"—are all bookended with field recordings of rowdy strikers on the march or picket line, and the B-side, a Country Joe and the Fish song retooled by Workers' Combine organizer Ed Emery, draws international connections to older counter-cultural movements. It's also worth mentioning that this record was made with the support of the Local Radio Wokshop, a group active in the late '70s and early '80s both helping local groups create radio, but also pushing for true community radio and the democratization of the dominant centralized, top-down broadcasting system in the UK.

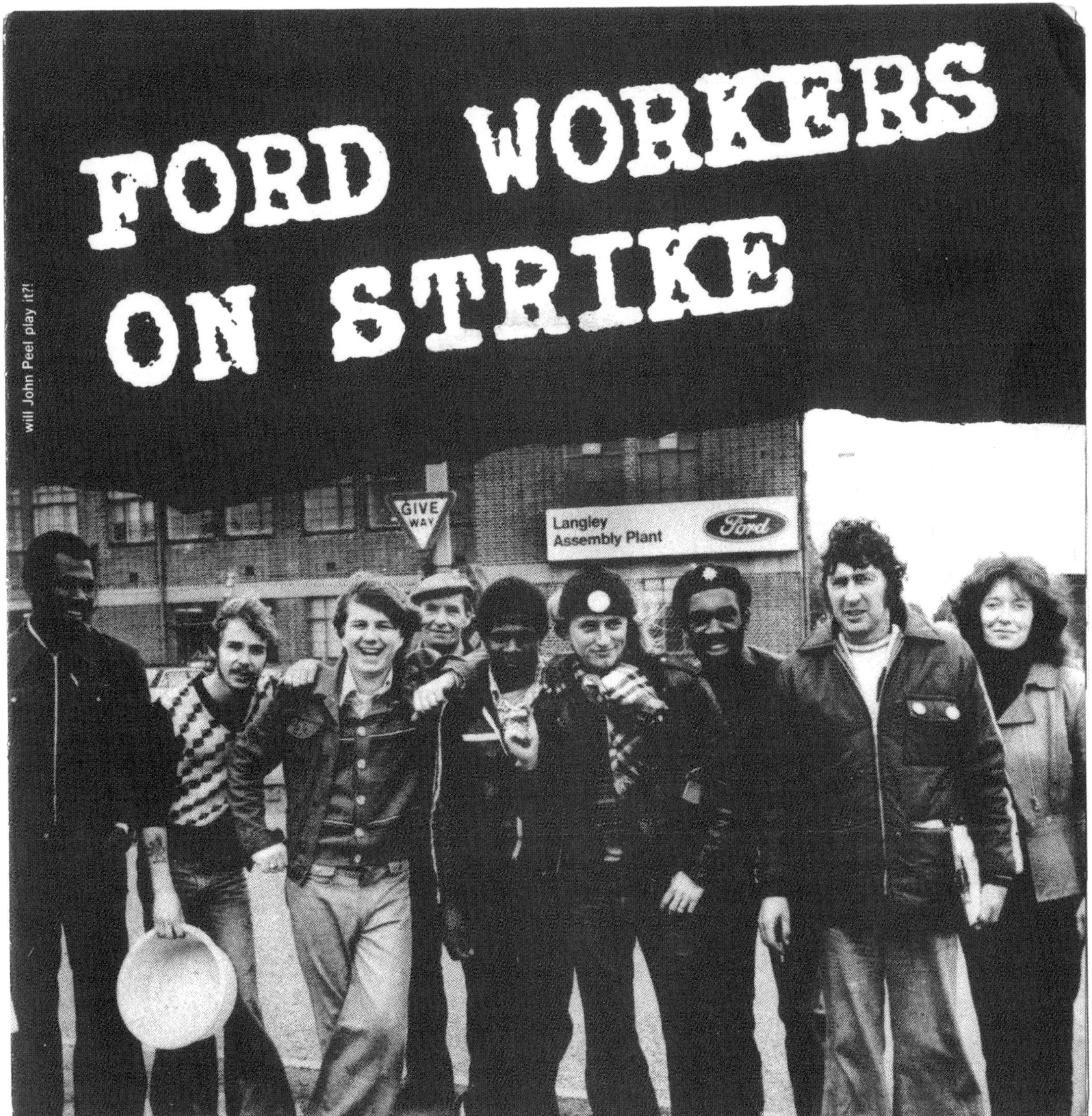
FORD WORKERS
ON STRIKE
will John Peel play it?!
GIVE WAY
Langley
Assembly Plant
Ford

THE FORD STRIKE SONG

This song was written at the start of the strike, by members of the Ford (UK) Workers' Combine. We wanted to make a record of it. We produced the "Fraud" T-shirts, and sold them to raise funds. Then we got into a recording studio and made the record - in 3 weeks flat! We're selling it to raise funds for our leaflets etc. The tune of the 'Ford Strike Song' is 'Fixin' to Die' by Country Joe McDonald. The tune for the middle bit is "There was I, waiting at the church", courtesy of Jim Callaghan. We've included guitar chords. The other side was recorded when the Ford workers marched through London on October 11th 1978. Thanks to everyone who helped. Hope you like it.

1. Well, come on all you women and men, Henry Ford's in trouble again!
   He's got himself in a terrible jam, with strikes at Halewood & Dagenham,
   We put down our tools and out the gate, for £20 on the basic rate!

Cho: And it's 1-2-3 - what are we fighting for?
You can stuff your five per cent, 'cos that won't pay the rent.
And it's 5-6-7 - picketing the factory gates,
It's one in the eye for Sunny Jim, Whoopee, we're goin' to WIN!

2. The Company's offer was quite diabolical. But our reply was categorical;
   When the Halewood lads heard the offer from Beckett, they went round the plant and started to wreck it.
   At every mass meeting you could hear them shout - All Right...It's Everybody Out!

Chorus.

3. There was I, quietly working away, Just an average day,
   When I heard the Company say,
   "Five per cent is all you'll get on pay." - Oh how it did UPSET me!
   So, I thought, why should we bother to wait, So I turned round to my mates
   And we walked right out the gate....
   We're staying out for a higher basic rate - Henry, we Love you!

4. The Union leaders tell us that they feel they could negotiate a productivity deal.
   They'll cut your mealbreaks & your teabreaks too, and the next in line they'll want to cut
   So we tell'em in the name of the working class you can stuff it right up your arse!

Chorus.

5. Eight hours on the line, it may sound funny. We don't do it for the funny, we do it for the money!
   Take a look around you friend, and you'll agree, the only way we'll win is UNITY!
   We're black, we're white, we're hand in hand, And together we'll make our stand!

Chorus.

6. The day will come - it may seem outrageous - we'll have the bosses working for starvation wages,
   And for full effect - we wouldn't want to spoil it - we'll have 'em begging for permission to go to the toilet.
   We'll expropriate the bastards of all their plunder - and get 'em back for keeping us under!

Chorus.

END

• The Ford Workers March Through London.

JOHNNY STRIKA

This one's dedicated to the Vultures of the Tory Press who hang round the edge of our struggle trying to slander us, put us down, divide us, and make us out to be mindless morons.

1. They call me Johnny, Johnny, Johnny Johnny Strika,
   But I'm no radical man.
   I'm an 'A' Shift, Day Shift, Ordinary Harry
   From Motor City Dagenham
   They call me TV headlining, newsmaking Johnny,
   Inflated stories of deflated pay.
   I do a new job every 27 seconds,
   A mechanical Travolta covered in Grease, Grease, Grease.

Cho: I'm a fully trained, fully skilled, automatic worka,
I'm a fully trained, fully skilled, self-propelling worka,
Bring no brain, take the strain, Motor City worka.

2. But they call me Johnny, Johnny, Johnny Johnny Strika,
   Tho' I'm a trade union man,
   I'm a 'B' Shift, Three Shift, Production Operator,
   From Motor City Dagenham
   They call me redline, deadline, non-productive Johnny,
   But that's not me okay.
   I do a new job every 27 seconds,
   A mechanical Travolta covered in Grease, Grease, Grease!

Cho: I'm a fully trained, fully skilled, automatic robot,
I'm a fully trained, fully skilled, self-propelling robot,
Need no brains, need no name, Motor City robot.

3. Still they call me Johnny, Johnny, Johnny Johnny Strika,
   But that's what they want me to be.
   But I'm a Harry, a Larry, an ordinary Garry,
   From Motor City Dagenham
   And not Johnny, Johnny, Johnny
   No not Johnny, Johnny, Johnny,
   No way am I Johnny, Johnny, Johnny,
   Please not Johnny, Johnny STRIKA!

Callaghan Out! Workers In! 19.60
We are the Ford Workers - On Strike!
TUC are Tragic! Rank and File are Magic!
Ford Workers OK! Five Per Cent No Way!
Upset your Foreman! Buy a Fraud T-Shirt!
2625.40
5% is Tragic
166.72
The Workers United Will Never Be Defeated!
50% is Magic!
Henry's in the Shit, Tra-la-la-la-la And we ain't goin' back till Xmas!
584.10
2591.38

What do we want? Twenty Pounds! How many hours? Thirty Five! Productivity? No Way!

The Ford Workers' Group (ex Ford (UK) Workers' Combine) is made up of rank and file workers and shop stewards from every major Ford plant across the country. Most of us are socialists. The idea for the Combine arose after the 1977 pay claim, which was drawn up by the Convenors and Officials without consulting the shop floor. To avoid a repetition this year we decided to get together and launch a campaign for a claim on the shop floor.

This is a new step forward in workers' organisation at Fords. And we have been very effective. We have produced a series of leaflets which have been distributed in all the plants. We have argued support for our claim (£20 on the rate; 1 hour off the day; no strings or productivity) in trade union branches, stewards committees, and on the shop floor. We produced badges, T-shirts, posters etc to spread the Campaign.

During the strike the Officials have neglected to do important things. We have made up for this, by organising ourselves. E.g. Keeping Ford workers informed of developments, by regular weekly Strike Bulletins all over the country; issuing Social Security information at the start of the strike; organising lobbies of the National Negotiators etc.

We think the workers and stewards still need a bigger say in Fords. The Combine is assisting this movement forward. If you agree with us, then why not join us? We organise national meetings of Ford workers, but we also have local groups meeting in their own areas (Dagenham, Halewood, Swansea etc). If you want speakers, badges, leaflets, T-shirts etc, or further details about how to get involved with the Combine, write to us: c/o The Secretary, 25 Dearmer House, London SW2.

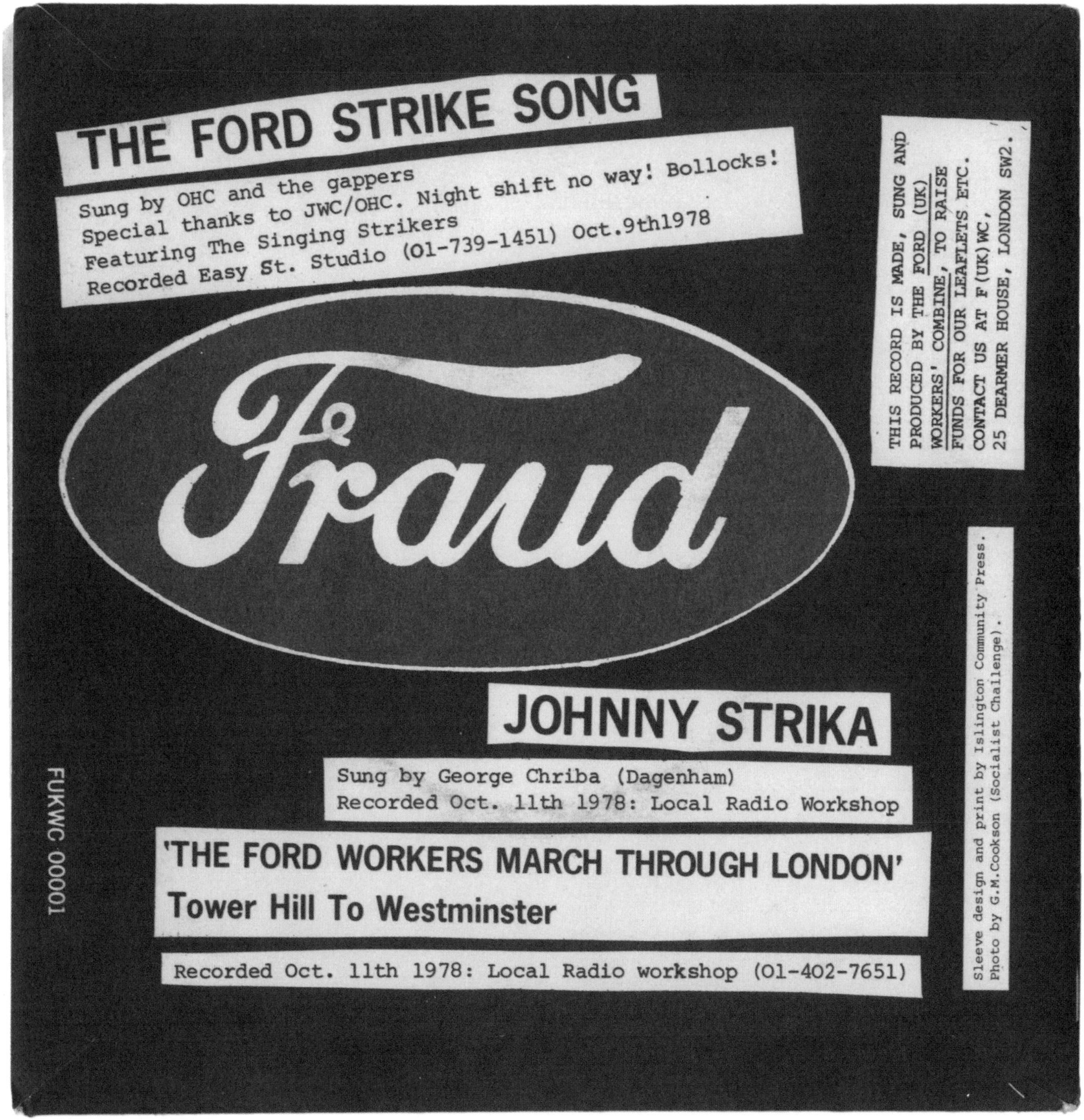
THE FORD STRIKE SONG
Sung by OHC and the gappers
Special thanks to JWC/OHC. Night shift no way! Bollocks!
Featuring The Singing Strikers
Recorded Easy St. Studio (01-739-1451) Oct.9th1978
Fraud
THIS RECORD IS MADE, SUNG AND PRODUCED BY THE FORD (UK) WORKERS' COMBINE, TO RAISE FUNDS FOR OUR LEAFLETS ETC. CONTACT US AT F(UK)WC, 25 DEARMER HOUSE, LONDON SW2.
JOHNNY STRIKA
Sung by George Chriba (Dagenham)
Recorded Oct. 11th 1978: Local Radio Workshop
'THE FORD WORKERS MARCH THROUGH LONDON'
Tower Hill To Westminster
Recorded Oct. 11th 1978: Local Radio workshop (01-402-7651)
Sleeve design and print by Islington Community Press.
Photo by G.M.Cookson (Socialist Challenge).
FUKWC 00001

Dare to Struggle, Dare to Win!
Six revolutionary songs performed in English by the League's Ontario cultural group.
CANADIAN COMMUNIST LEAGUE (MARXIST-LENINIST)
LIGUE COMMUNISTE (MARXISTE-LÉNINISTE) DU CANADA
Six chansons révolutionaires exécutées en anglais par le Groupe culturel de la Ligue en Ontario.
Oser lutter, Oser vaincre!

Canadian Communist League (Marxist-Leninist) Cultural Group

Dare to Struggle, Dare to Win!

7" EP

Canadian Communist League, M-L (LCC 78)

1978

Canada

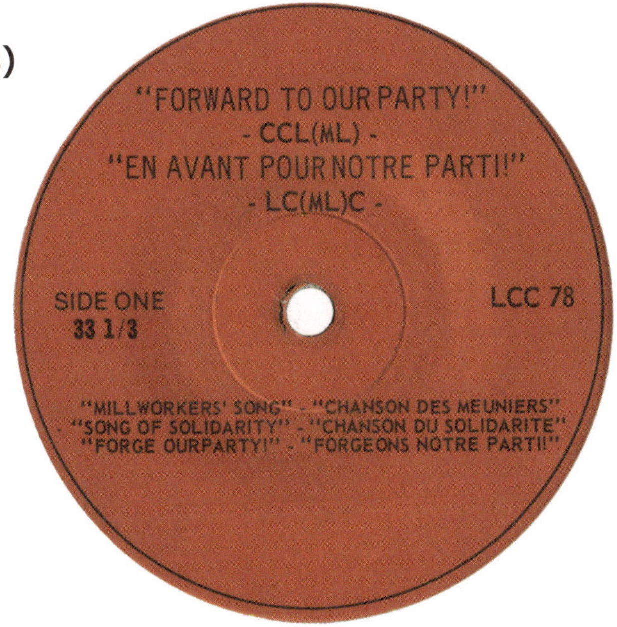

While this is not exclusively a strike record, this 7" produced by the Canadian Communist League (Marxist-Leninist) included two songs which document the party's participation in both the Robin Hood millworkers strike in 1977 and the 1976 Canadian general strike. The CCL (M-L) at the time was a Maoist-oriented communist party with cultural groups in both Ontario and Quebec, with this record produced in English by the Ontario section, with translations of all the lyrics also presented in French on an enclosed lyric sheet.

"Millworkers' Song" is a jaunty folk ballad that begins by presenting a fairly direct and didactic narrative about how on July 22, 1977, eight striking workers at Robin Hood Flour were shot by company thugs in Montreal:

The shotgun shells exploded
While the cops watched by the gate.
Eight workers fell down bleeding.
Peoples hearts were filled with hate.

It then quickly devolves into a sectarian rant:

There is one road to follow.
There's an answer that is real,
Socialist Revolution!
So all workers wounds will heal.

The second song, "Talking Union Bureaucrat Blues," is a talking blues-style track (à la Woody Guthrie or Country Joe & the Fish) criticizing mainstream Canadian union leadership for failing to support the first Canada-wide general strike held on October 14, 1976. Upwards of a million workers participated, with union heads pushing workers to stay home rather than take to the streets.

Multinationale
Chômage
Capitalisme
Capsuleries vivra!
SOLIDARITÉ

Le Groupe Musical des Capsuleries de Chaudfontaine

Capsuleries Vivra!

7" EP

Capsulerie (CAP 9378)

1978

Belgium

First, it needs to be said that this is likely the strike record housed in the most impressive sleeve of all time. Printed in two colors (blue and orange), the cover folds out into a giant and beautiful poster which chronicles the sale, closure, and almost immediate—and successful—occupation and self-management of a *capsulerie* (a factory that manufactures aerosol spray canisters, in this case butane lighters) in Chaudfontaine Belgium in the late '70s. A series of actions were held to celebrate and defend the occupation, including car parades, road closures, a launch of a solidarity raft on the Vesdre river inspired by a similar launch by workers at Mangé the previous year. Once the factory is up and running, the workers made a trip to LIP (the shining example at the time of worker self-management and production) and even contracted with them to produce boxes for their watches, an example of an emerging network of self-managed self-sufficiency. Similar to the Mangé/Groupe Expression records from the previous year (see above) this record was produced with the aid of the New Left magazine *POUR*.

Le Groupe Musical des Capsuleries de Chaudfontaine came together by performing at the opening day of the newly occupied factory and later connected with other politicized music groups, touring in Charleroi, Brussels, and Mons. The text on the sleeve ends on an heroically hopeful note: "From now on, the slogan Capsulerie Will Live is no longer just a slogan, but a dream that we must realize through struggle!"

Sous le ciel de Wallonie

Sous le ciel de Wallonie, même si nous n'avons plus de charbon
Il restait dans nos prairies des usines pour nos Wallons
Pour ne pas nous laisser faire il faut trouver une solution
Que nous soyons solidaires et qu'ensemble nous luttions

REFRAIN :

Nous voyons peu à peu nos usines se vider
Ils arrangent leurs combines pour tous nous licencier
Le chômage a augmenté les ouvriers sont déprimés
Ils en ont bien plus qu'assez et maintenant ils vont lutter

Comme les ouvriers d'autrefois qui nous ont montré le chemin à suivre
On va faire grève sur le tas pour gagner de quoi survivre.
Capsuleries de Chaudfontaine, Grand Bazar, Fonderies Mangé
Cela nous fait de la peine de ne plus travailler.

REFRAIN

Vous qui travaillez encore, luttez donc avec nous
Le travail ne veillera pas sur vous, luttez de plus en plus fort.
Pour ne pas nous laisser faire, il faut trouver une solution
Que nous soyons tous solidaires et qu'ensemble nous luttions.

De bons trav

Nous étions de bons tra
Nous avions le cœur au
L'Amérique est venue dé
Notre usine, elle va mou
Maintenant mauvais ges
Vous avez tout fichu en
Si nous occupons notre
C'est pour gagner notre

Si tu crois que c'est si f
De pouvoir garder nos m
Sans qu'ils mettent leur

Nous serons quand mêr

Non jamais nous ne lais
Nos usines aux mains d
Ils ne seront pas plus fc
Ils ne nous mettront pas

A quoi bon l'école aux e
Si plus tard le gouverne
Ne peut leur donner du
Pour eux continuons la
Nous devons payer TVA
Payer le fisc et le roi
Comme si cela n'était pa
Contributions il faut pay

C'est si triste dans notre
Le silence de nos machi
Que donnerons-nous au
Si nous n'avons plus d'a
C'est l'union que nous p
Dans nos cœurs unis sa
Il ne faut jamais oublier
Nous sommes tous dans

eurs

s

re

s
ins
dessus.
plus
têtus.

ons
nous
t.

e.

z

ts

ns
on.

me
panier.

La liberté

Tiens c'est drôle que se passe-t-il
dans cette usine?
Plus un bruit plus un écho
Est-ce une guerre, une épidémie,
une famine
Qui a vidé ces locaux?
On dirait un cimetière de machine
Et ça fait froid dans le dos.

REFRAIN:

Camarades soyez donc fiers
Pensez aux ouvriers d'hier
Qui comme nous ont dû lutter
Pour sauvegarder leur liberté
Oui la liberté, la liberté
Faut savoir la gagner, savoir la garder.

Tiens c'est drôle que se passe-t-il
dans ce pays?
Chaque forge est un flambeau.
Les cheminées ressemblent
autour des terrils
A des croix sur des tombeaux.
Les valeurs d'antan ne sont plus
que débris
Et notre espoir s'engloutit.

REFRAIN

Nous n'avions que nos deux bras
pour travailler
Ils suppriment nos emplois.
Nous n'avons que nos deux mains
pour demander
Ils baffouent tous nos droits
Mais il nous reste nos deux poings
pour lutter
Et gagner notre combat.

REFRAIN

Tiens c'est drôle que se passe-t-il
dans cette usine?
On entend que des chansons.
Filles et gars en liberté
sur les machines
Assureront la production
Car désormais ils ont une copine,
Elle se nomme autogestion.

REFRAIN

Les Ricains

REFRAIN:

Chassons de Wallonie les Ricains (2X)
Notre avenir est entre leurs mains (2X)

Nous lutterons toujours pour gagner
notre pain
Le travail subviendra sans cesse
à nos besoins
Ne perdons pas courage et peut-être
que demain
Le prix de nos efforts nous ôtera
nos liens.

REFRAIN

La liberté pour nous c'est d'abord
travailler
De contempler la réussite avec fierté
Et ne pas dire d'un air gêné «Je vais
chômer»
En rougissant devant notre inutilité.

REFRAIN

Hélas, nous ne sommes pas tous
à nous lamenter
Alors tâchons un peu ce soir
de nous évader
Tendons la mains à nos amis
des Fonderies Mangé
Gardons l'espoir un jour de nous voir
triompher.

REFRAIN SPECIAL

Chassons de Wallonie les Ricains (2X)
Notre avenir ETAIT entre leurs
mains (2X).

Pochette réalisée et imprimée
en soutien par le journal POUR

Historique de la lutte

En 1963 Reynolds reprend l'entreprise des Capsuleries de Chaudfontaine ; elle compte alors 400 travailleurs. En 1965, 250 emplois sont perdus, suite au transfert du laminoir et à la fermeture des départements « capsules » et « boîtes en carton ». Le 28 septembre 1977, la direction annonce la fermeture de l'entreprise. Aussitôt les travailleurs votent l'occupation en Assemblée Générale. Des actions sont menées : cortèges de voitures et blocage de la route, mise à flot d'un radeau sur la Vesdre, soirée de solidarité avec « Mangé » et « Expression ».

Le 23 octobre, c'est la première journée « portes ouvertes » : les lignes de production sont relancées pour fabriquer des aérosols. Plus de 1000 visiteurs défilent.

Le sigle Reynolds transformé provoquera la colère des patrons. Le 25 les travailleurs vont à l'Economie Régionale Wallone (ERW) et obtiennent une réunion entre les délégations syndicales, les dirigeants de Reynolds et l'ERW. Le 27 octobre, lors de cette réunion, ils se mettent d'accord sur le principe d'une analyse contradictoire sur la rentabilité de l'entreprise. Elle est confiée à la SNI, qui la confie officieusement à la Sobemap.

Le 19 novembre c'est la deuxième journée «portes ouvertes» avec en grande première le groupe musical des capsuleries. Fin du mois, coup de théâtre: les travailleurs prennent connaissance d'une lettre d'Urbain dans laquelle il déclare que «la SNI étant dans l'impossibilité de mener l'enquête, l'analyse n'aura pas lieu». D'autre part, dans une lettre adressée aux organisations syndicales il précise qu' «il n'est pas question

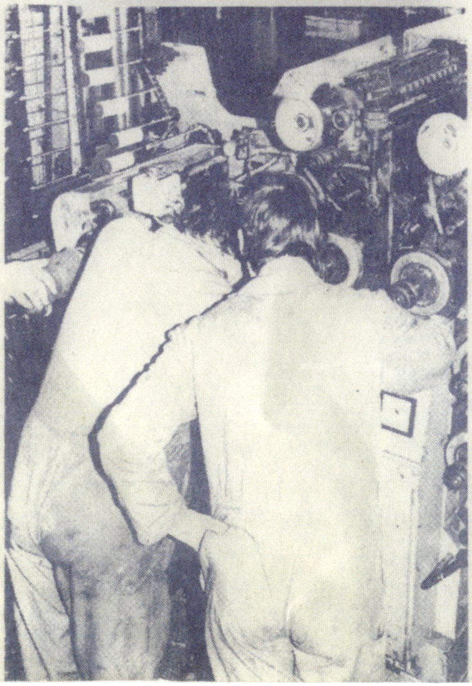

de la Sobemap». Il ne respecte d
pris!
Début décembre, des travailleurs
qui laissera des traces! En effe

début de l'auto-production de
1.000, 2.000, 5.000 briquets so
musical multiplie ses déplacem
Mons... Les visites de solidari
enfoncée dans un tube d'aéros
parlementaires. L'Economie R
(dans le bon sens cette fois)
effectue l'enquête.
Le patron, s'inquiétant subitem
abandonné un peu vite, fait
finalement de venir visiter l'er

L'ENGRENAGE SE BLOQUERA
IL SUFFIT DE LEVER LE BRAS !

LOCO

GAM
LOCO
7" single
Self-produced (GAM 100)
ca. 1978
Belgium

This has been a tricky record to research the context for. It is undated, and although produced by GAM, it doesn't have the robust documentation that many of their other records have included.

The 7" features the same track on both sides, with one side in French, the other in Dutch. The translated song title is "When Your Train is Not on Time..." and the lyrics tell the story of frustration with the train system, and how that should be blamed on the rail authority, not the drivers/engineers. The song also references in detail the demands of the machinists, who are underpaid, overworked (13 hour shifts are mentioned), and have no control over their schedules. To make matters worse, the unions refuse to listen.

Although the lyrics never explicitly state it, the implication is that large sectors of the rail industry are on a wildcat strike, and the goal of the song is to explain why to both other workers and the broader public. LOCO is the name of the new union created by the machinists after they were abandoned by the two major Belgian unions (the Catholic CSC/ACV and the Democratic Socialist FGTB/ABVV).

Like most GAM records, for this one they collaborated with railworkers and their families on the lyrics, and include a note about their specific political position. In their words: "it seems therefore clear to us that any supporter of democratic and working-class unionism must provide support (and sometimes critical support) to the machinists movement." In a recent interview, GAM members had little to say about this record other than considering it a failure. It's worth noting that the cover illustration on the sleeve is a reproduction of a print Dutch artist Albert Hahn made during a railway strike in 1903.

De Røde Raketter

Idag Activ Stilladser, imorgen dig

7" single

Stilladsarbejdernes Brancheklub AF 1920 (SBK - 1)

1978

Denmark

What does a record made by striking Danish scaffolding workers sound like? Exactly as you'd expect! This is an amazing audio document, with jaunty, schlager-tinged sing-a-longs, one titled "The Battle Song of the Scaffolders," recorded by De Røde Raketter [The Red Rockets], a communist folk-rock act from Copenhagen. In April 1978, the Stilladsarbejdernes Brancheklub [Scaffolding Workers' Industry Club] struck for the re-hiring of four fired union workers, against the speed up of work, against the criminalization of the picket line and blockading of work sites, and more.

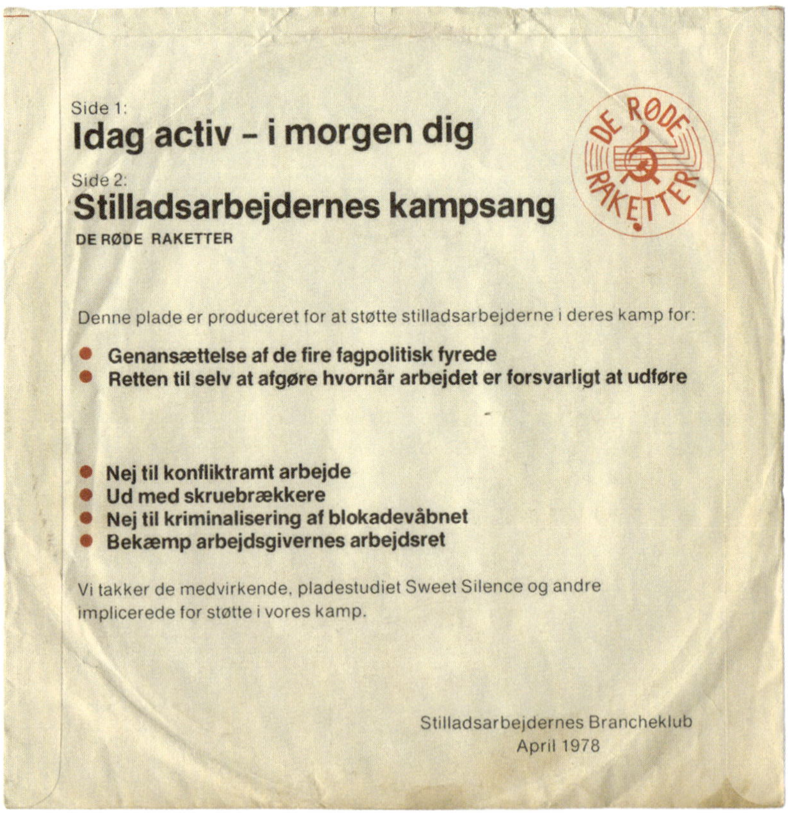

IDAG ACTIV STILLADSER
IMORGEN DIG
PER

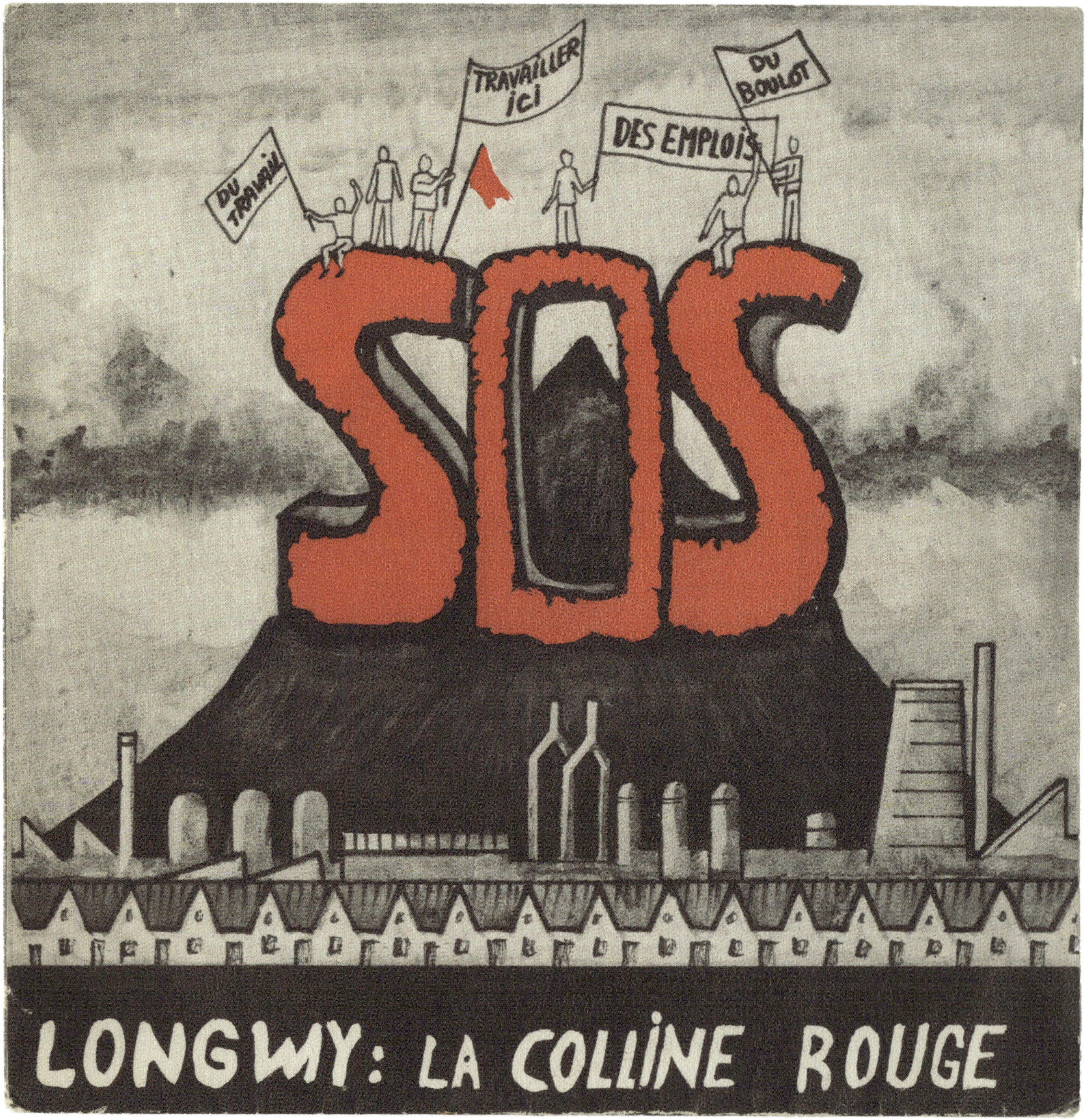
DU TRAVAIL
TRAVAILLER ici
DES EMPLOIS
DU BOULOT
SOS
LONGWY: LA COLLINE ROUGE

UIS CFDT de Longwy
<u>**SOS Longwy: La Colline Rouge**</u>
7" EP
Vendémiaire (VDES 041)
1979
France

This record was made as part of a 1979 struggle across the Longwy region. Nestled on the border of both Belgium and Luxembourg, Longwy and its main city Lorraine is an historic iron mining area. In the late 1970s, pressure from the European Economic Community and free market policies led to a massive reduction of the workforce, with 1.5 million foundry workers out on the street. In response the French Democratic Confederation of Labor (CFDT) and Unions Interpro de Syndicats (UIS) led a massive worker and community response, surrounding and shutting off access to the entire city of Lorraine. The A-side of the record here is the key track, "La Colline Rouge" (The Red Hill, or Red Slagheap), written and performed by Denis Menard, a militant worker, and recorded by Radio S.O.S. Emploi, the local worker's radio station. The song documents, in verse, the history of the region and small-mindedness of the government, regional business organizations, and mine owners, ending in a rousing verse about how yesterday 20,000 took to the streets under the red flag, tomorrow, who knows what can happen.

The Slag Heap Song
Red Hill

I
The land of three borders
It's the high land
In the valley of the Chiers
From the blast furnace factories
The metalworker is getting angry
It's unemployment, there's no more work
In the land of three borders
In the high land

II
Pyramid of ashes
Slag heap of toil
I'm not going to tell you
It was the worker's sweat
And even at the converter
It's not the prole who made his beer
Who's toasted in the song
Obviously he's not the boss

III
In the land of three borders
In the high land
Since yesterday
Longwy looks up
It's on the red hill
Sending out the SOS
It's the union that's on the move
The high land cries its distress

IV
In the land of three borders
There's no more work
Comrade worker
You may be entitled to a better life
The infernal pace
The little boss thinks it's normal
But you want to live in the country
Even if it's not paradise

V
In the land of three borders
The worker doesn't want to die
Today as yesterday
He'll fight again
On the molehill
The fight's just beginning
In the land of three borders
That they wanted to strangle

VI
They took the employee's money
They took from the public treasury
A little gift to the companies
Which they also bailed out
Today's forge masters
Want to grab us by the throat
Their capitalist system
With unemployment lengthens the list

VII
We've got to be competitive
In the common market
You're too old for steel
We'll sweep you away in a jiffy
Smelters in the dustbin
Here comes the company of tomorrow
Jobs are gone
And there's nothing to replace it

VIII
They say it's no longer profitable
It's the foreigners' fault
In Japan or Germany
Everything has to be restructured
We kick the Algerians out
When they're no longer needed
Then it's the older ones' turn
To early retirement

IX
Don't get political
There's misfortune for other reasons
No quarrels between factions
Thank you Bigeard for Neuves-Maisons
Giscard-Barre remain quiet
Eyes fixed on the horizon
On the horizon of the year two thousand
They take us for fools

X
In the land of three borders
The people have risen
Red flag for banner
We must unite
In the streets 20,000 yesterday
Tomorrow we must continue
We'll find a way
To save the High Land.

CE disque a été réalisé par l'UIS CFDT de LONGWY,

avec des militants,
avec l'équipe de Radio SOS Emploi,
avec des travailleurs,

La chanson du crassier

Colline rouge

I
Le pays des trois frontières
C'est le pays haut
Dans la vallée de la chiers
Des usines des hauts fourneaux
L'métallo s'met en colère
C'est l'chômage. y a plus d'boulot
Au pays des trois frontières
Dans le pays haut

II
Pyramide de cendre
Crassier du labeur
Je ne vais pas vous l'apprendre
D'l'ouvrier c'était la sueur
Et même au convertisseur
C'est pas l'prolo qu'y a fait son beurre
Qui qui trinque dans la chanson
'Videmment c'est pas l'patron

III
Au pays des trois frontieres
Dans le pays haut
Il y a depuis hier
Longwy regarde là-haut
C'est sur la colline rouge
Qui lance des SOS
C'est le syndicat qui bouge
L'Pays haut crie sa détresse

IV
Au pays des trois frontières
Y a plus de boulot
Camarade travailleur
L'as p-t'être droit une vie meilleure
Les cadences infernales
Le petit chef trouve ça normal
Mais tu veux vivre au Pays
Même si c'est pas l'paradis

V
Au pays des trois frontières
L'ouvrier veut pas crever
Aujourd'hui comme hier
Il va encore lutter
Monté sur la taupinière
Le combat fait qu'commencer
Au pays des trois frontières
Qu'on a voulu étrangler

VI
Du salarié on a pris le fric
Puisé dans le trésor public
P'tit cadeau aux sociétés
Qu'on a aussi renflouées
Aujourd'hui les maitres de forge
Veulent nous prendre à la gorge
Leur système capitaliste
Du chômage allonge la liste

VII
Faut ben être concurrentiel
Dans l'marché commun
Sidérurgie t'es ben trop vieille
On t'balaye en un tour de main
Les fondeurs à la poubelle
V'la la société d'demain
Les emplois s'sont envolés
Et y a rien pour remplacer

VIII
Y parait qu'c'est plus rentable
C'est d'la faute des étrangers
Au Japon ou a l'Allemagne
Il faut tout restructurer
On fout dehors l'algèrien
Quand on en a plus besoin
Puis c'est l'tour des plus âgés
A la r'traite anticipée

IX
Faut pas faire de politique
Y a l'malheur pour d'autres raisons
Pas d'querelles de boutiques
Merci Bègeard pour Neuves-Maisons
Giscard-Barre restent bien tranquilles
Les yeux fixés sur l'horizon
Sur celui de l'an deux mille
Ils nous prennent bien pour des cons

X
Au pays des trois frontières
Le peuple s'est levé
Drapeau rouge pour bannière
Il faut faire l'unité
Dans la rue 20 000 hier
Demain il faut continuer
On va trouver la manière
L'Pays haut pour le sauver.

Denis MENARD
MILITANT CFDT

Vendémiaire VDES 0.41

Bertus en de Posters
Oh, M.E., wat doe je nou?
7" single
Red Air Productions
1979
Netherlands

Bertus and the Posters is one of Bertus van der Horst's diverse musical groups (he appears to have also played bass in a heavy metal band called Scarface!). Not much info on Bertus is easily accessible, but I do know that he used the "Bertus and the Posters" moniker to self-release a couple protest singles in the late seventies/early eighties. The first was this one, a solidarity record in support of striking dockworkers at the Rotterdam harbor. The two sides of the record are a 1-2 punch, with the A-side—"Oh, M.E., Wat Doe Je Nou?" [Oh, M.E., what do you do know?]—an indictment of the violence of the Mobiele Eenheid (mobile unit aka riot squad) of the police in their repression of the workers. The song starts with a field recording of the chanting of this slogan by dockworkers outside the Rotterdam jail, and then evolves into a jaunty folk-rock protest tune. The B-side—"Kom op Mensen, Maak een Vuist!" [Come on People, Make a Fist!]—is a call for the workers to rise up, directly in opposition to corrupt union officials who are always failing them. The second record by the band was released in 1985, and was an attack on Margaret Thatcher and in support of the Miners' Strike in the UK (more on that later).

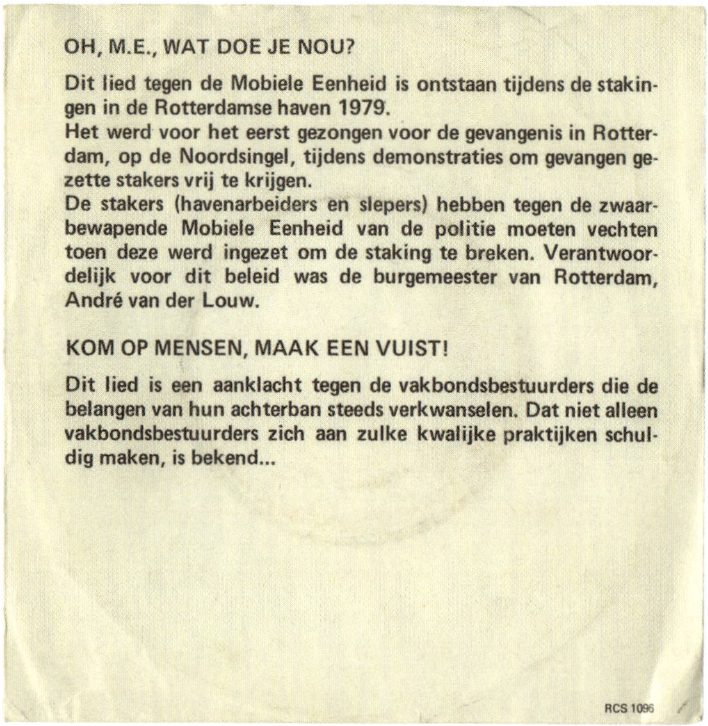
OH, M.E., WAT DOE JE NOU?

Dit lied tegen de Mobiele Eenheid is ontstaan tijdens de stakingen in de Rotterdamse haven 1979.
Het werd voor het eerst gezongen voor de gevangenis in Rotterdam, op de Noordsingel, tijdens demonstraties om gevangen gezette stakers vrij te krijgen.
De stakers (havenarbeiders en slepers) hebben tegen de zwaarbewapende Mobiele Eenheid van de politie moeten vechten toen deze werd ingezet om de staking te breken. Verantwoordelijk voor dit beleid was de burgemeester van Rotterdam, André van der Louw.

KOM OP MENSEN, MAAK EEN VUIST!

Dit lied is een aanklacht tegen de vakbondsbestuurders die de belangen van hun achterban steeds verkwanselen. Dat niet alleen vakbondsbestuurders zich aan zulke kwalijke praktijken schuldig maken, is bekend...

RCS 1096

BERTUS EN DE POSTERS
Oh, M.E., wat doe je nou ?
Kom op mensen, maak een vuist !

CORBY
MIKE CARVER

Mike Carver
<u>Save Corby</u>
7" EP
Hot Metal (SRTS/79/CUS 517)
1979
Great Britain

In 1979, British Steel announced plans to close their plant in the town of Corby, which was expected to lead to a loss of 10,000 jobs. This record of folky alternative rock by singer-songwriter Mike Carver was sponsored by Retention Of Steelmaking At Corby (ROSAC) and all proceeds from its sale went to ROSAC to "help build the fight against closure." Off the back of this struggle, Corby became a center of the three month national steel strike in 1980—the first major industrial conflict of the Thatcher era—which was led by the 100,000 strong Iron and Steel Trades Confederation and the National Union of Blast Furnacemen. The unions' and ROSAC's fight was lost, however, and the plant eventually closed, leading to 30% unemployment rates in Corby throughout the eighties. This dismal state was the inspiration for a much more popular record from 1984, "Steeltown" by alt rockers Big Country.

Frank Penn

<u>**It's History: "The Teachers Strike" Closed Bay Street Down**</u>

12" single

G.B.I. Recording

1981

Bahamas

This record is about, rather than for, a strike. Frank Penn, a popular Bahamian junkanoo (similar to calypso or soca) performer uses song to document a teacher's strike in the Bahamas led by the Bahamas Union of Teachers, which lasted for about a month at the beginning of 1981 and resulted in the largest per annum salary increase for all teachers in the union's history. The song highlights mass action (the closing down of Bay Street, as per the title) and the foundational place of teachers in the reproduction of society. "We educate doctors, lawyers, politicians, and priests" repeats the chorus, sung from the perspective of the teachers. There's no mention on the sleeve of organizational affiliation, intentions, or profit distribution, so while supportive of the strike—it is sung from the perspective of the teachers—the record isn't an extension of it, instead it appears to by capitalizing on its popularity (especially as it is pitched as "An Extended Souvenir Disc").

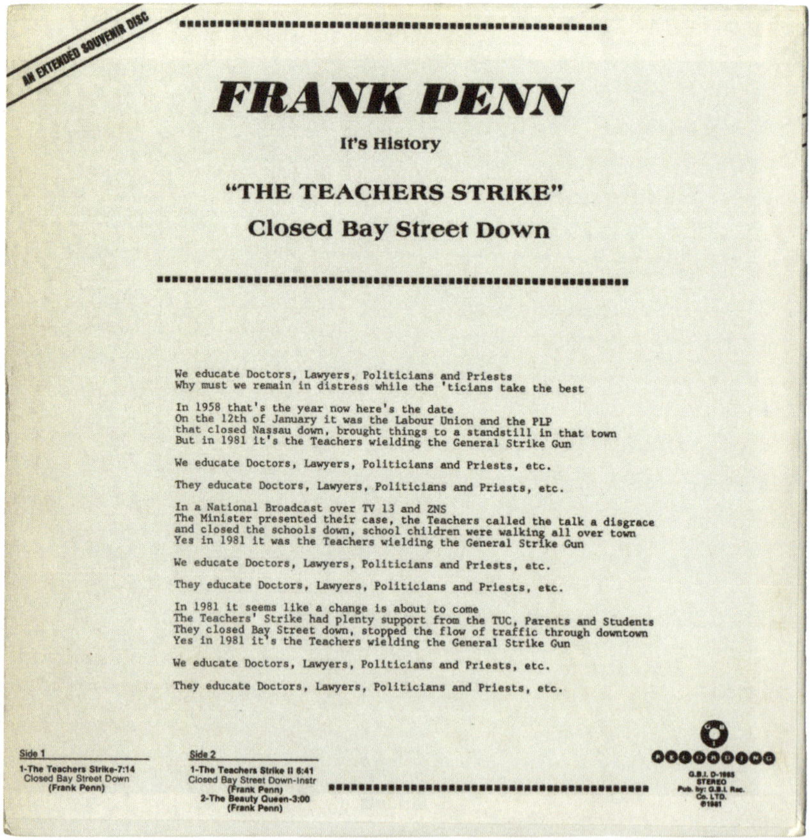

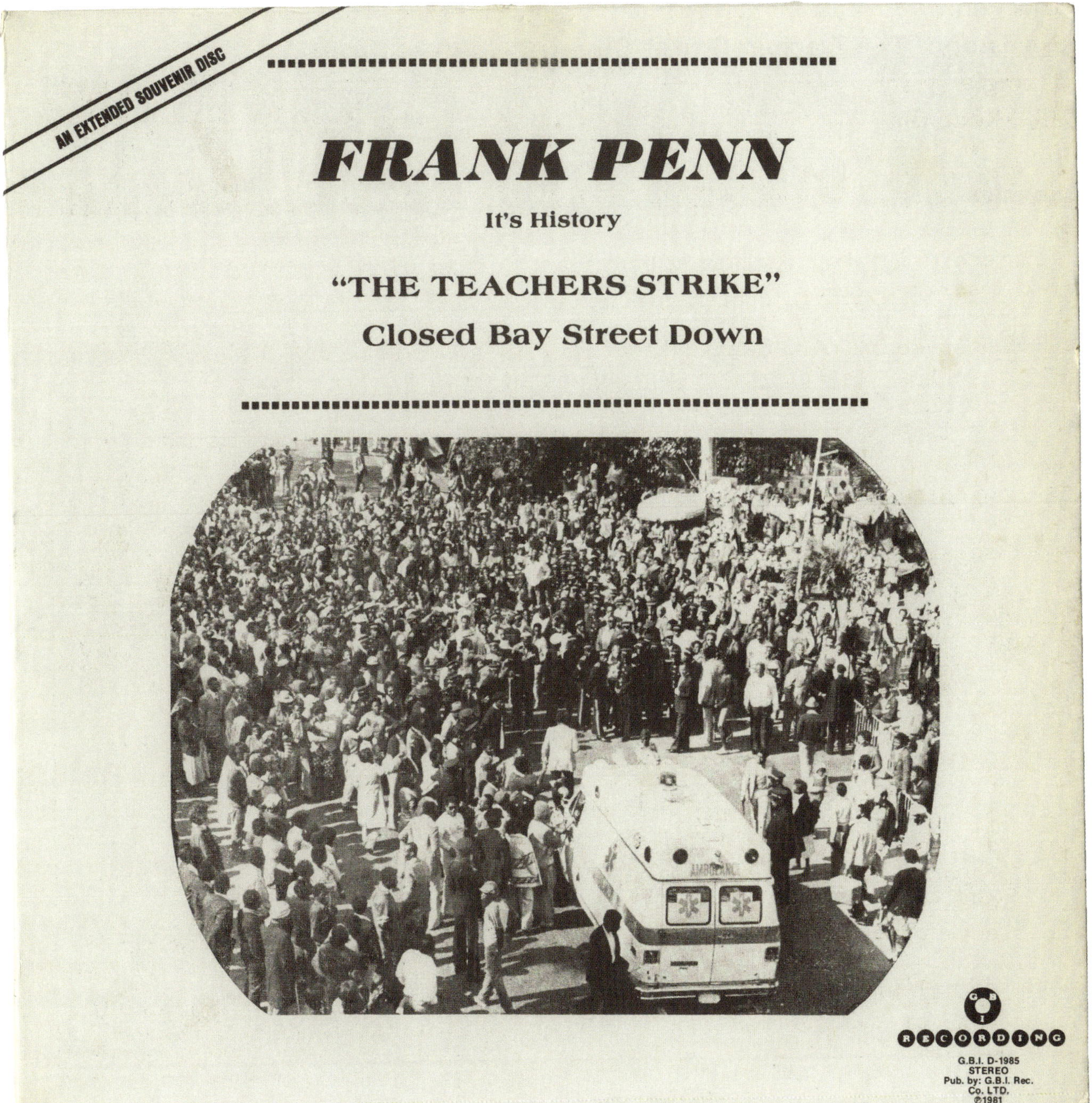
AN EXTENDED SOUVENIR DISC
FRANK PENN
It's History
"THE TEACHERS STRIKE"
Closed Bay Street Down
AMBULANCE
RECORDING
G.B.I. D-1985
STEREO
Pub. by: G.B.I. Rec.
Co. LTD.
℗1981

UN GRAND COMBAT
LADRECHT
VIVRA!
Des mines qui travaillent
un pays, des région qui VIVENT
CGT

Etienne Canonge et ses Camarades de Ladrecht
<u>Un Grand Combat</u>
7" single
Disques Fugato (H.A. 45025)
1981
France

This record was produced in solidarity with coal miners in Languedoc-Roussillon, the southernmost portion of France and seat of the Occitania, both the language and the people. In the late 1970s, the decision was made to close the Houillères du bassin des Cévennes mine, which at its peak had employed 20,000 workers. When all else failed, on May 5th, 1980, the miners occupied the Ladrecht vein of the mine, then shortly after, the Destival vein. At Destival, the miners not only occupied but reopened the mine, and began running it themselves. The mine occupations seem to have been amazingly dynamic, but that isn't really captured on the record, which is one of the most traditional (i.e., old left) ones here. Just two songs, both are straightforward renditions of historic labor standards, "l'Internationale" and "la Carmagnole." The words of each have been rewritten by Nury Maximilien, a retired miner, and performed by Etienne Canonge, a miner active in the Ladrecht occupation.

Polibio Mayorga con los Montoneros de Ecuador
La Huelga
7" single
Profona (100357)
1982
Ecuador

Beyond the raised fist and the words "La Huelga" printed on the cover, there is no other contextual information about what this record is about. Polibio Mayorga is one of the most prolific Ecuadorian musicians, releasing over 50 albums and 75 singles from the mid-1960s through the early 1990s. We assume this record—with its rousing choruses of "*¡Viva la huelga!*"—was produced in support of the general strike that swept across Ecuador in October and November of 1982, organized by the Frente Unitario de los Trabajadores [Workers' United Front], the largest coalition of major trade unions in the country. Sort of like the AFL-CIO in the US, it pulled together a massive coalition to strike in opposition to the government's proposed austerity measures. Unlike other 7" singles released on Profona, all distributed in generic paper sleeves, this record came in a unique letterpress-printed manila envelope, likely intended to take advantage of the popularity of the strike and boost sales.

LA HUELGA
PROFONA
TELEFONO: 265 930
PROHIBIDA LA
REGRABACION DE ESTE DISCO
QUITO - ECUADOR

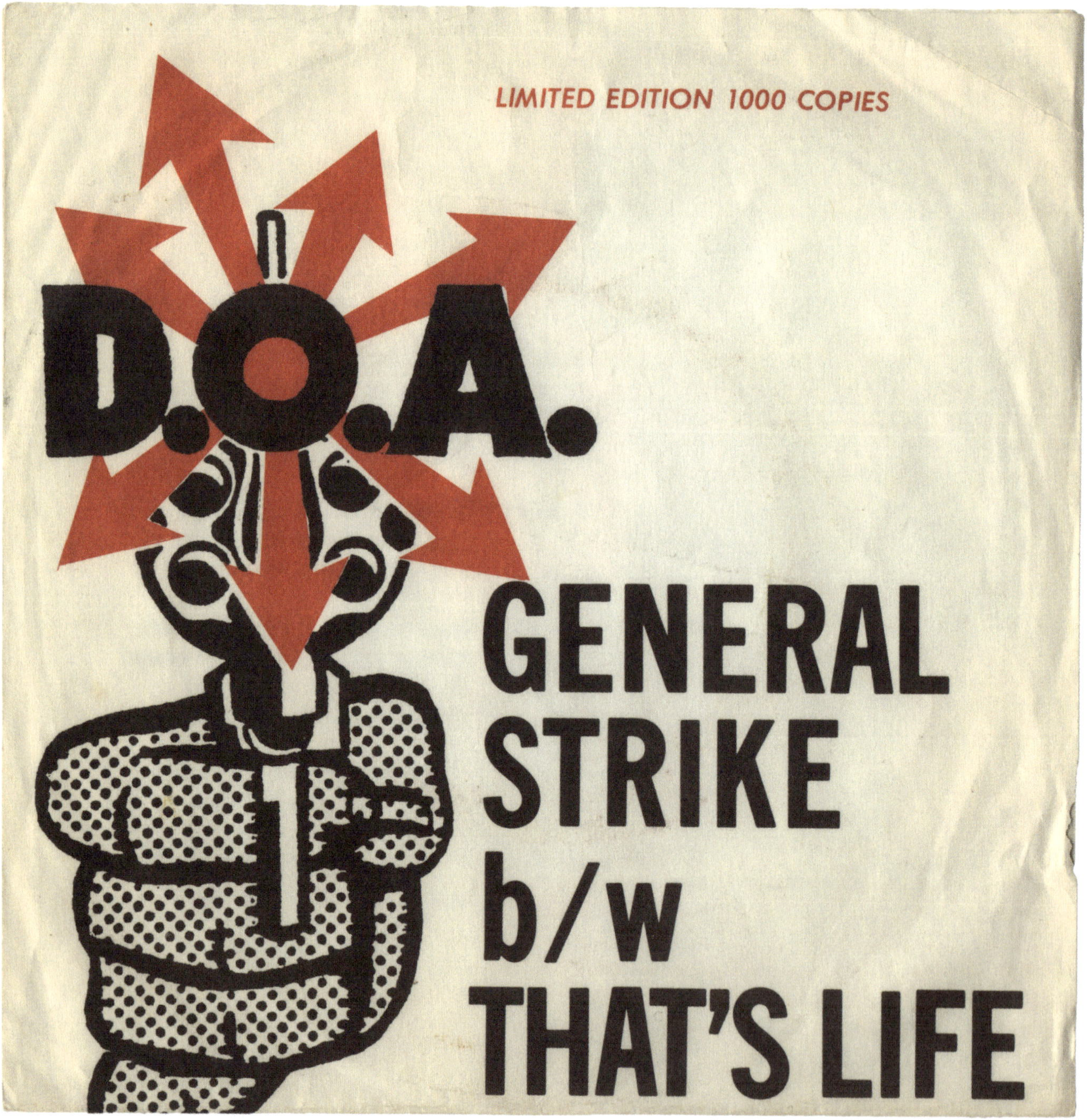
LIMITED EDITION 1000 COPIES
D.O.A.
GENERAL
STRIKE
b/w
THAT'S LIFE

D.O.A.
"General Strike" b/w "That's Life"
7" single
Sudden Death Records (SD004)
1983
Canada

The first and only punk record that's part of this landscape. These tracks were recorded by the paradigmatic Canadian political punk band D.O.A. in the midst of an escalating series of strikes across British Columbia, leading up to the region's Solidarity Coalition general strike of November 1983. The Solidarity Coalition was a labor-led amalgam formed to 'unite the left' and excite maximum involvement from the rank and file, as well as formal and informal community groups like tenant unions and churches. The goal was to build mass opposition to repressive anti-worker, pro-austerity legislation, and while the unions didn't want to call publicly for a general strike, it was clearly on the table. With their song "General Strike," D.O.A. is both echoing and helping shape that popular goal within the movement. The recordings were made the first week in November 1983, about four months into the action, which was sadly halted just days later on November 13th, before the record could actually be pressed and distributed. A private backroom deal led to a lukewarm agreement with labor that the government was later able to ignore. (The deeper story is pretty tragic, the most militant leader of the Coalition was out on the picket so much he got pneumonia and had to go to the hospital, and the punter who stepped in sold them all out.)

The sleeve for the record is an interesting exercise in contradictions, possibly due to the movement collapsing before it saw release. On the one hand, it's brutally direct and aggressive, the band's logo being shot at the viewer out of a revolver. On the other hand, it happily states "limited edition 1000 copies." The crass commercialism reads at odds with its otherwise punk aesthetic, especially since nowhere does it say its raising money for the Solidarity Coalition or any other political activity. In addition, our guess is that very few of the records included here were pressed in numbers much higher than 1,000 copies, so "limited," of course, always has to be seen in the context of demand!

The Hindle Pickets & T.B.E.
"Part of the Union" b/w "Year and a Bit"
7" single
Catch 22
1984
Great Britain

In 1983, workers at Hindle Gears initiated the first strike in their company's 50 year history under the Amalgamated Union of Engineering Workers. It's the first for some of the workers, too, who narrate the fact in the opening line of a surprisingly good post-punk track: "This is the first time I've been on strike in my life." After one month, management illegally fired them.

The strike lasted for over a year and was still ongoing when this record was released, with its primary goal of "drawing attention to the plight of the striker in this country." "In January," they write, "we decided to make a record. We didn't have sufficient knowledge of the record business to realise it had to be a plastic one for the D.J.'s to play it. We thought a cassette was good enough, but it wasn't. So began the task of raising the money to cut the record." Amongst the many inserts is a facsimile of a letter of support from Neil Kinnock, leader of the opposition and Labour Party. We've been unable to find evidence of the result of the strike, but in 2006 Hindle largely moved their operations to China. Outcomes aside, this is one the most enjoyable records here, both songs holding their own as solid, angular pop songs with just the right amount of experimentation.

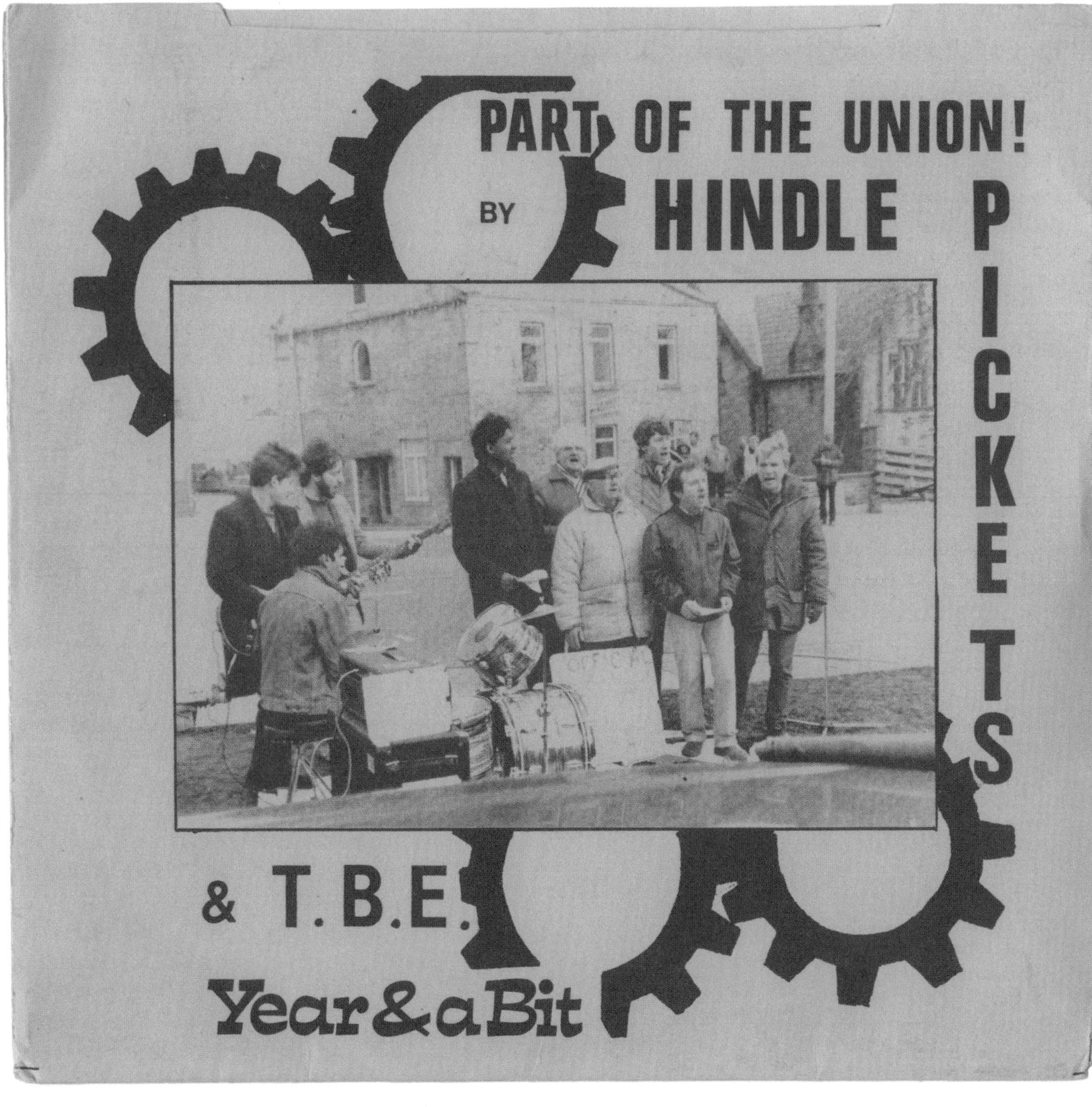
PART OF THE UNION!
BY HINDLE PICKETS
& T.B.E.
Year & a Bit

HINDLE DISPUTE

MARCH 11th 83

This was the day we came out on strike, OFFICIAL strike, may I add. This was the first strike that the company had to deal with in 50 years of existence. In way of settlement they gave us the sack, through a ballot form, which quite simply read, 'Tick this box if you want your job, or tick that box if you don't. Failure to do either, your contract will be terminated' We did not take any notice of this, under UNION INSTRUCTIONS.

PRETRIBUNAL

September the 9th was the day we went to Court. It was the pre-tribunal to determine whether or not we were wrongly dismissed but this shouldn't matter. All we were doing was exercising our rights as working men and women and withdrawing our labour. Surely, if they can sack you and get away with it LEGALLY, the working class have no rights left. We will be reduced to slave labour once again.

STRIKE PAY

Strike pay was keeping us going all this time, but along came that dreaded day when they stopped it, owing to the A.U.E.W. Rule Book. We started this dispute without money and it looks as though that's how it's going to end. But we will see it through.

POP GOES THE PICKET

In January we decided to make a record. We didn't have sufficient knowledge of the record business to realise it had to be a plastic one for the D.J.'s to play it. We thought a cassette was good enough, but it wasn't. So began the task of raising the money to cut the record. We began to raise it through sponsorshop forms.

PICKETING

At one of the firms, in the same Group, we were threatened with secondary picketing and on union advise WE LEFT.

BACK IN COURT

The Hindle Management appealed in the High Court against the verdict of the pre-tribunal, which we won. For the whole day we listened to their barrister talk about nothing, he even went as far back as 1880 but the only difference was in that case the man involved was hung. Anyway, it was adjourned until June 14th and 15th and July 2nd. Reserved Decision.

April the 13th is the day we were sacked. This came as a surprise. WE thought you could not be sacked when you were on strike.

JUNE

In this month we occupied the building but after 4 days we left the building on union advice. Plus, the management had taken out a court injunction. It is funny how fast the law works for the bosses and how slow it works for the WORKERS.

RE-ENFORCEMENT

Three days after we came out of the building, our wives decided to join the men on the picket line and then set up the Wives Support Group. This hadn't been done before, nevertheless, we were extremely proud of the wives getting involved in the dispute.

HOUSE OF COMMONS
LONDON SW1A OAA

The Office of the Leader of
the Opposition

July 5th 1984

MESSAGE FROM NEIL KINNOCK FOR HINDLE GEARS RECORD SLEEVE

The struggle by Hindle Gear workers in Bradford, dismissed in March 1983 by their employers when they went on strike in support of a pay claim, is in the vanguard of the fight back against anti-union laws.

For month after month the strikers at Hindle Gears – with the support of their families on and off the picket line – have defended the right of all free men and women to withdrew their labour.

Their struggle is determined and principled. It is an inspiration to others. It is in the tradition of those pioneers, many from places like Bradford, who made such great sacrifices in the past in order to create the Labour and Trade Union Movement so that individuals could combine and defend each other.

I salute the strikers at Hindle Gears whose voices are raised for free Trade Unions and for liberty.

Neil Kinnock

NEW RELEASE

DESCRIPTION: Single (7" 45r.p.m.).
ARTISTS: Hindle Pickets & T.B.E.
TRACKS: 'Part of The Union' s/w 'Year & a Bit'.
LABEL: Catch 22.
RELEASE DATE: 23rd July '84
DISTRIBUTION: Red Rhino/Cartel.

Drastic Measures Promo-Co. ... West Yorkshire

(PLEASE SEND A COPY OF ANY REVIEW TO ABOVE)

Having been on strike since MARCH 1983 (over 15 months) the strikers from Hindle Gears have joined forces with local musicians to publicise their plight & continuing legal battle...

This release is on the artist's own CATCH 22 label... the strike involving 22 men stuck in a catch 22 situation.

'PART OF THE UNION' is the old Woodie Guthrie song ('Union Maid') as reworked by The Strawbs. 'YEAR & A BIT' is an original by Firth & Clayton

THE HINDLE PICKETS ARE:- STUART FIRTH, MALCOLM BARKER, DAVID HOBBS, LES HOLLAND, JOGINDER SINGH, AUSTIN DODDS, ERIC GORST
–Vocals on both tracks...

...T.B.E. are... Mian Rahman (drums + vocals), Kevin McDade + Mark Clayton (guitars + vocals)

CONTACT ADDRESS: FOR FURTHER INFORMATION ON EITHER THE RECORD OR THE INDUSTRIAL DISPUTE CONTACT.... HINDLE GEARS STRIKE COMMITTEE c/o STUART FIRTH, 21 THROXENBY WAY, CLAYTON, BRADFORD BD14 6EU. TEL 0274-816157

The Hindles pickets + the three musicians all come from Bradford. The money to release this single on the strikers' own label was collected from supporters & sympathisers who donated into a fund. Many smaller strikes go virtually unreported in the national press. The main purpose of this record is to draw attention to the plight of the striker in this country. Regardless of political issues, strikes cause real suffering in human terms. Lack of money & loss of a stable lifestyle combine with the undermining of pride, security, morale and normal family life in a way that's hard to appreciate from the outside.

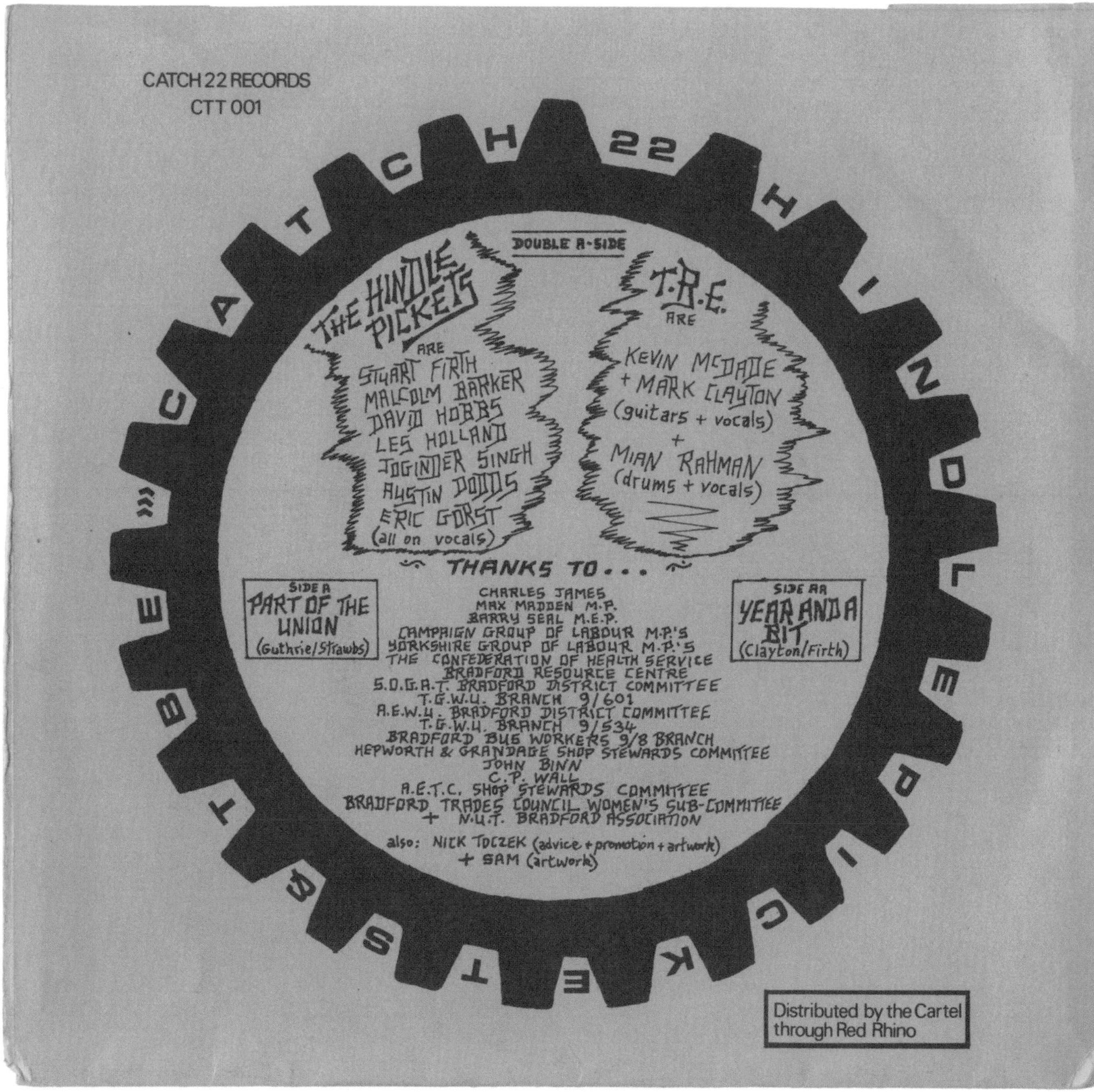

CATCH 22 RECORDS
CTT 001
"CATCH 22" HINDLE PICKETS
DOUBLE A-SIDE
THE HINDLE PICKETS
ARE
STUART FIRTH
MALCOLM BARKER
DAVID HOBBS
LES HOLLAND
JOGINDER SINGH
AUSTIN DODDS
ERIC GORST
(all on vocals)
T.R.E.
ARE
KEVIN McDADE
+ MARK CLAYTON
(guitars + vocals)
+
MIAN RAHMAN
(drums + vocals)
THANKS TO...
SIDE A
PART OF THE UNION
(Guthrie/Strawbs)
SIDE AA
YEAR AND A BIT
(Clayton/Firth)
CHARLES JAMES
MAX MADDEN M.P.
BARRY SEAL M.E.P.
CAMPAIGN GROUP OF LABOUR M.P.'S
YORKSHIRE GROUP OF LABOUR M.P.'S
THE CONFEDERATION OF HEALTH SERVICE
BRADFORD RESOURCE CENTRE
S.O.G.A.T. BRADFORD DISTRICT COMMITTEE
T.G.W.U. BRANCH 9/601
A.E.W.U. BRADFORD DISTRICT COMMITTEE
T.G.W.U. BRANCH 9/534
BRADFORD BUS WORKERS 9/8 BRANCH
HEPWORTH & GRANDAGE SHOP STEWARDS COMMITTEE
JOHN BINN
C.P. WALL
A.E.T.C. SHOP STEWARDS COMMITTEE
BRADFORD TRADES COUNCIL WOMEN'S SUB-COMMITTEE
+ N.U.T. BRADFORD ASSOCIATION
also: NICK TOCZEK (advice + promotion + artwork)
+ SAM (artwork)
Distributed by the Cartel through Red Rhino

UK Miners' Strike of 1984/85

The miners' strike, which started in 1984 (sometimes dubbed "The Great Strike") is one of the most impactful labor actions of the late 20th century, pitting the relatively powerful and organized British working class against the oncoming wave of neoliberal economic discipline embodied by Margaret Thatcher and her Tory government. It was a massive, year-long strike across the country taken up by coal miners under the banner of the National Union of Mineworkers (NUM). It came a decade after a massively successful—and much shorter—strike by NUM against a weaker conservative government. The strike was characterized by dogged and creative worker action (for example, flying pickets—where workers travel to join others' picket lines) met with extreme police violence. As an example of scale, "The Battle of Orgreave" was a clash between 5,000 picketers and 6,000 police. Thatcher made breaking the union—and hopefully the broader working class—her central goal, deploying both direct repression and intense rhetorical framing (she famously called the miners, "The Enemy Within").

The strike ended in a decisive win for Thatcher and the ruling class, determined as they were to safeguard the ascendancy of neoliberalism with mass police violence. By the end of 1985, the strike was over yet hundreds of miners were still in prison, and thousands more out of jobs. Mines were closed, communities crushed, and the union movement severely weakened.

In contrast to our other records—where fundraising plays a background role to foreground experimentation in culture, popularization, and research—almost every one of the seventeen records in this mini-collection states unequivocally that it was made to raise money, and often for the same centralized strike fund overseen by NUM (though you'll notice there are no records put out by NUM itself). This makes sense given the sheer scale of the strike, where not hundreds, but tens of thousands of workers were on pickets and needed funds to feed

themselves and their families. This would swamp almost any strike fund. We often find ourselves doing a lot of fundraising, and in this series of records we get to explore the fine grain variation in method and argumentation for something as clear and direct as donating to an official, centralized fund.

While the records reflect the structure of a national struggle centering a canonized and idealized "coal miner" and led by a single union, cultural experimentation and autonomy still pulse reliably in the background. There is an embracing of both traditional working class culture in the form of worker choirs and marching bands as well as newer forms of experimental pop music, often on the same record, and sometimes even the same song.

REMEMBRANCE
KELLINGLEY COLLIERY
BAND

Kellingley Colliery Band
<u>Remembrance</u>
7" single
Miner Hits (MHR001)
1984
Great Britain

It was regular practice for colliers—coal miners—to have a band, and the Kellingley Colliery Band was a relatively new one, working to provide "musical opportunities for the youngsters of the mining community." The title track, "Remembrance," is "a new arrangement of the famous hymn 'Abide With Me,' as played by the band at the funeral of Joe Green, Kellingley miner, who died on picket duty in June 1984." Joe Green was crushed by a scab lorry while on the picket line, which the miners held as murder and the conservative press labeled an accident. The final track is a miners' hymn dedicated to all miners who have perished in mines—thus the arc of the record braids martyrdom, both on and off the job, into the popular history of the struggle.

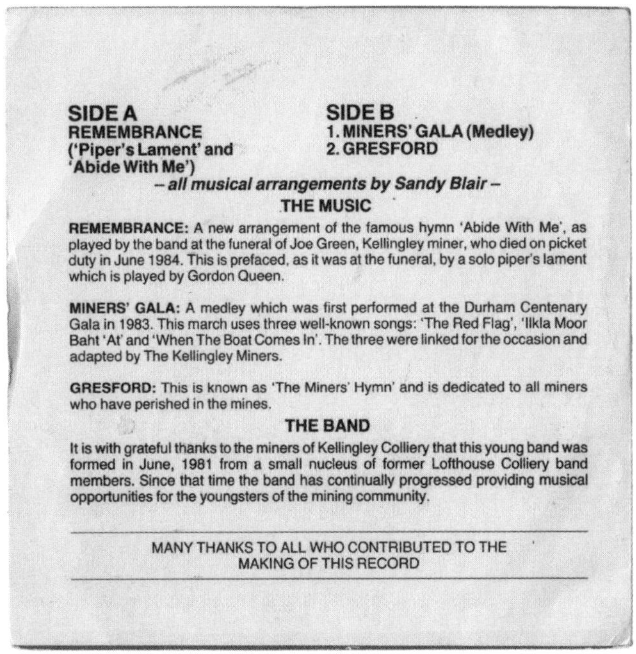

SIDE A
REMEMBRANCE
('Piper's Lament' and 'Abide With Me')

SIDE B
1. MINERS' GALA (Medley)
2. GRESFORD

– all musical arrangements by Sandy Blair –

THE MUSIC

REMEMBRANCE: A new arrangement of the famous hymn 'Abide With Me', as played by the band at the funeral of Joe Green, Kellingley miner, who died on picket duty in June 1984. This is prefaced, as it was at the funeral, by a solo piper's lament which is played by Gordon Queen.

MINERS' GALA: A medley which was first performed at the Durham Centenary Gala in 1983. This march uses three well-known songs: 'The Red Flag', 'Ilkla Moor Baht 'At' and 'When The Boat Comes In'. The three were linked for the occasion and adapted by The Kellingley Miners.

GRESFORD: This is known as 'The Miners' Hymn' and is dedicated to all miners who have perished in the mines.

THE BAND

It is with grateful thanks to the miners of Kellingley Colliery that this young band was formed in June, 1981 from a small nucleus of former Lofthouse Colliery band members. Since that time the band has continually progressed providing musical opportunities for the youngsters of the mining community.

MANY THANKS TO ALL WHO CONTRIBUTED TO THE MAKING OF THIS RECORD

Charlie Livingstone
"Get Off Your Knees (Unity)" b/w "Propaganda"
7" single
C. Miner Records (CMR 001)
1984
Great Britain

This is one of the few records here released without a picture sleeve, which makes it hard to know many details about Charlie Livingstone and these songs. The A-side of the single addresses fellow miners in the first person, talking about "our wives" unwavering support, and the experience of talking to "new comrades" on the picket. The song implies Livingstone was a miner himself, and his call to "get off your knees / stand up and fight / like our fathers did before" is a good faith rallying cry to fellow workers. While "Get Off Your Knees" is clearly intended as a Miners' Strike anthem, the flipside is not a miners song, but a track about the IRA and British Army violence in Northern Ireland—speaking to a broader politicization of miners and wider context for the strike.

Livingstone actually makes a cameo appearance in the Ken Loach documentary about the Miners' Strike, *Which Side Are You On?* It's a strangely awkward scene in the film, when Livingstone is performing what he clearly feels is a rousing rendition of "Get Off Your Knees" to a polite yet extremely bored looking audience of workers and families in a union hall or church basement.

C. MINER RECORDS
CHARLIE LIVINGSTONE
CMR 001
45 R.P.M.
SIDE A
STEREO
GET OFF YOUR KNEES (UNITY)
(Livingstone)
Produced by : COLIN GODDARD
Distributed by :
AUDREY SMITH
26, Sandileigh Ave.
Withington, Manchester
P 1984
ALL RIGHTS OF THE MANUFACTURER AND OF THE OWNER OF THE RECORDED WORK RESERVED · UNAUTHORIZED PUBLIC PERFORMANCE BROADCASTING AND COPYING OF THIS RECORD PROHIBITED
MADE IN FRANCE

THE MINER'S STRIKE RAP!
PROFITS TO THE MINER'S FAMILIES

Michael Rosen
The Miner's Strike Rap
7" single
Pit Records (PIT 100)
1984
Great Britain

An early rap record in support of the miners, this is about what you would expect from a white leftist children's book author and professor of children's literature with a post-punk backing band taking a turn at hip-hop (pssst, it's not great). Given that this is the only non-children's music and storytelling release in Rosen's discography (which also includes albums such as *Centrally Heated Knickers*), it speaks to the broad impact of the Miners' Strike and the level of mobilization that happened, not just amongst miners and their families, but the broader society. The aforementioned backing band includes members of A Popular History of Signs and To Finland Station.

Although no competition for Rakim or KRS-One, you can't accuse Rosen of not trying, and there is something compelling about his amateur rhymes over rudimentary Casio beats:

Come on everybody, wanna hear your voice
Now is the time that we gotta make a choice
Ain't no such thing as a pit that loses money
While the bees do the work and the boss gets the honey
A hip-hop — a hip hop hap
I'm giving you all the miner's strike rap

We have no idea how this record was received, although I don't think most of the miners in 1984 were rap fans. This record seems clearly aimed at mobilizing a broader audience to support the miners, and taking a chance on a pop style rather than sticking to either labor standards of the rock music likely popular with the miners themselves.

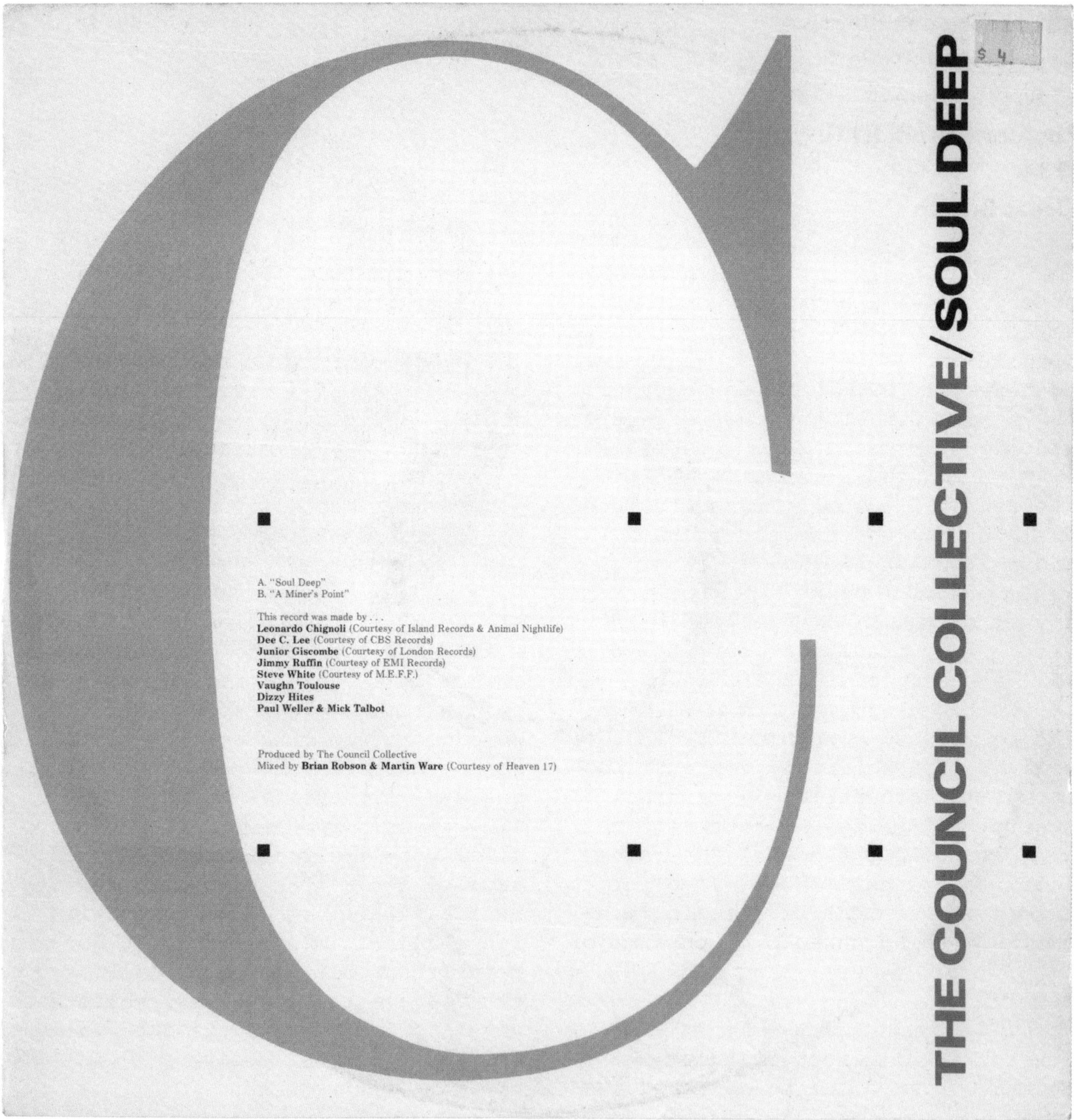
THE COUNCIL COLLECTIVE/SOUL DEEP
A. "Soul Deep"
B. "A Miner's Point"
This record was made by . . .
Leonardo Chignoli (Courtesy of Island Records & Animal Nightlife)
Dee C. Lee (Courtesy of CBS Records)
Junior Giscombe (Courtesy of London Records)
Jimmy Ruffin (Courtesy of EMI Records)
Steve White (Courtesy of M.E.F.F.)
Vaughn Toulouse
Dizzy Hites
Paul Weller & Mick Talbot
Produced by The Council Collective
Mixed by Brian Robson & Martin Ware (Courtesy of Heaven 17)

The Council Collective
Soul Deep
7" & 12" singles
Polydor (MINE 1/MINE X1)
1984
Great Britain

The Council Collective was a supergroup of sorts, organized by Paul Weller and Mick Talbert of The Style Council with support from Martin Ware of Heaven 17, Tommy Ruffin (brother of David Ruffin of the Temptations), and Dee C. Lee (backing vocalist for WHAM!). This was the moment of the emergence of socially conscious pop music mega-projects such as Band Aid and We are the World, so here Weller—a well known lefty—is trying to bridge his indie credibility with his major label clout. Polydor, who released this, is the only corporate label reflected in this book. The record saw significant radio play and was pressed in a dozen editions in multiple countries, including Australia, Ireland, the Netherlands, and Japan. An extended 12" version featured on the B-side a long format interview between two striking miners, something unheard of on a major label record, never mind a dance record.

The stated intention of the record is "to raise money for the Striking Miners and their families before Xmas. But obviously in the light of the tragic and disgusting event in South Wales," the writing on the back continues, "resulting in the murder of a Cab driver, some of the monies will also go now, to the widow of the man." This event would have been known to those at the time without further explanation, as the murder of cabbie Dave Wilkins was widely publicized by the Tory media and used as a wedge against the strike. Two strikers in South Wales had dropped a concrete block from a footbridge onto a taxi as it shuttled (with police escort!) a scab to work. "We do support the miners strike but we do not support violence. It helps no one and only creates further division amongst people." This back-pedaling was likely demanded by the label, and it's worth noting that the B-side interview acknowledges violence against management, but condemns the media manipulation of it, not the events themselves, which are understood by one of the interviewees as part of class warfare.

The Enemy Within
Support the Miners
7" & 12" singles
Rough Trade
1984
Great Britain

While folk and rock music were long-time formal standards for union songs, in mid-'80s United Kingdom it was dance music that was increasingly the voice of youth culture. The Enemy Within was a one-off project headed by Adrian Sherwood, the producer and brainchild behind On-U Sound, an avant-garde merger of dub music, post punk, and other emerging forms of dance music. This track consists of heavily chopped samples of speeches from Arthur Scargill (leader of NUM) laid over an electro groove. While the record states, "All proceeds to the Miners' Solidarity Fund," it also proclaims that you can "play this record at six"—an attempt to generate collective action "to create a surge of demand for power at six o'clock every evening." "The enemy within" is what Thatcher called the miners' union, and the taking up of the phrase as a name is both a recuperation and a youthful thumb in the face of authority.

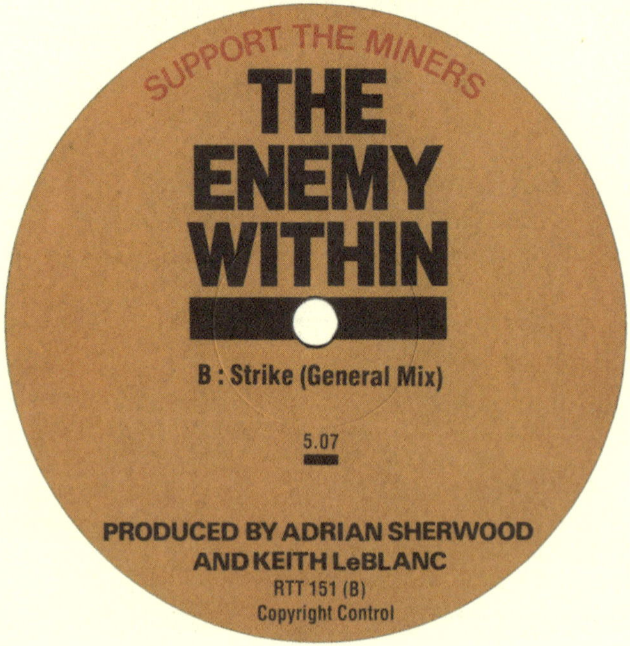

SUPPORT THE MINERS
THE ENEMY WITHIN
RTT 151

SUPPORT
THE
MINERS'
STRIKE
This record has been made to raise money! Money for the striking miners i.e., as the proceeds from the sales will be sent directly to British mining communities. Money they so urgently need in their fight to give a future to their communities, to themselves and to their children. They deserve our support because they've got the courage to oppose their oppressors. Oppressors using the ultimate weapon to silence the oppressed: starvation! Therefore solidarity means money means food means new energy in the miners' fight to survive.
This record is the memory of 15 miners benefits (which raised about £2000), done between September 6 and October 2, 1984. The first 3 gigs were done by Zowiso, The Ex and Vacuüm, the latter 12 by Zowiso, The Ex and Morzelpronk + Nico. The sound quality isn't perfect, the recordings more or less took place by accident. So what? The meaning of this record is to express solidarity with the miners' strike, not to get into the charts. If this isn't your cup of tea, get another record. But do you know at this very moment there are people who can't even afford something as simple as a cup of tea? At least you've got a choice!
FL 10,-
THE EX
MORZELPRONK+NICO
ZOWISO

The Ex, Morzelpronk + Nico, and Zowiso
Support the Miners' Strike
LP
Records Against Thaatchism!!! (RAT 001)
1984
Netherlands

A Dutch solidarity record, the result of fifteen recorded benefit shows and the first record we've found of musicians recording in support of a strike in another country. While the early eighties was a key moment of interconnectedness between political punk bands (for example, The Ex, featured here, were close friends and often touring mates with the British band Chumbawamba, themselves often out on the miners' picket lines) this record still provides a glimpse of a growing international character of working class resistance in the face of capitalist globalization.

The bands give a clear picture of this record purpose, with a fundraising frame which centers the miners themselves as protagonists: "This record has been made to raise money! .... Solidarity means money means food means new energy in the miners' fight to survive." Regarding the music, they write,

> The sound quality isn't perfect, the recordings more or less took place by accident. So what? The meaning of this record is to express solidarity with the miners' strike, not to get into the charts. If this isn't your cup of tea, get another record. But do you know at this very moment there are people who can't even afford something as simple as a cup of tea? At least you've got a choice!

Not wanting to waste space or opportunity, The Ex (who pressed this record under the one-off label name "Records Against Thaatchism!!!") included a foldout, two-color, two-sided offset poster. The image of a photographer swung at by a cop on horseback takes up most of one side, with "Support the Striking Miners" above and a bank routing number for an Amsterdam-based Miners' Strike Support Fund below. This inclusion of a "giro" or public banking account number is common on Dutch political records, with fundraising culture a consistent and direct feature of the international solidarity movement. The back of the poster is a collage of Dutch newspaper reports on the strike. In addition, included is a single sheet of paper that breaks down all money spent and made on their tour, including where the resulting revenue went! In recounting the organizing for the tour they mention that they showed videos about the strike while on tour, and even mounted a photo exhibition in one city.

The attention from the official media was nil. We had sent press releases to all eligible magazines and radio programs, but there was hardly any response. . . . It is therefore all the more pleasant to notice that we do not even need the bourgeois media. . . . Locally, the various halls were able to stimulate enough people through squatter and/or other alternative magazines.

One collaborator reportedly "pretended to be a miner injured in the picket line, and collected a lot of money [to send to the strikers]!"

STEUN DE BRITSE MIJNSTAKERS

Nou, hier dan eindelijk ons stukkie over de mijnstakerstoernee van de Ex en Zowiso en Morzelpronk en Vacuüm. 't Liefst hadden we gezegd: "Het was grandioos, we hebben 8000 piek opgehaald, doeg!, er zijn weer andere dingen te doen". Maar ja, die mensen van de BLUF kúnnen zeuren zeg!

INKOMSTEN:

Den Haag	f 881,50
Wageningen	1150,--
Arnhem	680,--
Nijmegen	1369,--
Amsterdam (BOC)	500,--
Dronten	550,--
Bergen Op Zoom	599,--
Amsterdam (Pleinwerker) ..	1064,35
Delft/Rijswijk	487,50
Deventer	688,--
Wormer	840,--
Helmond	1021,--
Hulst	475,--
Hanna Paulowna (d'r zus) .	900,--
Haarlem	478,--
+ nog wat los geld	32,--
	f11958,35

UITGAVEN:

trein, diesel, busje, benzine 6/7/8 september	f 475,--
buspreparatie	200,--
huur snoeren 20/9	125,--
diesel touringbus	530,--
diesel Ex-busje	95,--
benzine auto	20,--
bus onderdelen	100,--
drumsticks/-vellen	238,50
cassettes	60,--
foto-rolletjes, batterijen	46,--
veerpont	39,--
snaren	62,--
eten	155,--
kopieën persberichten	30,--
stencils, postzegels	125,--
p.a. speakers	665,--
huur video 15 dagen	175,--
afsluitingsfeestje	200,--
mikrofoonstaander Deventer	100,--
	f3560,50

inkomsten	f11958,35
uitgaven	3560,50
OPBRENGST	f8397,85

Overgemaakt op de diverse giro's:

steunfonds wageningen	f 400,--
nijmegen-deal	700,--
steunfonds mijnstakers ...	7000,--
er resteert nog	297,50
	f8397,50

Hier komt nog ± f500,-- bij, zijnde de opbrengst uit de verkoop van de bladen, platen en affiesjes e.d.

"Geen gelul, er moet geld komen", dachten we, toen duidelijk werd dat er mensen honger moesten lijden in hun strijd om niet aan de kant te worden geschoven. Mensen die vechten voor hun manier van bestaan, die de moed hebben om in het geweer te komen tegen de belangen van grootkapitaal-Thatcher-rechts-kernenergie, die verdienen het om gesteund te worden, op wat voor manier dan ook.

En wij hebben een bandje en daar kun je geld mee verdienen, simpel. Dus snel plannen gemaakt. Vrienden van de Zowiso, Morzelpronk en Vacuüm zagen het ook gelijk zitten, dus dat was het programma. Een oproep in Bluf leverde optredens op in Den Haag, Wageningen en Arnhem. De andere twaalf hebben we zelf gebeld, wat verbazingwekkend makkelijk ging. Die rare maandagen, dinsdagen en woensdagen zaten zo vol. Het was wel vreemd om nu 'zoveel mogelijk' geld te vragen, als je normaal voor onkosten speelt. Maar alles went.

Om duidelijk te maken dat de avonden om meer gingen dan de muziek draaiden we ook video's over de stakingen, was er een foto-tentoonstelling over de staking in Deal, gemaakt door twee vrouwen uit Nijmegen, en verkochten we bladen, pamfletten, affiesjes en onafhankelijke platen, waarvan de winst voor het goede doel was. Het was een heel circus.

Een vriend van Dolf had nog een touringbus, die we wel mochten gebruiken. Die vriend zat echter in Egypte en ... afijn, om een lang verhaal kort te maken (een motoragent die ons aanhield deed alsof hij het allemaal wel snapte), we hadden dus een touringbus, en dat maakte het reizen goedkoop, gezellig en comfortabel ('t lijkt Neckerman wel!).

De aandacht van de 'officiële' media was nihil. We hadden persmappen gestuurd naar alle in aanmerking komende bladen en radioprogramma's, maar reactie was er nauwelijks. Vara's Popkrant kwam notabene op de laatste toerdag nog even een keer aankakken! Wel verscheen er een paginagrote advertentie in de OOR, waar wij niets van afweten.(hi hi..)

Het is daarom des te leuker om te merken dat we de burgerlijke media niet eens nodig hebben. De belangstelling voor de hele toer was echt overweldigend. Plaatselijk konden de diverse zalen genoeg mensen wakker porren via kraak- en/of andere alternatieve bladen. Zonder de enorme inzet en enthousiasme van al die mensen hadden wij het nooit kunnen redden. Mensen in Arnhem maakten zomaar even 4000 affiesjes en verspreidden die door het hele land!

6, 7 en 8 september waren de eerste drie optredens, in De Blauwe Aanslag in Den Haag, de 10 Zilverlingen in Wageningen en Willem I in Arnhem. En dat begon hoopgevend. Na aftrek van de kosten hadden we al f2000,- over. Eugene van Serious Drinking, toevallig op vakantie, met een bepleisterd hoofd van de Yag-Yum demonstratie, gaf zich uit voor een in de picket-line gewond geraakte mijnwerker, en kollekteerde heel wat geld bij elkaar!

En toen begon de grote ruk, van 20 september tot en met 2 oktober, met Morzelpronk in plaats van Vacuüm. We zagen er toch wel een beetje tegen op, want 12 dagen elke dag spelen is niet niks. En ook nog: reizen, sjouwen, opbouwen, soundchecken, drinken, laat te bed, alles er om heen in de gaten houden, en dan nog elke avond de appels van de bomen spelen! Gelukkig waren er mensen mee voor de plaatverkoop, video enzovoort, zodat alles eigenlijk toch zeer gesmeerd liep. Op de meeste plaatsen hadden ze ook voor ons gekookt, dus werden we niet àl te bleekjes. Voor Zowiso was het af en toe wel even doorbijten, want eigenlijk moesten ze elke ochtend weer naar school, maar met een beetje slaap-smoesjes-spijbelen en een extra dosis vrolijkheid liep ook dat goed af.

De gratis (!) door Holland P.A. ter beschikking gestelde P.A. was perfect, al was het wel effe paniek in Nijmegen toen we het snoerenkistje vergeten bleken te zijn. Om half elf, met een volle zaal, volop in aller ijl geleende snoeren solderen is bepaald niet rustgevend. Maar aan het eind van de avond hadden we zo'n f1500,- en er waren mensen geweest die liefst honderd piek gaven.

Natuurlijk waren er ook avonden met minder mensen en minder geld. Maar alles helpt. Zo is Dronten nu niet bepaald een flitsende stad. De helft van het publiek was een soort brommerrockertjes die voor het eerst van hun leven 'echte krakers' zagen: "Dus jullie zijn krakers die benefieten houden om de huur te kunnen betalen?" Iets te veel bier op dènk. Anderen haalden hun neus op (Dolf had ook niet zo'n schone broek aan), maar hun geld ging ondertussen toch mooi naar de miners!

Deventer was een beetje een dieptepunt, als de staf ons 100 gulden in rekening brengt voor een microfoonstaniaard die gemold zou zijn. In de daaropvolgende diskussie over dat dit toch geen normale rock-avond is en dat mensen in Engeland niet te vreten hebben en dat die 100 piek van hun geld afgaat, durft die stomme klootzak te zeggen "van idealisme kan ik niet vreten"!!!

GGGRRRRRRRRRRRRRRRRRRRRRRRR Buiten het feit dat het een reparatie van een paar piek zou zijn, is dat zo in en in zielig!!! Vooral als je bedenkt dat het Burgerweeshuis ooit uit idealisme gekraakt en grootgemaakt is en dat die boerenlul aan dat idealisme een dikbelegde boterham heeft overgehouden. Het wordt tijd dat de medewerkers daar, die verder vreselijk hun best hebben gedaan, eens kijken wat er aan de hand is met hún centrum.

Overigens was het ook nog feest in Deventer, want Zowiso deed hun honderdste optreden: bloemen-confetti-serpentines-ballonnen! In Helmond hadden Jos en ik feest, wij hadden al tweehonderd keer herrie gemaakt. Ik ben met augurken bekogeld en uitgegleden over een stuk taart, geloof ik. Over uitglijden gesproken: in het gekraakte CLD in Delft was de vuurspuwer, die onder Morzelpronk een portret van Thatcher in vlammen spuwde, iets te royaal met de dieselolie aan het kwatten geweest. Het pogoën bij Zowiso leek meer op vrij worstelen, en Sabien ging met TV en al tegen de vlakte. Zij bleef heel, de TV niet. Die avond ploften er ook nog drie speakers, maar gezellig was het wel. De vuurvreter brandde later op de avond nog z'n bek aan de soep! (Of heb je dat verzonnen, Sok?)

Het ritme reizen-spelen-reizen-slapen zat er goed in. De ene rustdag is eigenlijk vervelend, maar iedereen is toch blij als het laatste optreden, in Haarlem, er op zit. Maar iedereen is vooral blij dat er zo waanzinnig veel geld is opgehaald. Met alle onkosten erafgetrokken meer dan 8000 piek! En iedereen is opgelucht dat we het er zo goed afgebracht hebben, en vooral ook dankbaar voor alle medewerking en enthousiasme.

En het laat ook weer eensgzien hoe je muziek óók kunt gebruiken, voor meer dan alleen vermaak of ter verhoging van de baromzet. Hoe belangrijk dat kan zijn, want dat wordt nog wel eens veregeten.

Veel tijd om uit te rusten (of stukkies te schrijven) kregen we trouwens niet, want er moest getrommeld/gezwaaid worden in Dordrecht, muziekgemaakt bij de blokkade bij het gerechtsgebouw aldaar, herrie gemaakt in de gracht bij de ontruiming van de Singel. En nu zitten we weer opgescheept met het resultaat van de mijnstakersbenefieten. Duizenden Engelse kinderen hier op vakantie, die het op mij gemunt hebben help!

ho!!

stop!!!

(we blijven lachen) doeg!

Terrie

GIRO 4568706

SIDE 1

THE EX:
- Oops! wrong goverment (Mine your own business, Thaatcha!) .... (+)
- Crap-rap .... (+)
- Squat! .... (o)
- Fire and ice .... (o)
- Blueprints for a blackout .... (-)

MORZELPRONK+NICO:
- During times of confusion .... (-)
- De kuur .... (+)

SIDE 2

MORZELPRONK:
- De koeienwals .... (+)
- Pielharmonies no. 1 .... (+)
- SKAAS .... (+)
- Prélude voor een blauwe indiaan . (+)

ZOWISO:
- New present day offers .... (o)
- Stiffy smile .... (o)
- Blacks prison .... (o)
- The truth lies midway .... (o)
- Bruises .... (o)
- F.A.O.-show .... (o)
- Tied hands .... (o)

All recordings caught live on cassette tapes by Crazy William (o), Arthur Wouters (+) and Kees Z'walkman (-) between September 20 and October 2, 1984. Mixed by Don and Dolf on November 30, 1984. Released in February 1985.

Bedankt: Vacuüm, Annoesjka, Will, Kees, Cobie, Ferrie, Beat (bus), Don (Music Farm), Arthur (Polyfoon productions), Patrick, Simon, Asla, Johann Feuerspeier, Tejaas & Annie (foto's), grachtenbus, Holland P.A., Oktopus, Villa Zuid, M.A.L., Hotel Bosch-Arnhem; en verder iedereen die heeft geholpen met de optredens in De Blauwe Aanslag-Den Haag, 10 Zilverlingen-Wageningen, Willem I-Arnhem, Doornroosje-Nijmegen, S.O.C.-Amsterdam, Labri-Dronten, Botte Hommel-Roosendaal, Pleinwerker-Amsterdam, CLD-Delft, Burgerweeshuis-Deventer(dus géén dank aan de leiding: dieven!), Plus-Wormer, Werkwinkel-Helmond, Kontrast-Hulst, Ark-Anna Paulowna, Patronaat-Haarlem. (...eh psst: HALBGR RELEASE!)

Morzelpronk, Van Diemenstraat 6,
1013 NH Amsterdam;
Zowiso, Knollendammerstraat 98,
1531 BG Wormer 02982-3783;
The Ex, Galgenstraat 4 a', 1013 LT
Amsterdam 020-278640/075-286795;
De Konkurrent (distributie), postbus
14598, 1001 LB Amsterdam 020-181646.

STEUNKOMITEE BRITSE MIJNSTAKERS, AMSTERDAM
GIRO 4568706 - GIRO 4568706 - GIRO 4568706

in tijden van verwarring
is het goed om duidelijk te zijn
laat ik dus zeggen:
ik ben 36 jaar en
ik heb nog nooit voor een baas gewerkt
laat ik dus zeggen:
het laatste waar ik aan zou denken is
om onder de grond te kruipen en
voor iemand anders kolen te gaan graven

in tijden van verwarring
is het goed om duidelijk te zijn
laat ik dus zeggen:
ik vind het onzin
mensen werk te laten doen
dat ook door machines gedaan kan worden
laat ik dus zeggen:
ik vind het absurd om te gaan staken
voor het recht jezelf kapot te mogen werken

in tijden van verwarring
is het goed om duidelijk te zijn
laat ik dus zeggen:
ik weet dat de vakbonden
de arbeiders
al duizendmaal hebben verraden
laat ik dus zeggen:
vrees dat het ditmaal weer zal gebeuren

in tijden van verwarring
is het goed om duidelijk te zijn
laat ik dus zeggen:
ik steun de britse mijnstakers
omdat hun vijanden
ook mijn vijanden zijn
laat ik dus zeggen:
ik steun de britse mijnstakers
omdat de machtelozen altijd gelijk hebben
laat ik dus zeggen:
ik steun de britse mijnstakers
omdat ze geloven dat
vooruitgang nooit kan zijn:
dat wat mensen overbodig maakt
maar altijd is:
dat wat mensen bevrijdt

CRAP-RAP

here i was
i was down in the street
i was feeling blue
suede shoes on my feet
i nearly cracked down
under this pressure
too much of my time
seemed to be dull leisure

i wasn't going anywhere
or just hanging around
i was looking for an answer
with the question still unfound
i had to search for something
find a clue
i didn't know yet what
but i had something to do

whatever i was looking for
i searched it everywhere
every place i'd been
i couldn't find it anywhere
i realized
this could be a clue
if someone wants to lie
he won't tell what's true

there had to be a reason
for hiding the truth
then i saw the answer
hanging underneath the roof
wall to wall ads
things we're told to buy
and when you can't afford it
they'll make shure you'll try

i'd like to turn my back
on the system i am faced with
but the next problem is the one
that is going to replace it
anyway
they don't need me anymore
now they say i'm trash
but i've heard that once before
they thought i'd feel
unhappy and ashamed
as they pushed me off the wagon
of their money-making train
okay, they don't want me
though i don't mind to work
i just don't wanna be exploited
or treated as a jerk
so here i am
i'm down in the street
i do what i wanna do
and that's okay by me
i'm not gonna crack down
under any pressure
i won't fall in that crap-trap
of hating my leisure

FIRE AND ICE

how do you compare
bad with bad?
do you subtract
the dead salvadorians
from dead afghans?
do you subtract
tortured chileans
from vanished czechs?
and with whom do you exchange
the exterminated vietnamese?

he who calculates with a bad memory
he who tells lies from lies apart
he wants to compare evil with evil
deserves the war he gets

and the off-writers sharpen their pencils
like the military sharpen their bayonets
on balances of power
they weigh corpses by the million
they divide fear by honour
and deduct radiation from profit

he who's in the red
finds no mercy in their eyes
and he who pays his debt
he's considered by them as weak

they measure everything
in valuations and prognoses
except
the shortest way from their office
to the underground shelter
they measure it in mm./sec.

they've got tongues like split atoms
with which they lick
their pens of rocket-steel
before they balance their books

they work day and night
they work fire and ice
they write off:
cities against oil-wells
children against money-lenders
freedom against-power

they work day and night
they work fire and ice
they write off
and end up at zero

SQUAT!

there's plenty of room
for 30,000 people
there's 30,000 people
looking for a home
empty buildings, all over the city
empty buildings, for hire and sale
empty buildings, isn't it a pity
empty buildings, so don't sit and wait:
squat!

BLUEPRINTS FOR A BLACKOUT

blueprints for a blackout
like a mass-murder in a far-away town
it can be even worse when it's your home-town
but no one will notice when the lights are out

blueprints for a blackout
like a call for arms against the peace threat
living off this world war three threat
seems there's nothing to be worried about

blueprints for a blackout
like public opinions that divide the crowd
demagogues leading the lonely crowd
waiting for volunteers to drop out

blueprints for a blackout
like planned heart-attacks stab by stab
a booming business behind your back
down-to-earth boxers in a knock-out

blueprints for a blackout
or how to sell the next disease
tragic proof of human inhumanity
this sort of things has become epidemic
it seems to be the only way
to settle disagreements

blueprints for a blackout
governments promise to consider our doubts
blueprints for a blackout
their answers hidden in the background
blueprints for a blackout
no one will notice as the lights are out
blueprints for a blackout
flexible like cartboard cut-outs
like blueprints for a knock-out

blueprints for a blackout
seems there's nothing to be worried about
no one will notice as the lights are out
blueprints for a blackout
like blueprints for a knock-out

DURING TIMES OF CONFUSION

during times of confusion
it's better to be explicit
so... i will say:
i'm 36 years old and
i've never been employed
so... i will say:
the last thing i would do is
to go underground and
dig somebody else's coal

during times of confusion
it's better to be explicit
so... i will say:
i think it's a waste
to have people doing work
that can also be done by machines
so... i will say:
i think it's sad to go on strike for
the right to work yourself to death

during times of confusion
it's better to be explicit
so... i will say:
i know that the unions
made suckers out of the workers
a thousand times over
so... i will say:
fear this time it'll be the same

during times of confusion
it's better to be explicit
so... i will say:
i support the striking miners
because their enemies
are my enemies
so... i will say:
i support the striking miners
because the powerless are always right
so... i will say:
i support the striking miners
because they believe that
progression can never be:
that which makes people redundant
but always is:
that which sets people free

NEW PRESENT DAY OFFERS

consecrate the new threat
they do it steady, steady on
masking military manoeuvres
yanks' chute-drop in honduras

here are the new offers
here is the new threat
this is the sphere of influence
surrounded by deads

exercise or preparation
we all know what the curse is
this is military provocation
the interest of the dollar purse

here is the new threat
u.s. hey here they come
new present day offers
under the new sun

STIFFY SMILE

pick it up by observing the others
come along with your set of tastes
choose the most acrobatical bastards
confetti smiles covering the waste

image and image, style and style
is it stiffy walter's or gary's smile

image and image, style and style
i know it for certain, the voters pay
their smile!

BLACKS PRISON

white man on white bench
in white park there's no dark
black man in full bus
white man drives mercedes
black majority white authority
crack of 'shell'-tank certain security

homeland is a blacks prison
homeland's racism
homeland is a blacks prison
homeland's practised racism

white man on white bench
in white park there's no dark
black woman housekeeper
negrophobia, white man's feeder

THE TRUTH LIES MIDWAY

is a middle course the way of safety
or tomorrow's internal policy
when rubber bullets become precursors
of the fire-arm society

well, the truth lies midway
rubber bullets pulverize the eye
the truth lies midway
development you have to pay
well, death is development today
oh, death is development today

is a middle course the way of safety
or tomorrow's internal policy
would you join a rally to die
would you join a rally to die
well, i ...
the truth lies midway
death is development today
today!

BRUISES

he shows signs of bewilderment
and truth after excessive drinking
he has lovers for leisure activities
he's the primitive
within his own 'free' thinking

he shall 'hit the dirt'
at least provoke
he's a primitive himself
in his own 'jokes'

bruises for the babies and wives
the subjects of his deliberation
bruises for anyone who cares
a pathetic creature in a 'social' nation

F.A.O.-SHOW

hungerfighters like to do it on their own
with diplomatic talks on a mock serious tone
they wipe away their conscience
talk about their social feeling
they appreciate the corruption
use bribes to deal with

stay a little longer, get rich of hunger
this is our charity appeal
and socially we do feel
get rich of hunger in the f.a.o.-show
keep the expenditures low
you're in the f.a.o.-show
keep the expenditures low
third world here we go

TIED HANDS

steady and sharp pressure
they try us to convince
of some new military treasure
which is full of nasty pins

dutch hands are tied
we're spinning like a wheel
it's not on us to decide
and you know how tied hands feel

tied hands, well my friend
is it your or is it my land

it's kill or cure
sink or swim, it's our task
to have the defence budget slimmed

tied hands, well my friend
is it your or is it my land

Various artists

The Last Nightingale

12" EP

Recommended/Rē Records (Rē 1984)

1984

Great Britain

A salvo from pop's more avant-garde wing. Rê Records is the label of Chris Cutler, organizer behind the independent prog band Henry Cow and brainchild of the Rock In Opposition movement against corporate control of music. What stands out on this record of quite experimental music (from Robert Wyatt and Fred Frith, both members/collaborators with Henry Cow) is the funding strategy. Unlike the traditional promise of a donation once the records are sold, here the label decided to donate the expected income upfront, before any money was actually made: "Because the miners need the money at once, the entire margin of the first pressing of 2500 has already been given to them. . . . So long as the strike continues, all monies from any future pressing will go the same way - *& in an unseizable form.*" That last bit refers to an attempt made by the courts to freeze and take NUM's assets after levying a 200,000 pound fine against them.

The LAST NIGHTINGALE

The *Why* of it.

For nine months now, miners & their families have had roofs, food, clothes & utilities to pay for - & no strike pay. Families living on £I2 a week. How can anyone believe that they'd put up with that kind of hardship if they weren't fully behind the strike ? A *political* strike, not a strike to be settled by pay negotiations. A strike to do no more than to uphold a signed agreement which the government want unilaterally to tear up. The miners are suffering their hardships to save not only their jobs but also the mining industry itself - a nationalised industry & therefore a national asset - for *us*, for the country as a whole. Not only are the miners & their families suffering to protect our national assets, but also, on 'our' behalf, the present government is busy trying to grab all the union assets (freezing millions against a £200,000 fine), offering Xmas bribes, importing expensive coal, paying for well over the odds oil & nuclear powered electricity, stunning policing bills, court costs &c.

&c. to the tune of more than £3 a week per head of us. This is an involuntary contribution we are all forced to make so that our leaders can renege on a signed agreement & waste our national assets. I took no part in any ballot to break the coal strike. This money is financing hardship. It seems clear that the least we can do is to give money *Voluntarily* to the miners & their families. It is them we *want* to support; their part is our part, unequivocally. Hence this record. Our work & all earned from it (from the record company & the distribution company too) are a concrete contribution to the miners' struggle. To this end, the entire income from the full pressing has been given, in advance, to the strike fund. So long as the strike continues, all monies from any future pressing will go the same way - *& in an unsiezeable form.* I hope this proves to be the first of many.

Finally, not only the money is dedicated to the miners & their struggle, so is the work, the quality of the work & the content of the work: it is all dedicated to them, with our respect & thanks. Rē. 84.

THE LAST NIGHTINGALE

A CELEBRATION OF THE FIRST YEAR OF
All Proceeds To The Miners!
THE U.K. MINER`S STRIKE 1984-1985
HERE WE GO

Various artists

<u>Here We Go: A Celebration of the First Year of the U.K. Miner's Strike 1984–1985</u>

LP

Sterile Records (SR 08)

1985

Great Britain

Another compilation album of pop music in support of the strike, this one on the punk/goth/industrial side of things, organized by the band Nocturnal Emissions and their label Sterile Records. Unlike many benefit pop records where a band donates a completely unrelated song to a compilation, here most of the tracks relate to the strike, with titles like "Maggy," "Picket the Safety Way," and "Bite the Hand That Fails to Feed You." The writing on the sleeve by the Here We Go Collective (likely Nigel Ayers of Nocturnal Emissions and friends), ties together the diverse tactics of the strike without condemning the more violent side:

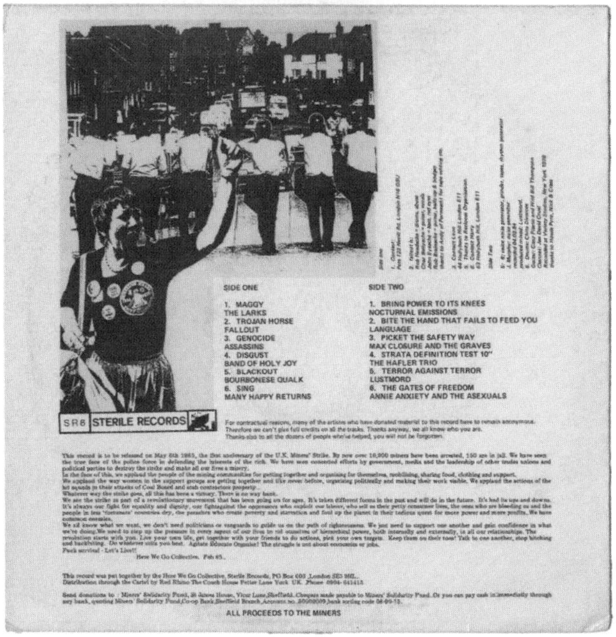

> ...we applaud the people of the mining communities for getting together and organising for themselves, mobilising, sharing food, clothing and support. We applaud the way women in the support groups are getting together and like never before, organising politically and making their work visible. We applaud the actions of the hit squads in their attacks of Coal Board and scab contractors property.... Whatever way the strike goes, all this has been a victory. There is no way back.

Various artists

<u>Heroes</u>

LP

Rock 'N' Dole (RDR 2)

1985

Great Britain

This record was produced on behalf of the Durham Miners Support Group by Consett Music Project, a local initiative that developed into a worker-run recording studio for young people in 1988 after the closure of the town's coal pit, and continued to thrive into the 2000s. "5 pound is a small price to pay for heroes!" proclaims the back—"All proceeds will go to help support the 625 sacked miners and their families." Again we have a fold-out poster, this one celebrating a working class family, much like the cover. The backside takes the tracklist and pairs each song with a quote, either from *Digging Deeper*, an edited collection of essays on the ongoing strike, or from the local bishop's 1985 Gala Day speech. Collaged next to them are pictures of every musician featured, most in the act of recording. When explaining the record in their own words, the support group write: "we needed to express, in musical terms, the reason why the miners went on strike and the reason why they were so well supported by wives and families."

The LP is impressive for how it ties together big name acts like Billy Bragg and The Flying Pickets (one of the stranger hiccups in mainstream pop history: an a cappella group of former miners who had participated in the 1970s miners strikes—thus the name of the group—who had a #1 hit in 1983) with local groups and choirs. The overall treatment of the record is one of respect for both the miners and the musicians, recognizing the importance of both and the power of working together.

HEROES

HEROES

HEROES

HEROES

HEROES

HEROES

HEROES

HEROES

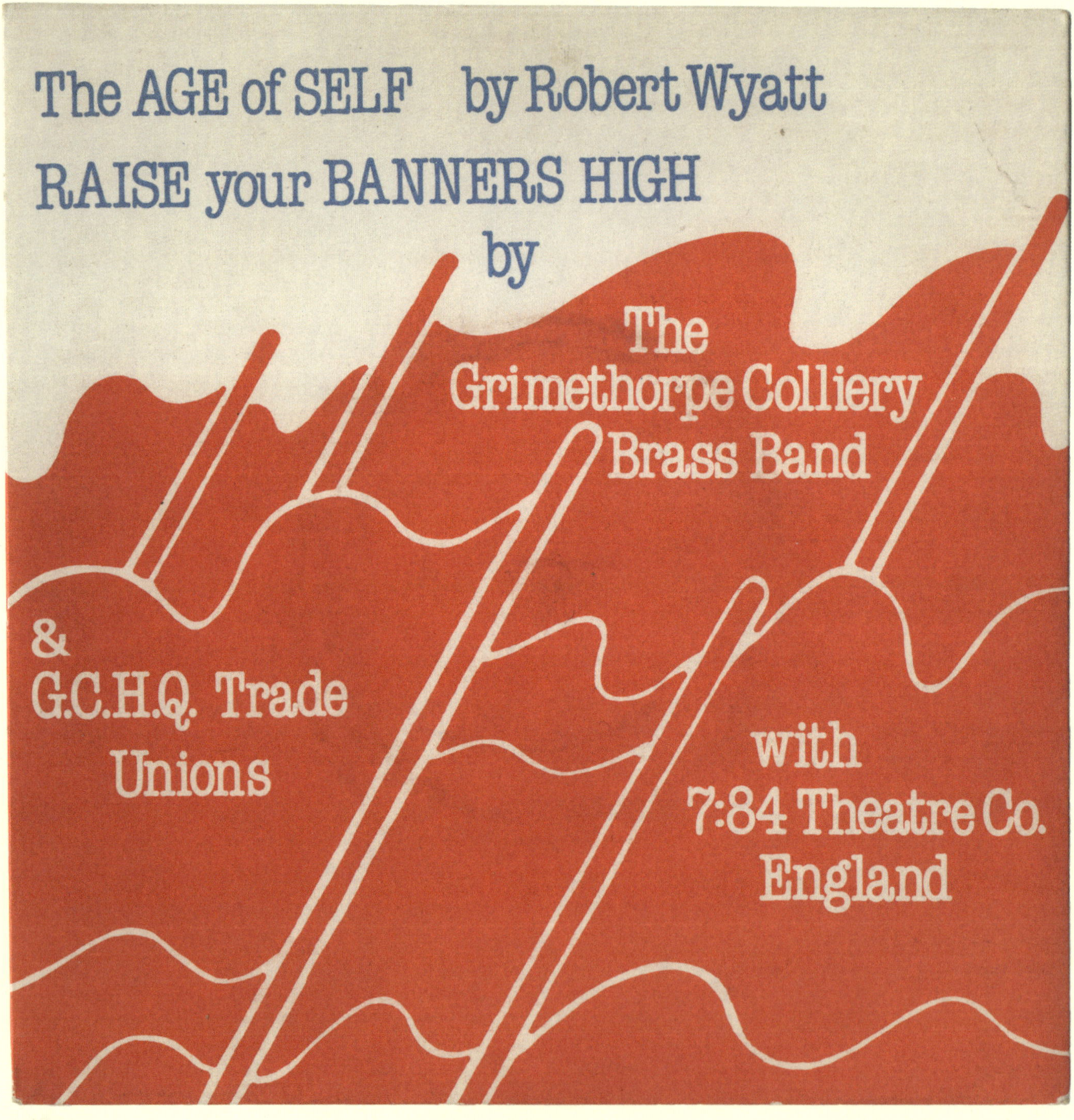
The AGE of SELF by Robert Wyatt
RAISE your BANNERS HIGH
by
The
Grimethorpe Colliery
Brass Band
&
G.C.H.Q. Trade
Unions
with
7:84 Theatre Co.
England

Robert Wyatt, The Grimethorpe Colliery Band, and G.C.H.Q. Trade Unions, with the 7:84 Theatre Co.
"The Age of Self" b/w "Raise Your Banners High"
7" single
Trade Union Congress (TUC 784)
1985
Great Britain

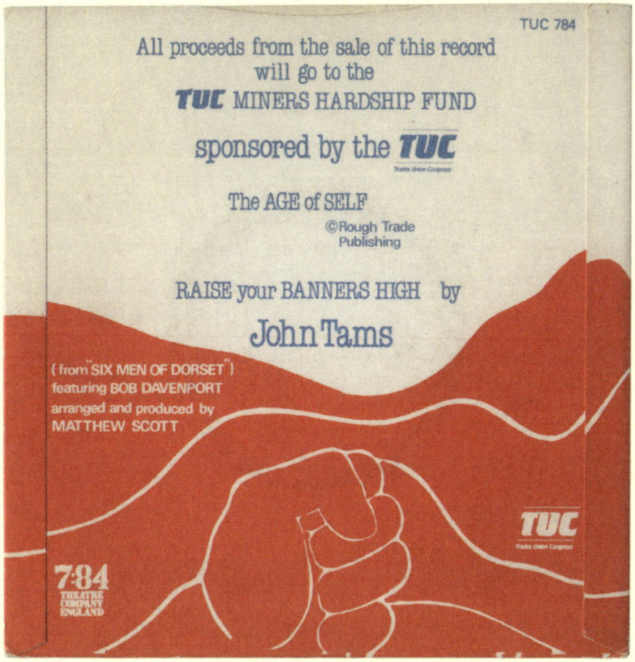

This record brings together a range of groups: the award-winning Grimethorpe Colliery Band, the left-wing theater group 7:84, indie musician Robert Wyatt, and the G.C.H.Q. Trade Unions. GCHQ stands for Government Communications Headquarters, a British intelligence listening center, where unionization had been outright banned a year earlier. The struggle against this ban developed into a mass campaign with the Trade Union Congress (TUC) and alongside the Miners' Strike became a touchstone for the trade union movement in Britain throughout the '80s.

In its own way, this is a very different version of a "supergroup" record like the one produce by the Council Collective. While Robert Wyatt had a long and illustrious career in more avant-garde rock circles (he had been the drummer of Soft Machine, and recorded a string of popular and heavily politicized solo albums), the miners' band and political theater group are almost anti-pop, rooted in performing directly with and for workers. The record is witness to this merger, juxtaposing a patriotic brass dirge and chorus on the A-side with a shockingly smooth, well-produced, and groovy track by Wyatt on the flipside. Wyatt's "Age of Self" is a wry undercutting of the narcissism facilitated and encouraged by neoliberalism, but the contrast between the two tracks is still sharp, and hard to read.

Test Dept. and the South Wales Striking Miners Choir
Shoulder to Shoulder
LP
Ministry of Power (MOPI)
1985
Great Britain

The South Wales Striking Miners Choir was a temporary assemblage of three Welsh labor choirs, which

traveled to London with the intention of meeting people to generate support for our cause and to share our culture. We took part in a concert with Test Dept. and we were relieved and surprised how our way of singing was accepted by the younger generation, and as comrades in arms, a binding friendship was formed.... We gave another concert in Bristol in November and stood shoulder to shoulder again with Test Dept. like the stout hearted men ["Stout Hearted Men" is a song on the album] we are comrades together."

Test Dept. were one of the most consistently left-wing of the eighties British industrial bands, known for clanging on big pieces of metal inside disused industrial infrastructure with projections covering the walls. The back of this record winks at that multi-media reputation with a series of film strips depicting moments from the struggle, and there's the promise of a video of the national tour being available in the spring, which sadly doesn't appear to have ever been released. The cover's constructivist style harkens to a time when avant-garde art was put in service of labor and is an interesting choice, as by the mid-'80s Soviet Constructivism was far more likely to be found on an arty punk or new wave record (Generation X's "Your Generation" 7" and Age of Chance's *Crush* LP are both good examples of this) than anything connected to working class struggle. At the same time, most of the back cover is given over to a first person narrative written by the miners in the Choir. Partisan pop culture (albeit an extreme version) and working class culture continue to rub up against each other on the record itself, as choral songs, speeches, and blasts of industrial noise follow one another but never quite fuse together, holding out the promise of some new form, but never actually fulfilling it.

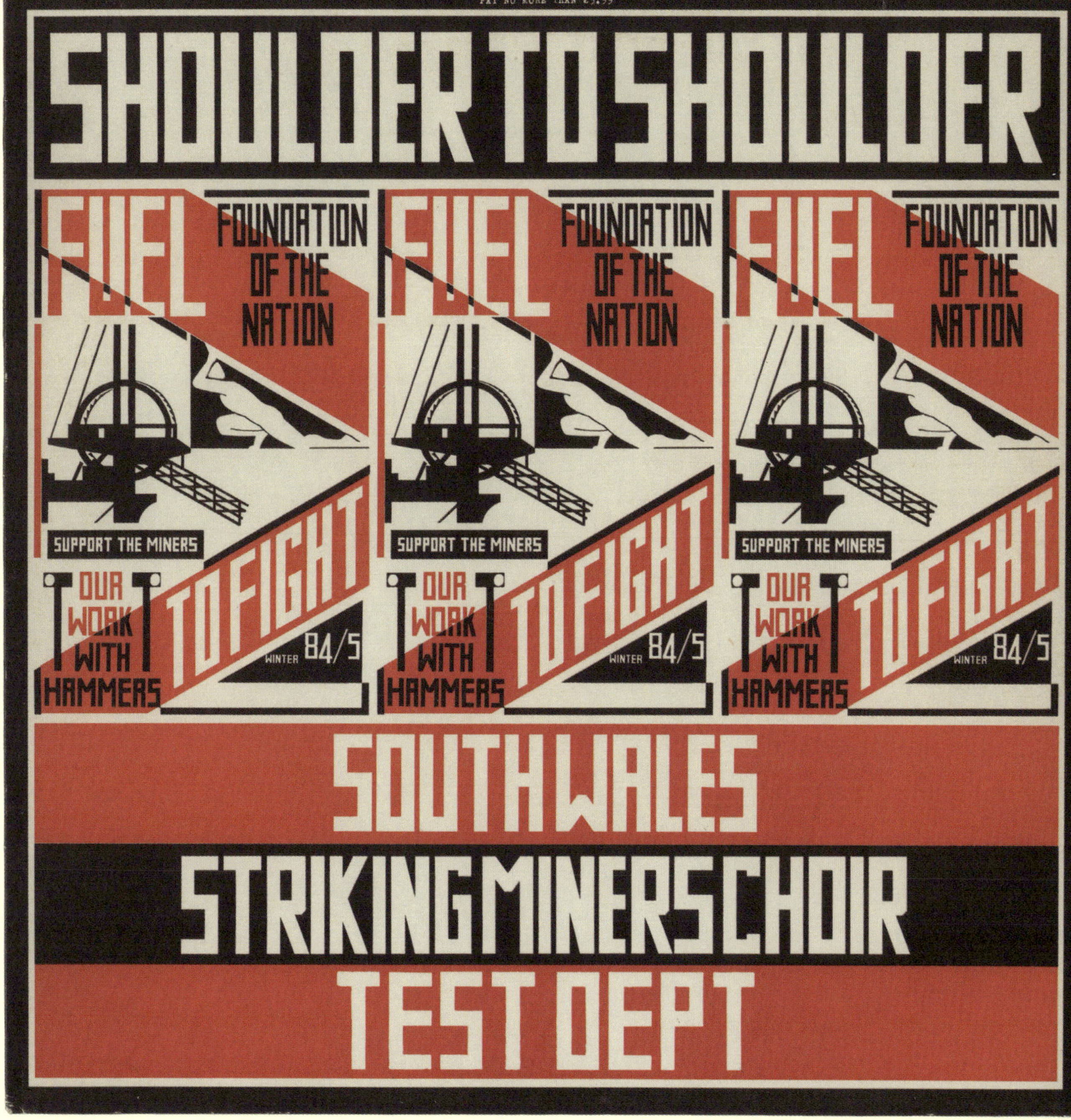
PAY NO MORE THAN £3.99
SHOULDER TO SHOULDER
FUEL
FOUNDATION OF THE NATION
SUPPORT THE MINERS
OUR WORK WITH HAMMERS
TO FIGHT
WINTER 84/5
SOUTH WALES
STRIKING MINERS CHOIR
TEST DEPT

E
P
BETWEEN THE WARS
BILLY BRAGG
Pay no more than One pound and twenty-five pence

Billy Bragg
Between the Wars
7" EP
Go Discs (AGOEP 1)
1985
Great Britain

Bragg has often said that it was his experience playing on the picket lines of the Miners' Strike that he learned how to write about people's complex lives and connect to working class audiences, not just pop fans. This record mixes two original tracks with two pointed covers: Florence Reece's classic miner and union song "Which Side Are You On" and Leon Rosselson's "World Turned Upside Down" telling the story of the Diggers during the English Revolution. The record is dedicated to "the work of the Miners' Wives Support Groups." Bragg's deep involvement in the miners' support movement is evident in his presence on two additional Miners' Strike records included in this book.

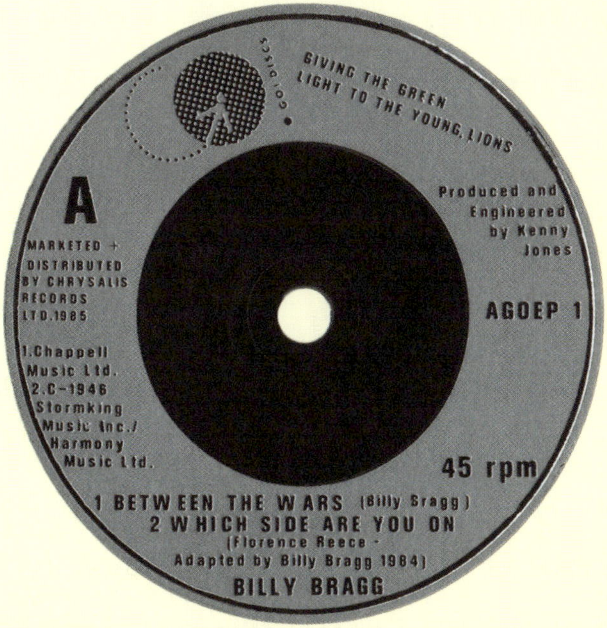

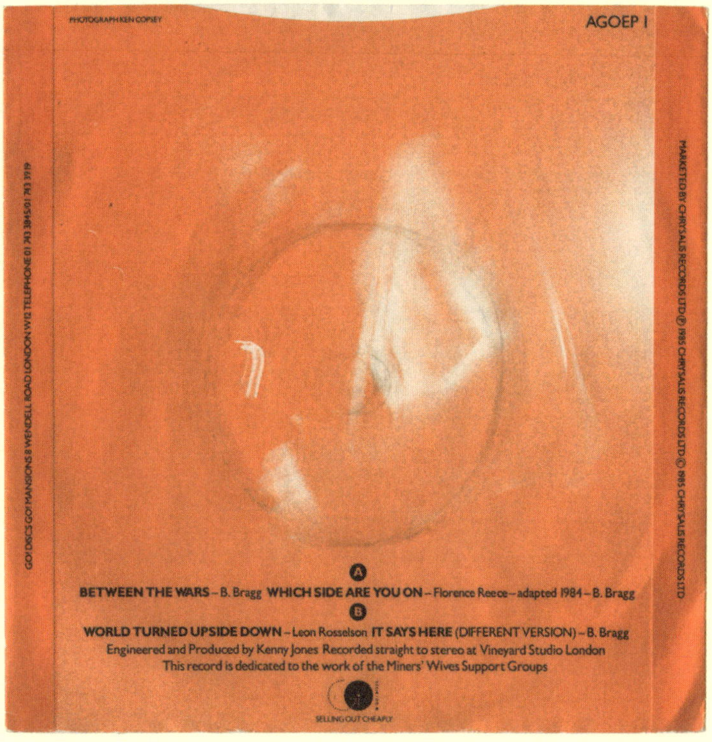

Easterhouse
Whistling in the Dark
12" single
Rough Trade (RTT 164)
1985
Great Britain

Easterhouse was a popular new wave/alternative rock act from Manchester. They swam in the same sea as New Order and The Smiths (guitarist Ivor Perry actually played with The Smiths on their final tour before breaking up), but never quite made it internationally. Singer and songwriter Andy Perry was a member of the Revolutionary Communist Party, and gave the band an ardent leftist bent. This record is evidence of that, with three songs dedicated to the miners that rebuke the Labour Party for abandoning them. In addition to the lyrics, the back cover also features a lengthy treatise on the state of the UK and need for the struggle against Thatcher to continue.

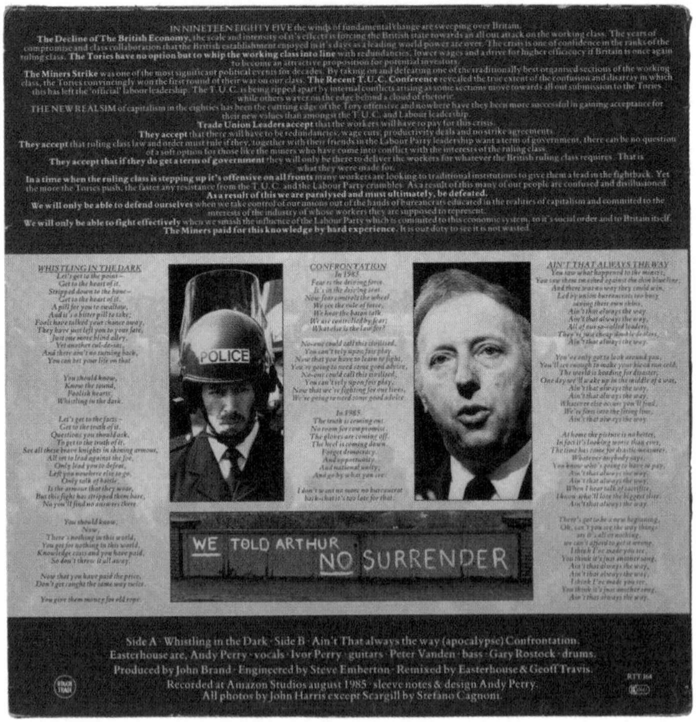

EASTERHOUSE
WHISTLING IN THE DARK

WHICH SIDE ARE YOU ON
MUSIC FOR THE MINERS, FROM THE NORTH EAST

Various artists

Which Side Are You On: Music for the Miners, from the North East

LP

Which Side Records (WSR 1)

1985

Great Britain

Rather than broadcast support, this record specifically focuses on the coal mining communities of Northumberland and Durham, and the musicians who supported them during the strike. Unlike the more pop-oriented records, most of the music here is solidly folk (written specifically about the local aspects of the strike) and working class standards (like "The Red Flag" and "The Internationale." With the record coming out after the end of the strike, there was more time to not only collect enough songs for a full length album, but also to pack the record with additional information, from an oversized foldout insert (which contextualizes the record within the strike, gives specific background to each song, and includes extensive information about the recipient of the funds the record raised: Women Against Pit Closures) to a giant wall poster featuring a photo of the Easington Miners Wives Support Group out on the picket. It also seems important to point out the lack of a question mark in the title, whether intentional or not. "Which side are you on" is not a question here, but a statement—class struggle was at the core of life in these communities, not something you opted in or out of.

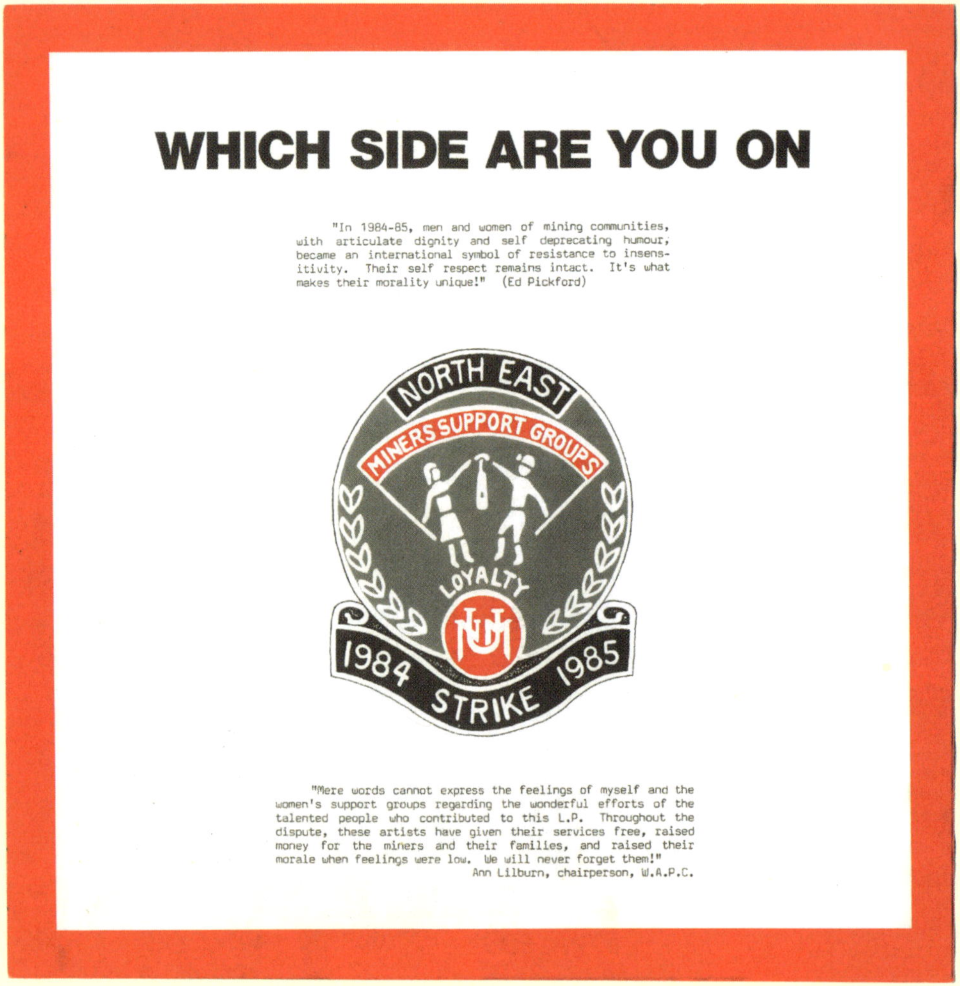
WHICH SIDE ARE YOU ON
"In 1984-85, men and women of mining communities, with articulate dignity and self deprecating humour, became an international symbol of resistance to insensitivity. Their self respect remains intact. It's what makes their morality unique!" (Ed Pickford)
NORTH EAST
MINERS SUPPORT GROUPS
LOYALTY
NUM
1984
STRIKE
1985
"Mere words cannot express the feelings of myself and the women's support groups regarding the wonderful efforts of the talented people who contributed to this L.P. Throughout the dispute, these artists have given their services free, raised money for the miners and their families, and raised their morale when feelings were low. We will never forget them!"
Ann Lilburn, chairperson, W.A.P.C.

EASINGTON MINERS WIVES SUPPORT GROUP by

cyk

H SIDE ARE YOU ON

R THE MINERS, FROM THE NORTH EAST

Various artists
<u>Dig This (A Tribute to the Great Strike)</u>
LP
Forward Sounds International (Forward 002)
1985
Great Britain

Another compilation album, this one from a more anarcho-punk slant with tracks from Chumbawamba, Poison Girls, Omega Tribe, and the Ex (as well as a cover illustration by the paradigmatic anarchist artist Clifford Harper). Released after the strike was crushed, note the subtitle: a tribute. This record is a negotiation between, on the one hand, the immense outpouring of political, economic, and cultural support for the miners, and on the other, acknowledging the failure of the strike and the real continued needs of sacked miners. As stated on the back:

Benefits, meetings, songs, poems, collections, arguments. The miners strike inspired a great wave of cultural solidarity! The media orgy is over. The miners have returned to work to be met with an extremely vindictive management. <u>640 miners have been victimised</u>. . . . All the money raised by this album will go to the Miners Solidarity fund. . . . WE URGE YOU TO REMEMBER AND SUPPORT THE VICTIMISED MINERS.

The need to recognize the sense of empowerment that the strike engendered—including, and maybe especially, in non-miners—is palpable on the record, with its cover featuring three singular protagonists that look more punk than worker standing off on an empty street against a long line of riot cops. It's a powerful image because of its romanticism, yet strange because of its evocation of an old Western duel.

DIG THIS
A TRIBUTE TO THE GREAT STRIKE
POISON GIRLS · MEKONS · MEN THEY COULDN'T HANG
AKIMBO · STEVE LAKE · LENINGRAD SANDWICH
· THE EX · OMEGA TRIBE · CHUMBAWAMBA ·
C·H

side a.
'amnesty'
banner theatre
side b.
'picket line parodies'
keresley pit women
'holloway song'
mal finch
AMNESTY
REINSTATE
AND
SET THEM FREE
ALL PROFITS TO JAILED + SACKED MINER'S FUNDS.

Banner Theatre Song Group with Keresley Pit miners, Keresley Pit Women's Support Group, and Mal Finch
<u>Amnesty: Reinstate and Set Them Free</u>
7" single
T.U.R.C. (TURC 002)
1985
Great Britain

Released in the wake of the Miners' Strike, this record is squarely aimed at supporting the miners that had been fired and jailed for their participation in the strike. The A-side, "Amnesty," is a didactic track using song to explain how strike organizers were framed for attacking scab workers, this being a popular way to punish the organizers and remove them from the struggle. The song is interspersed with recordings of the miners themselves, discussing being abducted from their homes and sent to prison on false charges, in the face of overwhelming evidence in their favor. The B-side consists of a collection of picket line ditties penned and sung by the Keresley Pit Women's Support Group, as well as Mal Finch's "Holloway Song," which describes conditions at the Holloway women's prison. It is a great intersectional track about both the women imprisoned for their ongoing antinuclear protest at Greenham Common as well as those sent to jail for their support of the Miners' Strike. The entire record is produced by the Banner Theatre, a community theater project based in Birmingham with a strong working class character (similar to the 7:84 Theatre featured on a record above). It still exists, and continues to produce plays with the community around contemporary struggles.

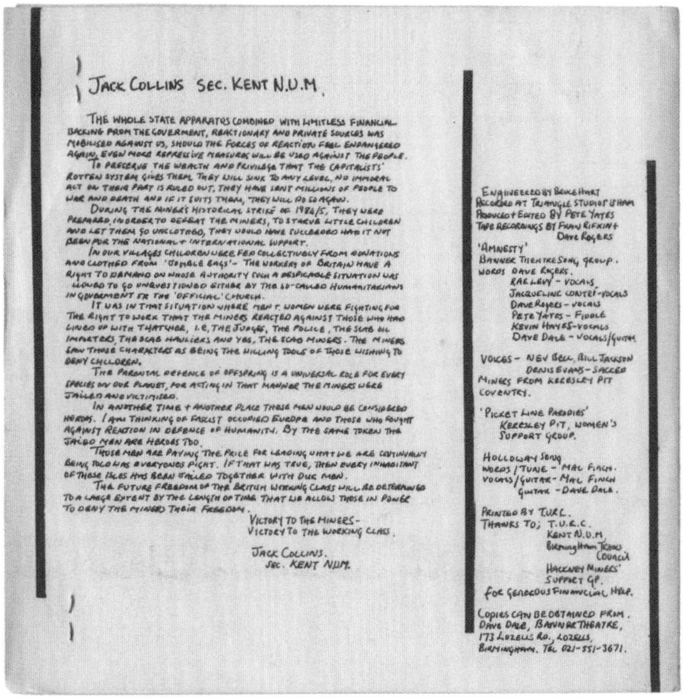

JACK COLLINS SEC. KENT N.U.M.

THE WHOLE STATE APPARATUS COMBINED WITH LIMITLESS FINANCIAL BACKING FROM THE GOVERNMENT, REACTIONARY AND PRIVATE SOURCES WAS MOBILISED AGAINST US, SHOULD THE FORCES OF REACTION FEEL ENDANGERED AGAIN, EVEN MORE REPRESSIVE MEASURES WILL BE USED AGAINST THE PEOPLE.

TO PRESERVE THE WEALTH AND PRIVILEGE THAT THE CAPITALISTS' ROTTEN SYSTEM GIVES THEM, THEY WILL SINK TO ANY LEVEL, NO IMMORAL ACT ON THEIR PART IS RULED OUT, THEY HAVE SENT MILLIONS OF PEOPLE TO WAR AND DEATH AND IF IT SUITS THEM, THEY WILL DO SO AGAIN.

DURING THE MINERS' HISTORICAL STRIKE OF 1984/5, THEY WERE PREPARED, IN ORDER TO DEFEAT THE MINERS, TO STARVE LITTLE CHILDREN AND LET THEM GO UNCLOTHED, THEY WOULD HAVE SUCCEEDED HAD IT NOT BEEN FOR THE NATIONAL + INTERNATIONAL SUPPORT.

IN OUR VILLAGES CHILDREN WERE FED COLLECTIVELY FROM DONATIONS AND CLOTHED FROM 'JUMBLE BAGS' – THE WORKERS OF BRITAIN HAVE A RIGHT TO DEMAND ON WHOSE AUTHORITY SUCH A DESPICABLE SITUATION WAS ALLOWED TO GO UNQUESTIONED EITHER BY THE SO-CALLED HUMANITARIANS IN GOVERNMENT OR THE 'OFFICIAL' CHURCH.

IT WAS IN THAT SITUATION WHERE MEN + WOMEN WERE FIGHTING FOR THE RIGHT TO WORK THAT THE MINERS REACTED AGAINST THOSE WHO HAD LINED UP WITH THATCHER, I.E. THE JUDGES, THE POLICE, THE SCAB OIL IMPORTERS, THE SCAB HAULIERS AND YES, THE SCAB MINERS. THE MINERS SAW THOSE CHARACTERS AS BEING THE WILLING TOOLS OF THOSE WISHING TO DENY CHILDREN.

THE PARENTAL DEFENCE OF OFFSPRING IS A UNIVERSAL ROLE FOR EVERY SPECIES ON OUR PLANET, FOR ACTING IN THAT MANNER THE MINERS WERE JAILED AND VICTIMISED.

IN ANOTHER TIME + ANOTHER PLACE THOSE MEN WOULD BE CONSIDERED HEROES. I AM THINKING OF FASCIST OCCUPIED EUROPE AND THOSE WHO FOUGHT AGAINST REACTION IN DEFENCE OF HUMANITY. BY THE SAME TOKEN THE JAILED MEN ARE HEROES TOO.

THOSE MEN ARE PAYING THE PRICE FOR LEADING WHAT WE ARE CONTINUALLY BEING TOLD WAS EVERYONE'S FIGHT. IF THAT WAS TRUE, THEN EVERY INHABITANT OF THESE ISLES HAS BEEN JAILED TOGETHER WITH OUR MEN.

THE FUTURE FREEDOM OF THE BRITISH WORKING CLASS WILL BE DETERMINED TO A LARGE EXTENT BY THE LENGTH OF TIME THAT WE ALLOW THOSE IN POWER TO DENY THE MINERS THEIR FREEDOM.

VICTORY TO THE MINERS –
VICTORY TO THE WORKING CLASS.

JACK COLLINS.
SEC. KENT NUM.

ENGINEERED BY BRUCE HART
RECORDED AT TRIANGLE STUDIOS B'HAM
PRODUCED + EDITED BY PETE YATES
TAPE RECORDINGS BY FRAN RIFKIN + DAVE ROGERS

'AMNESTY'
BANNER THEATRE SONG GROUP.
WORDS DAVE ROGERS.
RAE LEVY – VOCALS
JACQUELINE CONTRÉ – VOCALS
DAVE ROGERS – VOCALS
PETE YATES – FIDDLE
KEVIN HAYES – VOCALS
DAVE DALE – VOCALS/GUITAR

VOICES – NEV BELL, BILL JACKSON, DENIS EVANS – SACKED MINERS FROM KERESLEY PIT COVENTRY.

'PICKET LINE PARODIES'
KERESLEY PIT, WOMEN'S SUPPORT GROUP.

HOLLOWAY SONG
WORDS/TUNE – MAL FINCH.
VOCALS/GUITAR – MAL FINCH
GUITAR – DAVE DALE.

PRINTED BY TURC.
THANKS TO; T.U.R.C.
KENT N.U.M.
BIRMINGHAM TRADES COUNCIL
HACKNEY MINERS' SUPPORT GP.
FOR GENEROUS FINANCIAL HELP.

COPIES CAN BE OBTAINED FROM. DAVE DALE, BANNER THEATRE, 173 LOZELLS RD., LOZELLS, BIRMINGHAM. TEL 021-551-3671.

AMNESTY! — BANNER THEATRE

JOHN HANSON ON THE PICKET STOOD,
THEY LIFTED HIM AT CORTONWOOD,
JOHN WAS A MAN THEY MEANT TO NAIL
NOW HE'S LOCKED IN ARMLEY JAIL.
(CHORUS.).
AMNESTY AMNESTY
THEY FOUGHT FOR YOU,
THEY FOUGHT FOR ME,
AMNESTY AMNESTY,
REINSTATE AND SET THEM FREE.

PETER MEYER OF LEA HALL MINE,
GAVE THOSE SCABS A REAL HARD TIME,
HE SAID TO PICKET IS NO SIN,
AND HE STUCK IT OUT THROUGH THICK + THIN.

COLIN WHITTLE OF ROSSINGTON,
THEY SAY HIS DIGGING DAYS ARE DONE,
THE BOSS WONT LET HIM DOWN THAT HOLE,
HE PAID THE PRICE FOR PICKING COAL.

I KNEW A LAD FROM BILSTON GLEN,
STOOD FIRM BEHIND THE N.U.M.,
SET FOOT ON COALBOARD PROPERTY,
NOW HE FIGHTS FOR AMNESTY.

JOHNNY LOWE OF GOLDTHORPE MINE,
ELEVEN LONG MONTHS ON THE PICKET LINE,
FOUGHT FOR THE RIGHT TO DIG THE COAL,
NOT A LIFETIME SIGNING ON THE DOLE.

CLIVE HAM DOWN AT KERESLEY PIT,
SACKED FOR A SCAB HE DIDN'T HIT.
THE JUDGE HE FOUND HIM NOT TO BLAME.
THE COALBOARD SACKED HIM JUST
THE SAME.

CHRIS TAZEY FROM THE KENT COALFIELD,
HE SAID "STAND FIRM WE MUST NOT YIELD"
HE SAW THE HUNGER PAIN + TEARS,
AND PRISON BARS FOR 3 LONG YEARS.

MICHAEL BOYLE OF SILVERWOOD,
GAVE THE UNION ALL HE COULD,
SOLD EVERYTHING HE HAD TO SELL,
DIDN'T LET THEM TAKE HIS JOB AS
WELL.

FROM SNOWDOWN UP TO BILSTON GLEN,
IT'S TIME TO ORGANISE AGAIN,
WHEN WE'RE UNITED WE ARE STRONG,
LET 'EM KNOW THAT THE FIGHT
GOES ON!

HOLLOWAY SONG

THE WALLS YOU PUT AROUND ME
DISSOLVE + FADE AWAY
THEY'RE ONLY STONE + METAL
+ THEY'RE ALL YOU HAVE.
I AM NOT ALONE HERE
THERE'S MANY YOU CAN'T SEE
THERE'S MANY GONE BEFORE ME
+ MANY MORE TO FOLLOW ME.
+ WHEN YOU LOCK THE DOOR BEHIND US
YOU ONLY FAN THE FLAMES
BY GIVING US A NUMBER,
YOU DON'T ROB US OF OUR NAMES.
(CHORUS)
NO THERE ARE NO WALLS TO HOLD US
NO LAWS TO KILL THE SPIRIT
AND YOU CAN'T TAKE AWAY,
NO YOU CAN'T TAKE AWAY,
YOU WILL NEVER TAKE AWAY,
OUR FREEDOM.

THERE'S NOTHING YOU CAN USE NOW
TO THREATEN OR CONTROL,
AUTHORITY IS HOLLOW,
WHEN IT'S ALL YOU HAVE.
OUR VOICES WONT BE SILENCED,
BY HIDING US AWAY,
IT'S YOU WHO ARE THE PRISONERS,
THOUGH YOU TELL YOURSELVES
YOU'RE FREE.
AND WHILE YOU NOURISH FEAR +
DESPAIR, WHILE YOU ARM FOR
NUCLEAR WAR,
WHILE YOU TAKE AWAY OUR RIGHTS,
YOU DARE TO PREACH TO US OF LAWS.
(CHORUS)

VOICES — NEV BELL, BILL JACKSON + DENIS EVANS —

SACKED MINER'S FROM KERESLEY PIT COVENTRY.

'PICKET LINE PARODIES'. — KERESLEY PIT WOMEN

YOU WON'T FIND US AT THE KITCHEN SINK
YOU WON'T FIND US AT ALL
COME ON OVER TO THE PICKET LINE
COS WE'LL BE PICKETING THERE.
COME ON OVER TO THE PICKET LINE
WE'LL BE PICKETING THERE.
. . .

WE WANT NO PIT CLOSURES,
WE SHALL NOT BE MOVED X2
JUST LIKE A PICKET STANDING
ON A PICKET LINE,
WE SHALL NOT BE MOVED.

REINSTATE OUR MINERS
WE SHALL NOT BE MOVED x2
JUST LIKE A PICKET STANDING ON
A PICKET LINE,
WE SHALL NOT BE MOVED.
. . .

THESE SONGS ARE AN EXCERPT
FROM A 'CABERET' ACT, ON THE
MINER'S STRIKE, WHICH THE
WOMEN TOURED + PERFORMED
DURING THE DISPUTE. FOR
FURTHER INFORMATION CONTACT;
LIZ SUGRUE, 79 BENNETTS RD.,
KERESLEY END.
TEL: KERESLEY 4439.

BLESS OUR LADS, BLESS OUR LADS
'COS OUR LADS NEVER SCABBED,
BLESS ALL THE PICKETS + THE N.U.M.
BLESS ALL OUR HUSBANDS, 'COS WE'RE
PROUD OF THEM.
AND WE'RE SAYING GOODBYE TO THE SCA[BS]
FOR THEY'RE NOT BRAVE LIKE OUR LADS
THE WIVES NOW SAY THANK YOU.
THEY'RE PROUD OF THE PICKETS,
WHO FOUGHT FOR THEIR JOBS ONE + AL[L]
BLESS YOU ALL, BLESS YOU ALL
YOU PICKETS WILL NEVER FALL,
YOU FOUGHT NOW WITH PRIDE
NOW SHOW ALL THE SCABS.
NOW GO BACK TO WORK + WALK TALL
. . .

WE ARE NOT AFRAID X3
TODAY
OH DEEP IN OUR HEARTS,
WE DO BELIEVE,
THAT WE SHALL OVERCOME.
SOME DAY.
WE SHALL OVERCOME X 3 RPT.

HOLLOWAY SONG.

. . . FOR THE WOMEN AT GREENHAM COMM[ON] WHO, DESPITE THE FACT THAT MANY HAVE GONE TO PRISON SEVERAL TIMES, REFUSE TO GIVE UP THEIR PROTEST. . . . FOR A[LL] WOMEN PRISONERS IN HOLLOWAY PRISON . . . FOR 'GREENHAM WOMEN EVERYWHERE' . . . FOR ALL THOSE JAILED FOR THEIR ATTEMPTS TO ENSURE THE SURVIVAL OF THEIR JOBS + COMMUNIT[IES] IN THE MINERS' STRIKE '84/'85.

THE SINGER, MAL FINCH, WROTE THIS SONG WHILE IN HOLLOWAY PRISON FOR NON-PAYMENT OF A FINE, HAVING BEEN FOUND GUILTY OF CRIMINAL DAMAGE AT USAF GREENHAM COMMON. SHE IS A MEMBER OF THE DERBYSHIRE BAND 'FLAMIN' NERVE' WHO, THANKS TO THE FINANCIAL SUPPORT OF 'WOMEN AGAINST PIT CLOSURES', ARE SOON TO RELEASE A TAPE FEATURIN[G] AMONGST OTHER ORIGINAL MATERIAL, THE SONG "HERE WE GO (THE WOMEN OF THE WORKING CLASS)" WHICH MAL FINCH WROTE A[S] A TRIBUTE TO WOMEN IN THE MINING COMMUNITIES.

THE TAPE CAN BE ORDERED DIRECT FROM:— W.A.P.C. C/O N.U.M. (WOMEN'S SECTION), ST. JAMES HOUSE, VICA[R] LANE, SHEFFIELD. OR FROM:— 'FLAMIN' NERVE' C/O 4, MA[...] RD., DARLEY BRIDGE, NR. MATLOCK, DERBYSHIRE. SEND £4.00 (£3.00 SPECIAL RATE FOR MINER'S FAMILIES) + 30p p+p. ALL CHEQUES + POSTAL ORDERS TO BE MADE PAYABLE TO 'WOMEN AGAIN[ST] PIT CLOSURES'.

side B
PICKET LINE PARODIES
keresley pit women
HOLLOWAY SONG
lyrics, music, mal finch
c all rights reserved

Bertus en de Posters
"Miner" b/w "He! Maggie Snatcher"
7" single
Red Air Productions (TBA 4408)
1985
Netherlands

This is the second Bertus record here, this one in solidarity with British miners. It's quite a strange disc, two very didactic country-folk tunes sung in English with a Dutch lilt. Although produced in the Netherlands, the audience the songs are written to appears to be the striking miners, with the original intent to distribute this in the UK. Yet it seems likely that the strike ended before the record could be produced and a Dutch translation sheet is included which has details about the repression and fallout against the most militant miners, and a statement that the record will raise funds for them. It's actually unclear if many copies ever actually made it over to the UK, as the only copies ever for sale on Discogs or eBay are always from Dutch sellers.

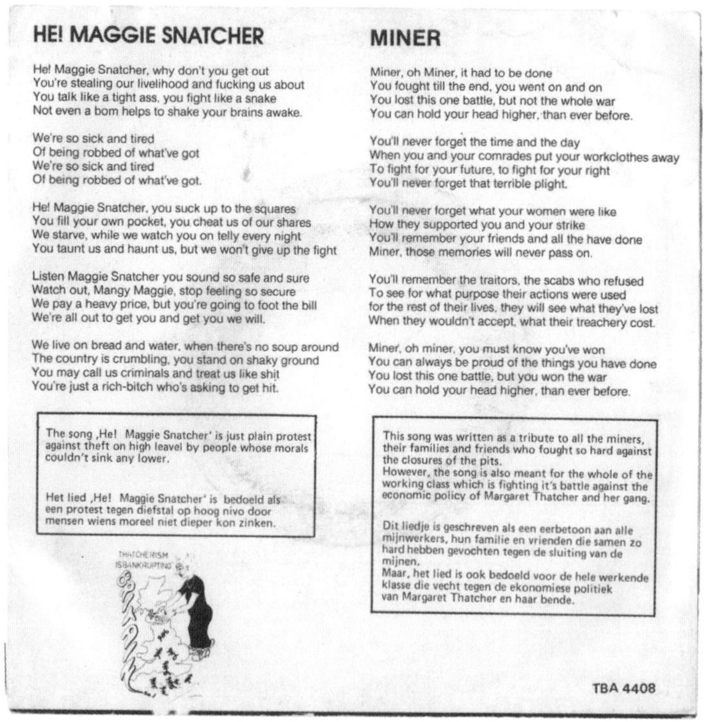

HE! MAGGIE SNATCHER

He! Maggie Snatcher, why don't you get out
You're stealing our livelihood and fucking us about
You talk like a tight ass, you fight like a snake
Not even a bom helps to shake your brains awake.

We're so sick and tired
Of being robbed of what've got
We're so sick and tired
Of being robbed of what've got.

He! Maggie Snatcher, you suck up to the squares
You fill your own pocket, you cheat us of our shares
We starve, while we watch you on telly every night
You taunt us and haunt us, but we won't give up the fight

Listen Maggie Snatcher you sound so safe and sure
Watch out, Mangy Maggie, stop feeling so secure
We pay a heavy price, but you're going to foot the bill
We're all out to get you and get you we will.

We live on bread and water, when there's no soup around
The country is crumbling, you stand on shaky ground
You may call us criminals and treat us like shit
You're just a rich-bitch who's asking to get hit.

The song ,He! Maggie Snatcher' is just plain protest against theft on high leavel by people whose morals couldn't sink any lower.

Het lied ,He! Maggie Snatcher' is bedoeld als een protest tegen diefstal op hoog nivo door mensen wiens moreel niet dieper kon zinken.

THATCHERISM IS BANKRUPTING BRITAIN

MINER

Miner, oh Miner, it had to be done
You fought till the end, you went on and on
You lost this one battle, but not the whole war
You can hold your head higher, than ever before.

You'll never forget the time and the day
When you and your comrades put your workclothes away
To fight for your future, to fight for your right
You'll never forget that terrible plight.

You'll never forget what your women were like
How they supported you and your strike
You'll remember your friends and all the have done
Miner, those memories will never pass on.

You'll remember the traitors, the scabs who refused
To see for what purpose their actions were used
for the rest of their lives, they will see what they've lost
When they wouldn't accept, what their treachery cost.

Miner, oh miner, you must know you've won
You can always be proud of the things you have done
You lost this one battle, but you won the war
You can hold your head higher, than ever before.

This song was written as a tribute to all the miners, their families and friends who fought so hard against the closures of the pits.
However, the song is also meant for the whole of the working class which is fighting it's battle against the economic policy of Margaret Thatcher and her gang.

Dit liedje is geschreven als een eerbetoon aan alle mijnwerkers, hun familie en vrienden die samen zo hard hebben gevochten tegen de sluiting van de mijnen.
Maar, het lied is ook bedoeld voor de hele werkende klasse die vecht tegen de ekonomiese politiek van Margaret Thatcher en haar bende.

TBA 4408

BERTUS EN DE POSTERS
Miner
(You can hold your head higher, than ever before)
He! Maggie Snatcher

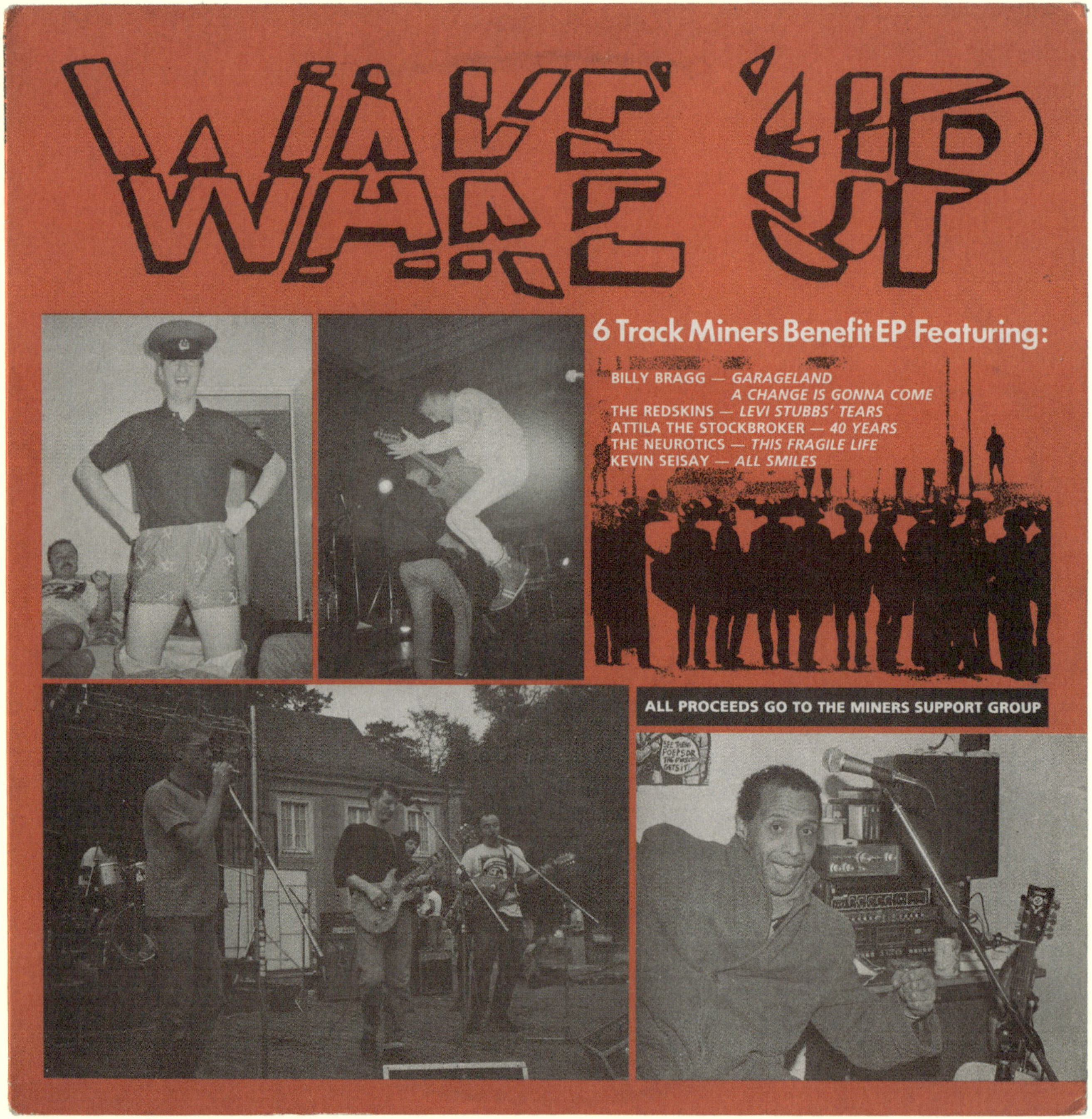
WAKE UP
6 Track Miners Benefit EP Featuring:
BILLY BRAGG — GARAGELAND
A CHANGE IS GONNA COME
THE REDSKINS — LEVI STUBBS' TEARS
ATTILA THE STOCKBROKER — 40 YEARS
THE NEUROTICS — THIS FRAGILE LIFE
KEVIN SEISAY — ALL SMILES
ALL PROCEEDS GO TO THE MINERS SUPPORT GROUP

Various artists
<u>Wake Up</u>
12" EP
Wake Up Records
1987
Great Britain

Another fundraising record, this one from the DIY punk scene, put out a full two years after the crushing of the Miners' Strike and in the name of those still jailed or not reinstated with all profits to the Miners Support Group. "The support of all socialists to repay [the miners'] sacrifices must never cease. The leadership of the Labour Party and the TUC have turned their backs. The lesson is plain—don't trust them. They've chosen their side—choose yours; WAKE UP and join the fightback." It collects live recordings from big name acts like Billy Bragg and Redskins during recent tours, with much of the in-between song banter addressing the Miners' Strike. The record does an unintentionally good job of capturing some of the tensions in the music scene's support of the strike—while some musicians supported the union structure and the backing of the Labour Party (Bragg), others were militant critics of both the NUM and Labour, and instead supported independent worker action (Redskins). This is captured in Redskins' lead singer Chris Dean calling Bragg "Neil Kinnock's publicity officer." Kinnock was then head of the Labour Party, and accused by many on the left of abandoning the miners (as well as kicking out the far left of the party).

The Fuse
Seattle 1919
2xLP
FUSE Music (SIS 003)
1985
USA

A power-pop double LP dedicated to the 1919 General Strike in Seattle? Absolutely. Imagine what Loverboy might have come up with if they were reading Marx on that weekend they were working for and you get the idea here. And that's actually not too far off. The ring leader of The Fuse was musician and then PhD candidate at the University of California Santa Barbara, Rob Rosenthal, who decided to pull together this group to turn his doctoral thesis on the 1919 strike into a rock opera. Most of the other players were local musicians without much recording experience, although a couple of them played drums and bass in the new wave act Major-Domo.

The 21 songs on the album trace the story of fictional character Peter Rinearson leaves his farm to ride the rails, landing in Seattle, securing a room on Skid Row, and stumbling onto the Industrial Workers of the World union hall. After joining the Wobblies, the songs trace his life working in the shipyards at a time of both increased exploitation and growing worker militancy. Peter then comes upon the offices of the *Union Record*, the first labor-owned newspaper in the US, and befriends real-life writer and organizer Anna Louise Strong. The backdrop of World War I both generates much work in the shipyards but also a utopian impulse in the international working class, leading to revolutionary movements in Russia, Germany, Chile, and beyond. The songs narrate Strong's reportage and promotion of these revolts, and her fiery speeches calling on Seattle's workers to follow suit. After shipyard workers are locked out, 65,000 of the city's workers going out on strike in solidarity

Seattle 1919
THE FUSE

The Story

Scene from a soup kitchen run by striking workers. *Photo courtesy of Museum of History and Industry, Seattle, Washington.*

"Peter Rinearson" is a fictional character, based on several real people. As for all the rest, THIS STORY IS TRUE.

On a cold fall morning in September, 1917, Peter Rinearson slips away from his family's farm, part of the great migration to the cities that swept the United States around the time of the first World War. Reaching Chicago, he quickly loses the little money he has to street hustlers, and so joins the thousands of footloose men riding the rails and looking for work. Life on the road, he writes home to his sister Katy, "can run a man pretty hard." ("Running Down the Road")

Arriving in Seattle in early 1918, Peter finds a city bursting at the seams. Workers stream into town to work in the booming shipyards, now turning out one of every four ships needed for the war effort. Jobs are easy to find and the pay is good, but the costs of food and shelter eat it all up, and city life seems strange to a farm boy on his own for the first time. He gets a room on Skid Row and, looking out, sees a carnival on the streets: shipyard workers, Alaskan miners, prostitutes, gamblers, sailors, Salvation Army bands. And always and everywhere, there are the soapboxers: labor activists speaking on streetcorners, spreading their visions of a new world to come. ("Winter in Seattle") Looking for companionship, Peter ducks into the local "Wobbly hall," headquarters of the radical Industrial Workers of the World. Here, for the first time, Peter hears the stories of men and women actively trying to bring about that new world. ("Roll in With the Union")

Work fills Peter's days. The shipyard owners, inspired more by the chances to make windfall profits than by their declared love of country, run their yards at terrific speeds. The workers, in turn, respond by meeting the schedule "for the sake of the boys Over There," but hold no illusions about their bosses' motives. ("Push")

But life isn't only work. After putting in five and a half days of labor each week, people head down to a large converted barn on Yesler Way. Peter joins them, to look for a face, share a drink with new friends, and dance to the band. Sweet, sweet Saturday night! ("Now the Other Way Turn")

One evening, walking by the Union Record, the country's first Labor-owned daily newspaper, Peter hears Anna Louise Strong, the paper's best-known writer, speaking to a crowd ("Street Speech"), and he's captivated by Anna and her words. At work, they ring in his ears, and resonate with the words of those around him in the shipyards. ("Anna Louise")

As the war finally ends in November of 1918, the shipyard workers learn they have been double-crossed by Charles Piez, the head of the government's Emergency Fleet Corporation, in league with the shipyard owners. Although Piez had promised them that the E.F.C. would grant a pay raise as soon as the war ended, he now

(continued on page 2)

in February 1919. The mainstream unions, afraid of anticommunist backlash—and actual rank-and-file workers' power—do everything to scuttle the strike, bringing it to an end after five days. The album's lyrics (all of which are included in an 8-page booklet) not only tell this story, but just as interestingly the story of the General Strike Committee, which reorganized life that week for workers and their families, functionally becoming a counter-power to the city government.

Although not a direct product of a strike, we've included this record because it is such a comprehensive and fascinating attempt to tell the story of one of the most militant moments in US labor history. Rosenthal was also clearly connected to social and labor movements, he helped assemble and produce a Folkways LP dedicated to the songs of the tenant rights movement and released another LP on his own label (FUSE Music) of songs against Ronald Reagan. In addition, he would eventually publish (in 2012, with co-author Richard Flacks) *Playing for Change: Music and Musicians in the Service of Social Movements*, one of the most comprehensive academic studies of the role of music in people's struggles.

18. **ON THE LINE**

Pass that jug!
I got to light me a fire inside
17 on the docks, oo-ee it's colder
than a polar bear's ass on the line tonight
But nothing's going in, nothing's coming out
Nothing's moving that ain't allowed
I'd rather be in bed
hugging that sweet love of mine
But there comes a time
when you gotta be walking the line

Back in Boston, out in Houston
down in New Orleans
Don't you be fools
don't you be tools
Remington Rifles don't make sewing machines
No, they're sowing terror and they're spitting fire
and the man who tells you different's just
a goddamn liar
Brothers, sisters,
You know we've reached that time
Off your seat, on your feet
It's time for walking the line

Do you remember, back in November
We asked for help from you?
Since that time we've lived a mighty big lesson
and now our days of waiting are through
We ain't loading no weapons bound for Russian land
We ain't putting no weapons into Kolchak's hands
There's a time for talking
Lord, we're past that time
It's time for walking, walking, walking
walking the line.

© Rob Rosenthal 1985

19. **CAUGHT IN THE MIDDLE**

I joined the IWW for a principle
and the AF of L for a job
Now I'm caught in the middle
Don't know which way to go
The lakes are half frozen
The shipyards are closing
The whole town's locking up tight
And those that fight
Gonna feel the cold

Carrying the world—it's a mighty big load
Blazing the future—it's a mighty dark road
You get tired when the wind in your sail
starts to die
Back home I've got a family
I can't clothe them in truth
or feed them dignity
By night I'll teach them the dreams I see
But by day I'll keep my peace

Live for tomorrow or live for today
Now what's it gonna be?
I'm caught in the middle
Don't know which way to go
Fight for it all
or live off the crumbs
And what if the future
don't never come?
Got to make it through today
to see tomorrow

© Rob Rosenthal 1985

Strike scene at the intersection of Seventh and Unic

20. **THE PROMISED LAND**

Peter get moving, grab your coat and hat
Going down to the harbor to the ticket shack
I'm going, going, going, fast as I can
Gonna book me a passage on an ocean queen
There's a new world coming that I've never seen
I'm going, going, going to the Promised Land

"The future works," that's what I've been told
Gotta see for myself what the future holds
I'm going, going, going, fast as I can
I've had enough of the Red Scare news
I've had enough of the back-biting blues
I'm going, going, going to the Promised Land

The people here are weary now
They've fought so well so long
They need some time to rest before
they're ready to move on
But I can't wait, my soul still burns
while there's so much to be done
I wish them luck as I change worlds
and join what's just begun

Some hear the calling of a Chosen Hand
I hear the calling of a Promised Land
I'm going, going, going, fast as I can
I want it here and now, not no pie-in-the-sky
I haven't got the patience to wait 'til I die
I'm going, going, going to the Promised Land

The chains of the past lie heavy
on this Promised Land
Orphan of the wartime
she may be too weak to stand
Wolves surround the new born child
and there's murder in their eyes
There's nowhere else I'd rather be
than fighting by her side

We've been up to the mountain and down to the sea
Seen the old world crumbling into history
Now I'm going, going, going, fast as I can
There's a home a-waiting on the other side
There's a comet blazing, gonna catch a ride
I'm going, going, going to the Promised Land

Weit droben im Land

Text und Musik: Bernd Köhler

Das Lied zum PROGAMMA-Streik

Bernd Köhler
<u>Weit droben im Land</u>
7" single
IG-Metall (JST-281)
1985
West Germany

The B-side of this single is a straight-to-tape, no frills overview of the strike—called "Der Streik bei Progamma" [The Strike at Progamma]—articulated by union rep Karl Maier. Spoken acapella until the very end, when a minor-key workers' chorus with guitar and accordion fades in as an outro; it's the same song which appears in full on the flip. Economical! The song has hints of tragedy, or maybe it's heroism—it conveys a difficult but just march ahead. Bernd Köhler, who both wrote the track and plays guitar on it, is a Mannheim-based folk rock singer-songwriter who became active in the labor movement through left-wing Christian circles and produced a number of other political records under the pseudonym Schlauch. The record feels quite "by-the-numbers," as if a very powerful union brought in a hired-gun to record a paradigamatic "strike song." It is effective, but doesn't carry the excitement of some of the more ad-hoc records included here.

The strike at Progamma was voted for by the workers of IG-Metall across multiple corporations in the auto industry. They sought a 35 hour work week, and the action was partially successful, with the 367,000 strikers eventually winning a 38.5 hour week and structured pay increases. They were joined by tens of thousands of workers in the Printing and Paper Union, again across the industry, and the Trade, Banking, and Insurance Union, as well as some Lufthansa workers, all also seeking reduction in hours without reduction in pay. The strike was an example of using cross-industry organizing to good effect.

Mijn-Alarm
<u>Mijn-Alarm</u>
7" single
Antler (Antler 044)
1986
Belgium

A pop supergroup, Mijn-Alarm (Mine-Alert, or My-Alert, there is a play on words here in Dutch) was a Belgian "We Are the World"-type project intended to raise funds and bring attention to coal miners who were on strike for 5 weeks in the Belgian province of Limburg. Formed just for this project, the band consisted of the bassist from metal band Killer, drummer from goth/industrial group Siglo XX, guitarist from new wave act TC Matic, and vocal turns from the singers of almost 20 groups. Intended to be "pop" music that would reach a mainstream audience, the record was quite popular in Belgium, being significantly less saccharine than many similar rock music benefit records produced at the time. It received significant local radio play and sales, raising money for the workers' support committee.

mijn-alarm
MINERS ON STRIKE
DE MIJNEN
AFBOUWEN
NOODLOTTIG
VOOR LIMBURG
TEN DIT NIET TOE
DE MIJNWERKERS
Solidariteits-single ten voordele van de «Mijnwerkers»

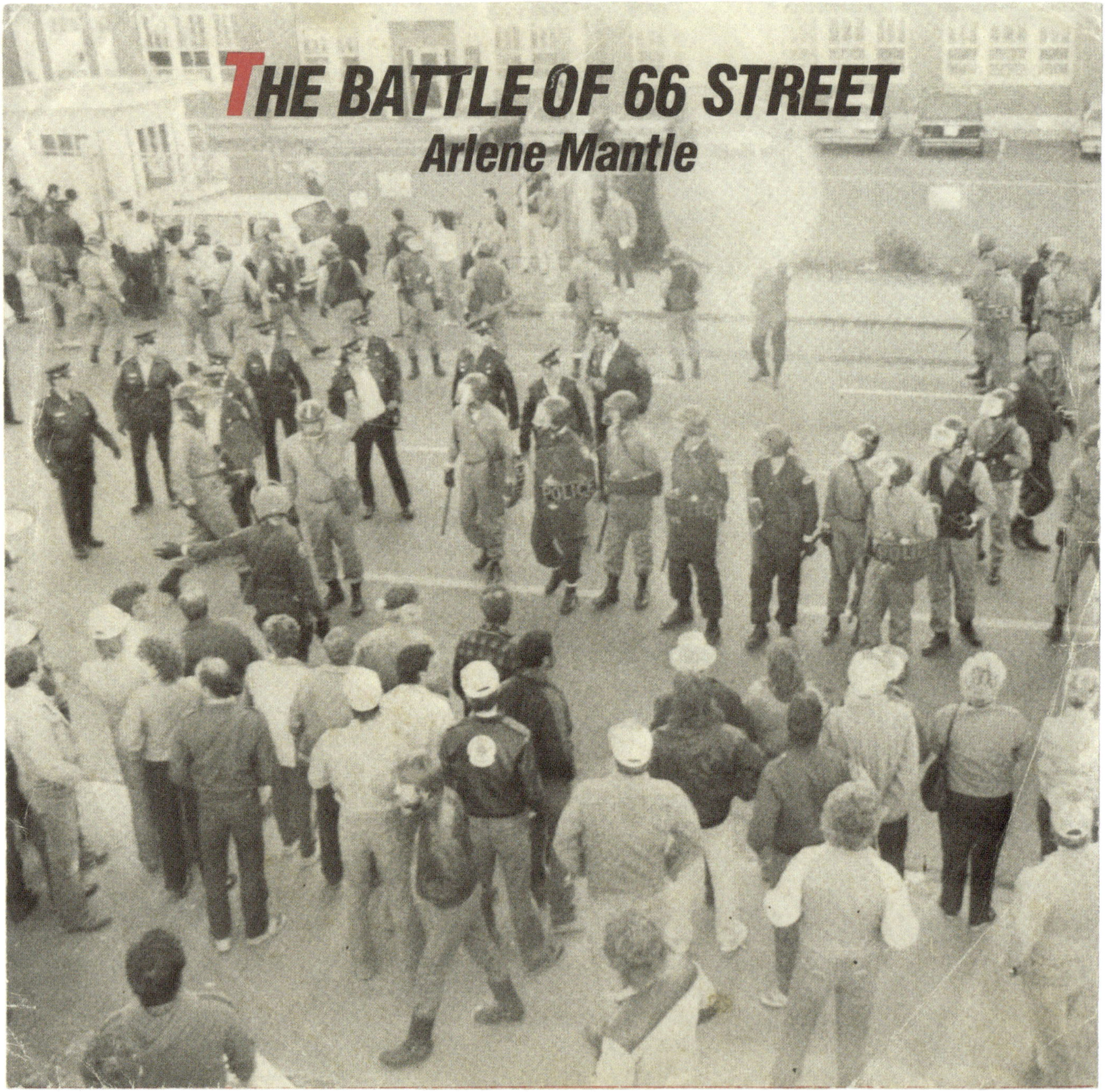
THE BATTLE OF 66 STREET
Arlene Mantle
POLICE

Arlene Mantle
The Battle of 66 Street
7" single
On The Line Music (WRC3-4775)
1986
Canada

The entrance to Gainers' meatpacking plant sat on 66 Street in Edmonton, the heart of Alberta's meatpacking industry. The battle referenced in the title, in the strike's spectacular first week in the summer of '86, was waged by over a thousand unionized United Food and Commercial Workers (UFCW) fighting—in the streets!—the scabs bussed in to be their replacements. Factory owner and hockey entrepreneur Peter Pocklington (who paid Wayne Gretzky, a single player on the Edmonton Oilers, the equivalent of $2 million US dollars/year) had ignored the successful contract fights at nearby factories and instead was demanding concessions at the bargaining table, nickel and diming the union for the second year in a row.

Over 5 minutes, the song builds up the image of Pocklington as their antagonist, recounting mistakes made by the union in the recent past as a product of his tricks, and goes on to describe some of the union's allies and tactics in broad strokes. The chorus of the song identifies the principal goal: "We'll be on this picket til the labour laws are changed." The record, written and recorded as a collaboration between Canadian folk-labor legend Arlene Mantle (think Pete Seeger of the North) and the strikers, contributed to general fundraising—presumably strike funds and legal funds. Mantle even pressed it herself, on her On The Line record label.

On the back of a successful nationwide boycott of Gainers, a settlement was reached just before Christmas 1986, six and a half months after those first street battles. The workers had won, but signed back on to lower than average wages in a town where social life and symbolic place had been rocked by several other packinghouse closures.

Janet Cook
Silentnight Strike EP
12" single
Cocomus Records & Tapes (CCM2)
1986
Great Britain

A brief three track record from Janet Cook, which appears to be her only release. The record supports a strike by workers with the Furniture, Timber and Allied Trades union in two factories of the Silentnight Mattress Co. At the time Silentnight was the largest mattress manufacturer in England, and its owner Tom Clarke—nicknamed "Mr. Wonderful" by his friend Margaret Thatcher—had reneged on a labor contract and sacked over 300 workers. The strike began just a few months after the defeat of the National Union of Mineworkers (see the section of records on this strike above) and lasted a staggering 18 months. Mattress strikers recall that post-defeat miners gave them great support, Labour MPs visited picket lines, and the local Labour Party in Barnoldswick provided office space after the union's previous office was firebombed.

The standout track, "Blue Monday (in a Northern Town)," is a trance/psych tune (reminiscent of the Velvet Underground) in which Janet presents detailed information about the strike and the company in the form of gossip—all in a pretty incredible working class Yorkshire accent. The listener gets drawn into an imagined conversation with the speaker:

And how long's it been going on for now? 17 months? What and he had 600,000 quid for his family that year? . . . Think about it! Some of them were working over 25 years. . . . There were! Eh, should be ashamed of himself. . . . What 2,000 shares? You're joking! Vested interest you say! Ha! He had more than his shirt on 'im and he took ours right off our backs! How long now? Over 17 months? It just makes me sick it does . . . just another Tory story I suppose. . .

The tone is high camp, and it's quite enjoyable. Although strange in form, the performance makes political stances in support of the strike appear as the common sense of an everyday working class person. The other main track is a zippy synth-rock number to the tune of "Silent Night," playing upon a British love for Christmas. It's quite easy to imagine this song being sung by carolers during the 1986 holiday season.

JANET COOK
HOW DO YOU SLEEP ?
THE WRITING'S ON THE WALL
NO MORE TORY STORIES
TIME'S UP T.C.!
SILENTNIGHT STRIKE
CLOSING DOWN
THE END IS NEAR
ONLY 7 DAYS TO GO
MASSIVE REDUCTIONS
½ PRICE DORMA LINEN
½ PRICE LIGHTING
½ PRICE CONTINENTAL QUILTS
BEDS ½ PRICE & LESS
PRINCIPLES
MAGGIE'S HERO SACKS HIS WORKERS
PLEASE DON'T BUY SILENTNIGHT BEDS MADE BY SCABS
Silentnight STRIKE e.p.

Kirk Thorne/Andy Clancy/Paul Elliott
<u>Songs from the NCU Strike</u>
7" EP
National Communications Union (NCUSTRIKE ONE)
1987
Great Britain

This record has no picture sleeve, but includes more info than usual on the label itself. It's "dedicated to all loyal NCU Members" in their strike against British Telecom. Or rather—on the heels of the breaking of the Great Miners' Strike—against Thatcher's privatization schemes. 110,000 British Telecom engineers walked out, starting the first indefinite national strike in the union's history. The music here is a fascinating melange of styles, all three tracks seemingly aimed at different sectors of the workers. First is a calypso track by Kirk Thorne that begins with the sound of a ringing phone from the telecom operator's point of view, and speaks from the perspective of the "we" of the workers. It chronicles the tactics used against the strike, connects it to other workers struggles, and an analysis of the industry—including concrete numbers on what the bosses are paid and how many people have been fired. If the A-side likely intends to appeal to Black workers, the flipside is decidedly more white, starting with a synth-pop ballad ("Victory Unite" by Andy Clancy) and then a classic labor folk tune ("The Ring Ring, Brr, Brr, Brr, Blues" by Paul Elliot, backed by a group of picketeers). The musical diversity is an interesting conceit, and a fairly unique one in terms of these strike records.

NATIONAL
COMMUNICATIONS
UNION
ncu
SONGS FROM
THE NCU STRIKE,
JAN - FEB 1987
Dedicated to all loyal
NCU members (E & C)
NCUSTRIKE ONE (A)
SIDE 1
℗ © 1987 The National
Communications Union
Pub. by
Nice Music
Prod. & Arr.
by Kirk Thorne
MORE PERCENT
(K.Thorne)
KIRK THORNE (Vocals / All Instruments)
(Backing Vocals by Alvin King)
ALL RIGHTS OF THE MANUFACTURER AND OF THE OWNER OF THE RECORDED WORK RESERVED UNAUTHORISED PUBLIC PERFORMANCE BROADCASTING AND COPYING OF THIS RECORD PROHIBITED

Lillian Allen • Aya • Pierre Fournier • Ginger Group • Clifton Joseph
Andrée Lemieux • Arlene Mantle • Eileen McGann • Stringband
Phil Vernon • Nancy White
A TIME TO STAND TOGETHER
LE TEMPS DE S'UNIR
CUPW 1965-85
STRENGTH & SOLIDARITY
JUSTICE POUR LES NETTOYEURS ET NETTOYEUSES
S.P.C.
The Crisis Continues
CUPE
END CONTRACTING OUT
Votre service Nos emplois!
Non à la privatisation
S.P.C.
DISCARD

Various artists

A Time to Stand Together/Le Temps de S'unir

LP

Slim Evans Recording (SE 001)

1987

Canada

The union this record centers around, the Canadian Union of Postal Workers (CUPW), was established after postal workers literally overthrew their old one in a country-wide wildcat in 1965. That militancy remained in 1987 when CUPW organized rolling strikes to fight a wave of neoliberal privatization and the consequent closure of sorting facilities. The rolling strikes were only partially successful, as total privatization was held off but many strikers lost their jobs. This record was put out after the strikes, with half the proceeds for postal workers fired and suspended due to militant action, the other half going to the Working Committee for Social Solidarity, a kind of think tank for labor policy, "to demonstrate our commitment to a wider need to stand together with others." Like the National Communications Union 7" discussed previously, this is the rare record that features a wide array of musical styles, from folk to reggae to rock, Celtic to dub poetry. In addition, it is presented in both English and French,

and claims to be the first record to ever present English Canadian and Quebecois labor songs together. This eclecticism seems to show a growing recognition amongst labor leadership that not only were their memberships increasingly diverse, but in order to appeal to the general public they needed strike songs created in popular idioms, not just iterations of historical labor songs.

MAIL SORTIN' MAN

When John Henry was a little baby
Sittin' on his daddy's knee
He picked up some letters
and threw 'em in a pile
Said, "sortin's gonna be the life of me"

Now they took John Henry to the mailroom
Just as soon as he could stand
Put him in the Union
Gave him $3.96 and hour
Said, "Son you're a letter sortin' man"

Well the memo said to John Henry,
"We're gonna bring that Steam Sorter round,
We're gonna put that Steam Sorter
Out on the job,
Gonna whop that mail on down"

Now John Henry said to the memo,
"A man ain't nothin' but a man,
Before I let
that old Sorter beat me down,
Gonna die with a letter in my hand"

Now the man who made the Steam Sorter
Thought he was mighty fine
But John Henry
Sorted out of 15 bags,
Steam Sorter only done 9

Now John Henry said to his hammer,
"Looky yonder what I see
You're Sorter down broke
And you're mail done choked
And you can't sort mail like me!"

Now the letters was flying in the mail room
John Henry was sortin' fire
But he sorted so hard,
He broke his poor heart
And he laid down his letters and he died

When the Union heard that John Henry
Had drawn his final pay
They put a black band
Around every mail box
And shut down delivery for the day

Now they took John Henry to the Rideau
And buried him in the sand
Now every single Postie
That comes rolling by
Says, "there lies a mail sortin' man"

(c Bossin, Froehlich CAPAC) Stringband's music is available on "Canadian Sunset"*, "National Melodies"*, "Live"*, and "Across Russia by Stage"*

LES MOTS DOUX

C'est avec des mots doux que nous tenons à dire,
Pourquoi il faut lutter, continuer encore
C'est avec des mots doux que nous voulons décrire
Nos combats acharnés pour changer le décor.

Ce décor où l'on joue le dur métier de vivre,
Qui réclame des yeux, des poumons et des doigts.
Qui réclame la peur et des comédiens ivres,
Pour qu'ils jouent ce qu'on veut, en silence et sans voix.

Mais la nôtre s'élève à chaque fois qu'on range
Naissance et privilèges et qu'on en fait des lois,
Qu'on paie mieux ceux qui ont acquis diplômes et livres,
Les autres, c'est connu, ont des besoins plus bas.

Alors toute douceur nous devient étrangère,
Nos mots prennent les armes, appellent au combat,
Nos liens se sont tressés en ces étranges guerres,
Que même un peu perdues, nous gagnons chaque fois.

Nos liens se multiplient malgré les lois, les armes,
Pour un crâne fendu: dix militants de plus
et beintôt le pouvoir, l'ambition et leurs charmes
Se tiendront dans leurs fiefs, et se sauront perdus.

C'est avec des mots doux que nous pourrons écr
Nous avons tant lutté, nous lutterons encore.
C'est avec des mots doux qu'on parlera de vivre
D'aimer, de travailler
Et pois d'aimer encore.

(c Andrée Lemieux, Isabelle Gusse)

OUR WORLD

One day I saw her walking, a picket line
And she was carrying, a great big sign
I asked her why, she said,
"It's 'cause I'm into making changes"
I saw her at a rally, way downtown
Whoa but that woman really gets around
I asked her why, she said,
"It's time for making changes"

And we got to stand together
Got to take a stand
Look at what they're doing to us
All across the land
And it's Our World! Our World! Our World!

He cleans at Canada Post, minimum wage
Unsafe conditions, fueling his rage

Halte à la sous-traitance

Non à la privatisation

He wants a union 'cause he knows
It's a way of making changes
We've heard our native peoples, proud and strong
Demand self-determination for so long
An end to genocide,
It's time for making changes

She's visiting Managua, in from the hills
So many hopes and dreams, yet to fullfill
She faces contra guns, cause Yankee dollars kill
It's time for changes
He's from South Africa, under attack
No rights or privileges, because he's black
We've got to join with him, 'cause he's fighting back
and making changes

(c Arlene Mantle PROCAN - ' used with permission of the Canadian 'utoworkers and On the Line Music Collective from a soon to be released \W album) Arlene Mantle's music is available on "Class Act"* and n the Line"

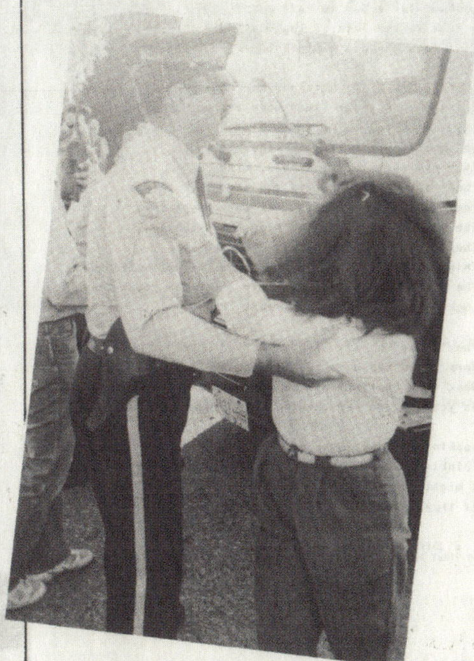

SIDE 1 / FACE A

WHY DO WE HAVE TO FIGHT
Lillian Allen (3:23)

TU N'ETAIS PAS DANS MES SOULIERS
Pierre Fournier (3:30)

GOOD GIRL
Nancy White (3:15)

HEATHER'S SONG
Aya (2:30)

NO CONTRACTING OUT!
Phil Vernon (3:00)

HISTOIRE DU 8 MARS
Andrée Lemieux (4:18)

MAIL SORTIN' MAN
Stringband (3:20)

SIDE 2 / FACE B

LES MOTS DOUX
Andrée Lemieux (3:00)

OUR WORLD
Arlene Mantle (4:20)

LOOKIN' FOR A JOB
Clifton Joseph (3:15)

MAN'S JOB
Eileen McGann (4:05)

UN ACCIDENT
Pierre Fournier (3:58)

A TIME TO STAND TOGETHER / LE TEMPS DE S'UNIR
Ginger Group (4:03)

PROFITS FORM THE SALE OF THIS RECORDING WILL BE DONATED TO:
- Postal workers fired and suspended in the 1987 strike
- The Working Committee for Social Solidarity.

PROFITS DE LA VENTE DU MICROSILLON SERA VERSE DANS UN FONDS POUR:
- Travailleurs et travailleuses congédiés et suspendus lors de la grève de 1987
- Comité de travail pour la solidarité sociale.

Technical Co-ordination
Coordonnation technique Si Garber
Artwork and Design/
Conception Atistique Doug Simpson
Special Thanks to/
Remerciements à Evert Hoogers and Caroline Lee

PRODUCED BY/PRODUCTION:
Julius Fisher and Gary Cristall
For Slim Evans Records and Tapes
2149 Parker Street
Vancouver, B.C.
Ph. (604) 253-6222

DISTRIBUTED BY/
DISTRIBUTION
Festival Records
3271 Main Street
Vancouver, B.C.
Ph/Tel. (604) 879-2931
Fax /Telecopieur (604) 879-4325

This collection of labour songs is CUPW's musical contribution to a theme postal workers have come to view as urgent. In these times of increasing victimization resulting from the neo-conservative drive to create a "free market" economy, it is especially important for workers, the unemployed, women, the elderly - all of us who are affected - to stand together in the struggle to create a different kind of society based on meeting human needs.

What makes these songs remarkable is how they convey this message at such a deep and emotional level. And for the first time ever, Canadian and Québécois labour songs are brought together in one album.

To demonstrate the necessity for postal workers to "stand together", part of the proceeds from the sale of this album will be placed in a fund for workers fired and suspended in our recent strike against privatization of Canada Post. To demonstrate our commitment to a wider need to "stand together" with others, the other part of the proceeds will go to the Working Committee for Social Solidarity.

Les chansons syndicales interprétées sur ce microsillon sont la contribution musicale du SPC à un thème que les postiers considèrent urgent. A notre époque de représailles croissantes entraînées par la poussée néo-conservatrice pour créer une économie de "marché libre", il est particulièrement important que les travailleurs et travailleuses, les sans-emploi, les femmes, les personnes âgées --- tous ceux d'entre nous qui sont touchés --- s'unissent pour créer un différent genre de société répondant aux besoins humains.

Les interprètes de ces chansons remarquables nous communiquent ce message profond avec chaleur et émotion. Pour la première fois, des chansons syndicales québécoises et canadiennes se retrouvent sur le même microsillon.

Pour témoigner de la nécessité que les postiers "s'unissent", une partie des profits de la vente du microsillon sera versée dans un fonds pour les travailleurs et travailleuses congédiés et suspendus lors de notre grève récente contre la privatisation de Postes Canada. Pour témoigner de notre engagement à un besoin plus profond de "s'unir" à d'autres, l'autre part des profits sera versée au Comité de travail pour la solidarité sociale.

In solidarity/Solidarité.

Jean-Claude Parrot,
National President/Président national,
Canadian Union of Postal Workers/
Syndicat des Postiers du Canada.

Music is a powerful tool for the labour movement and for all social movements. It helps us laugh. It helps us cry. It helps us feel the rage and solidarity we need to overcome injustice. It articulates our vision of a world where human needs come before profits and the market. Music humanizes a sometimes dehumanizing struggle.

Music is particularly powerful as an organizing tool. And we need every tool available today, to build a movement which can thwart greed and militarism.

It has been a honour for us to produce this album for the Canadian Union of Postal Workers. Postal workers have been on the front lines in defending public ownership of basic postal services as well as wages and conditions of all Quebecois and Canadian workers.CUPW has been exemplary in standing for women's rights and for other oppressed sectors of society.

We dedicate this recording to Marie Taylor (CUPW) and Gert Lefebre (LCUC), two postal workers who held the line in 1987 and who were crippled by the bosses and their scabs. Their bodies were broken but not their spirit.

La musique est un outil puissant pour le mouvement syndical et pour tous les mouvements sociaux. Elle nous fait rire. Elle nous fait pleurer. Elle nous fait ressentir la fureur et la solidarité nécessaire pour surmonter l'injustice. Elle donne vie à notre vision d'un monde où les besoins humains ont préséance sur les profits et le marché. La musique humanise une lutte parfois déshumanisante.

La musique est surtout puissante comme outil de mobilisation. Aujourd'hui plus que jamais auparavent, nous avons besoin de tous les outils disponibles pour bâtir un mouvement syndical qui peut contrecarrer l'avarice et le militarisme.

Ce fut un honneur pour nous de produire ce microsillon pour le Syndicat des postiers du Canada. Les postiers ont été au premier plan de la défense des services postaux comme services publics ainsi que des salaires et conditions de travail de tous les travailleurs et travailleuses québécois et tous les travailleurs et travailleuses canadiens. Le SPC a été exemplaire dans sa défense des droits des femmes et autres groupes opprimés de la société.

Nous dédions ce microsillon à Marie Taylor (SPC) et Gert Lefebre (UTC), deux travailleuses des postes ayant été estropiées sur les piquets de grève par l'employeur et ses briseurs de grève. Leur corps a été fracturé, mais leur courage est demeuré intacte.

Julius Fisher
Independent Canadian Transit Union/
Syndicat canadien indépendant du transport (CSC)
American Federation of Musicians/
Fédération des musiciens des États-Unis et du Canada (CTC)

Gary Cristall
Director/Directeur,
Vancouver Folk Music Festival

Reynald et Fernand
"Pouvoir Mieux Vivre" b/w "Partager"
7" single
RKFA (RKFA 8901)
1989
France

This record doesn't come directly from workers or a union, instead it was made by the synth-pop duo Reynald et Fernand in support of striking workers at two Peugeot factories near the Swiss border. Roughly 14,000 metalworkers from multiple unions (CFDT, CGT, FO) had walked out. Peugeot's parent company, PSA, was France's single largest privately held company at the end of the '80s, so the struggle was poised to set patterns for bargaining across the entire auto industry. It started as a wildcat, and developed over more than five weeks, capped with an occupation. This record was pressed with the support of the unions and sold during a solidarity march in Paris, with profits going to the strike fund for workers. Sadly the music is unbearable power ballads, although there is an earnestness which comes through that gives it a little charm. Just look at that grin on the cover image (and his open fly)!

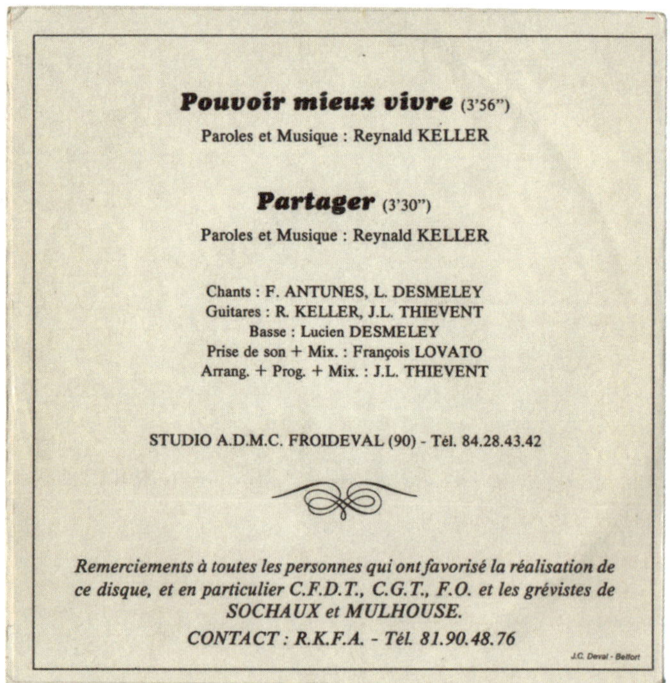

POUVOIR MIEUX VIVRE
PARTAGER

Lacky Streik
"Streik-Rap" b/w "Ab geht die Post"
7" single
His Masters Voice?/J&P (90206)
1990
Germany

Catching up with contemporary culture, here is another record that foregoes the folk and martial sonic landscape of labor movements past for an attempt at mainstream pop. In this case, a set of pop rap and pop rock songs in support of a German postal workers strike in 1990.

The level of involvement of rank-and-file striking workers is entirely unclear here as the music and lyrics are credited to individuals (Claus Blume and Thomas-Paul Jüttner, respectively) not the union or a workers' cultural group. At the same time, the lyrics are surprisingly impactful in their focus on the affective conditions of postal workers. There is a real focus on labor conditions in contrast to many of the records included here which dial in on either wages or worker control. Here we have lyrics like this:

If work is killing me, then it stops for me!
Because thinking ahead, and I pay attention to that,
means taking a break, I breathe a sigh of relief,
I have to have time to relax.
I want more time, I want it now.

The lyrics are more effective than the music, which feels designed to function as much like corporate jingles as it is the labor sing-a-longs of old. But while jingles get caught in our head, they're an imposition, not something we desire or fight for. "Streik-Rap" highlights the tension between attempting to be relevant to a modern, pop music-oriented audience while maintaining a politic that is rooted in solidarity and bringing workers together to engage in a culture that feels authentic and grassroots.

DIE
DEUTSCHE
POSTGEWERKSCHAFT
präsentiert:
STREIKRAP
AB GEHT DIE POST
LACKY STREIK

Lucha 90
Wes: "onderwijsstaking 1990,
hoogst uitzonderlijk en uniek van aard!"

SITEK
<u>Lucha 90</u>
LP
SITEK (no cat #)
1990
Curaçao

This record takes live recordings from a mass meeting of SITEK, the national union of education workers in Curaçao, at the time of a historic strike, and pairs them with studio recorded songs. Thanks to the island's impressive linguistic mix it's hard to tell exactly what the demands and grievances were—the quote on the cover translates clumsily to "education strike 1990, highly exceptional and unique in nature!"—but we can tell that the production values are high, and the tracks form a well executed collage of group singing that merges in and out of chants and speeches. The highlight is a call and response between speaker and audience with intricate staccato rhythms that the assembled education workers have absolutely no trouble navigating; as far as popular workers' songs go it's one the most technically accomplished we've come across and handled with the most life and ease. It drops you right into the action!

HET WAS GRANDIOOS!

nos ta keda rustig.....
CUROIL
Ban lucha pa igualdat total den Enseñansa
SITEK
NOTI-BOMBOSHI
JUFFROW DI SKOL OF SHISHI DI KAYA?
DIREKTIVA SITEK MESTER PIDI DISKULPA PA SUSESONAN DI DJALUNA
AKTITUT PORKERIA DI MAESTRONAN DI SKOL
MEI
21.30 OR
19.00 OR
MI NO TA BAI!
SITEK MESTER
TJE

Some Closing Notes

Kennedy Block

"If you and a few friends can make noise somewhere in public, be it with drums, a PA system and a generator, brass instruments, a choir of screaming children, or whatever else, you can join the rebellion against the state's control of the airwaves. Or maybe you cut the fence at a big corporate music festival in your town, making it free for whoever wishes to come. Maybe you disconnect the mic system so your fascist mayor can't project lies at a speaking event. Making detailed plans and taking precautions for renegade sound is great, but don't be afraid of doing something messy and imperfect. Ecosystems of resistance form around bold actions and creative experiments."
— Free Jack, Free the Airwaves*

While thinking about these records, notes to myself:

-Bring a field recorder to the barricade, to the march, to jail support, to the squat defense. We can document ourselves without worrying about product. Everything can be turned into something else, another occasion, another action, a cycle of collective cultural production. Slogans on the street can be turned into a listening party, a combative rave, a fundraiser—i.e., they can be turned into *collective understanding and action*. Use music to stage the next fight with the lessons you deem most important. In other words, your insights—learned from meetings or the street—can be circulated not as essays but as forms of culture: values, style, gestures.

-Take the time to come up with music and carry with you the means to circulate it—be that an instrument or a Bluetooth speaker or yelling through a paper cone. Let a playlist be part of your go-bag. During the 2020 uprisings in NYC I saw Pop Smoke's "Welcome to the Party" cohere a crowd; after a few cop cars got smashed up, one little speaker brought a hundred skittish protesters back into the street. The music's confidence, popularity, and ubiquity (at that point in the summer) helped to naturalize the proposal of smashing cop cars and throwing fireworks inside them. In bringing us physically back together in this mood Pop Smoke also prevented an aggressive police response.

-There is an online radio station that would be happy to play your friend's weird DJ set that collages street recordings of protest with popular songs, with rousing speeches, with chants, etc. You don't just have to get on the news to get on people's radar. Aim for places that aren't already thought of as political.

-Shove as much as you can into everything you sell. Every pamphlet can smuggle a poster, every poster can carry an essay on its back, every digital music sale can come with a downloadable pack of movement graphics. *Everything we make can have an invitation to join in the making*—whether as chord and lyric sheets for music or actionable steps for making contact. Include precise details: some of the best songs in this collection include the full names

of managers, exact numbers on pay, specific stories broken down step by step. . . P.S. in 2024, mixtapes (on cassette) were selling like hotcakes.

-Bands (or any collective) can be a cultural unit that travels and connects struggles. Music is a beautiful way to share lessons from one struggle to another.

-Form a band. Then form a new band at least once a year, with at least one person who has never played in a band before. If we want a scene to support us, we have to participate in making it.

-It is not the goal of someone doing cultural work to simply *support* a struggle outside of oneself, but to join the struggle and *be changed by it*. The most exciting of the musicians represented in this book, if they can even be identified as such, were in direct contact with strikers. Do not wait for permission to participate.

* Free Jack, Free the Airwaves is a 2024 zine which came out of the movements to Stop Cop City and Defend the Atlanta Forest. In 2021 locals blew the lid off of a proposal to clearcut a key South Atlanta forest and replace it with a police training facility. Over the next three years the ruling clique's attempt to somersault upright and armored out of the George Floyd rebellions was stymied by small groups of autonomous militants, their friends, children, out-of-towners, regular citizens, autonomous researchers, treehouses, molotov cocktails, rocks, soda cans, fireworks, and—importantly—music. The struggle has been a burning torch for class confrontation and subversive cultural innovation in the United States. It is also the current high-water mark for coordinated state repression. Democrats and Republicans have experimented with new legal techniques against protesters (RICO and Domestic Terrorism charges), voter suppression, and the targeting of support infrastructure like bail funds with raids and legislation. On January 18th, 2023, their footsoldiers in the Georgia State Patrol even ambushed and murdered Tortuguita, the nom de guerre with which we knew a 26 year old anarchist living in the woods. Free Jack, Free the Airwaves exemplifies a key tendency in the movement towards protagonism and self-organization. The "Jack" in the title is Jack Mazurek, a participant in the struggles who was arrested in one of four home raids against activists conducted by the FBI, GBI, and ATF on February 4th, 2024. To read the zine in full visit freejack.co. To donate to Jack's fundraiser, visit givebutter.com/tLAvDE. As of March 2025, they have raised $32,750 of a $40,000 goal.

THIS IS NOT A MUSIC FESTIVAL

Because we are not here as consumers or as mere spectators. This is not another photo-op, another "networking opportunity." We are here because our need for a free forest, culture, and existence can't be crushed by the police, nor can it be sold back to us as an image in an uninspired Hollywood rip-off. In a cave called Divje Babe, located in present-day Slovenia, archeologists have recently discovered a 60,000 year old flute. The human need for music has been with us since the very beginning. We are here to affirm that this deep and timeless desire, which has survived an Ice Age, the rise of empires and states, the advent of borders; slavery, war, famine and Holocausts, is an important part of the current struggle.

This movement is not just about a piece of land. It is not being fought between the police and their goons on one hand and some activists and their friends on the other. We are witnessing the collision of two competing ideas of life and the future.

If they win, they will pollute all of the rivers, destroy all of the forests, pave over everything beautiful, and they will use the police to assure unlimited profits as our civilization chokes out its dying breaths.

If we win: human needs will be measured against the imagination, against our collective ambitions and dreams, not held hostage by a system of artificial scarcity and waste. Our communities will not be held together by their ability to kill and maim enemies or heretics. **They will be held together by music, and the ability to generate common luxuries.**

So let's not say *"Oh THEY don't really care about the struggle, they are only here for the party"*; or, *"this is not about music and festivals and all of this crap, this is about serious politics and organizing."* Instead let's say the truth: this is only a glimpse of what we could give one another if we manage to outlive the oil-based economics of the current world system. **The emancipation of the senses, the free development of the imagination and the passions: this is precisely what we are fighting for.**

no cop city, no hollywood dystopia

The authors would like to thank everyone at Common Notions, including Erika for all the editing support, Rebecca, Jeff, and Sarah for promotion and getting the book into the world, Malav for all his unflagging support, and Carson for doing the unrecognized labor of packing and shipping; Chris Jones for passing the UK Ford strike 7″ on to Josh, which helped to spur this project; Erik Buelinckx for so much help with the context and translation around the Belgian and French records; Brage Aronson for the same with the Scandinavian entries, as well as publishing this book in Norway(!); Mat Callahan for support and conversation; Alessandro Delfanti for Italian translation support; Rosemary Grennan and Mayday Rooms for great info on the Ford strike 7″; Jonathan Melrod and Peter Olney for a very useful conversation about promotion; Kevin Van Meter for throwing himself into this project and opening the doors to contacts and support in the US labor organizing and education community; Jim and everyone at P.I.T. for being the coolest record shop in Brooklyn. Most of the records included in this book are from Josh's personal collection, but a number were borrowed from Interference Archive, for which we are extremely grateful. Josh would like to thank Monica and Asa for being forever patient with his obsessive collecting; and Kennedy would like to thank their parents for an immense amount of support on this project.

Strike While the Needle Is Hot
Josh MacPhee and Kennedy Block

ISBN: 978-1-945335-54-9
eBook ISBN: 978-1-945335-56-3
LCCN: 2025904577

10 9 8 7 6 5 4 3 2 1

Common Notions
c/o Interference Archive
314 7th St.
Brooklyn, NY 11215
www.commonnotions.org
info@commonnotions.org

Common Notions
c/o Making Worlds
210 S. 45th St.
Philadelphia, PA 19104

Discounted bulk quantities of our books are available for organizing, educational, or fundraising purposes. Please contact Common Notions at the address above for more information.

Cover design, layout, and typesetting by Josh MacPhee.